With A Little Faith

With A Little Faith

Jude Stringfellow

"Now faith is the substance of things hoped for, the evidence of things unseen."

Hebrews 11:1

To order additional copies of this book, contact:
Xlibris Corporation
1-888-795-4274
www.Xlibris.com
Orders@Xlibris.com
30205

Contents

Dedicated to Mom and Dad. They've been kissing each other for more than 50 years.

DISCLAIMER

At times, I felt it necessary to change the names of not only the guilty, but the innocent as well. At times, my friends asked me to change their names and this begs the question: Are they innocent or guilty? You decide. My brother has asked me if I have told the entire truth while writing the book, and I must say, that after reading it I can find two tales which are not all together truthful, but I'm not telling you which ones they are, thus giving me an out should I need one. Happy reading.

Thank You Page

I greatly thank anyone and everyone who helped me to get this book published by sending me donations from your heart. There are a few who need to be mentioned by name and they are: Ginger and Dennis Handy of Tennessee, who first read my inquest and responded immediately. Secondly, I wish to thank Ericka from Seattle, Washington, who not only showed tremendous faith by sending me a donation, she's a student who works part time at a hospital just to make ends meet. Thank you BIG TIME to Debbie Minshall, her husband and her two sons Matt and Evan. I met Debbie and the boys at the Harry Potter 6 party at Borders of Oklahoma City on July 15, 2005. Debbie and I talked briefly about the book, and she was so inspired about the idea, she literally paid every penny I had left to pay on the publishing costs. You can say what you want to say, but people are out there who want to make a difference. Thank you guys so much for your help.

Prologue

I was sitting there reading the latest cartoon captions of *Todd the Dinosaur*, minding my own business, because that is what I always do, and my son came into the house with that "look" on his face. He was smiling. He wasn't going to tell me why, but I knew that in the 17 years I had known him that there were very few reasons for this particular smile. Funny isn't it? I can tell which of my children has let gas in the closed car by the smell, it doesn't matter how well you've trained them, they all do it, and I find it a little disturbing that I can detect with just my nostrils which of my kids to blame. I'm never wrong . . . this smile, this barely showing the teeth, but all the dimples being exposed for optimal cuteness. What was he about to do? What was I about to get myself into? It was always unexpected and it was always unavoidable. In a flash my life would be changed. "It was true Mom", he began without missing an opportunity to look me square in the eyes, "Princess had a bunch of puppies and she had some of them without legs and one died because it couldn't fight off the others. Another one died when it walked into the snow I guess, and she didn't go out and get it. I found it, I buried it." A tragic story yes, but he hadn't stopped the excessive smiling. That's when it hit me. No! He didn't! He knows we can't have another dog in this house! We already broke the rules with Matrix, a beagle-dachshund mix that we had re-rescued from the shelter just a month before. Our landlord Frank would have my head if he thought we went out and got another dog.

It wasn't the first time. Reuben had already stepped over the line (again) when he had to have a cat, and when one cat comes another one finds its way into my house. I was already being asked to pay more each month to cover the deposit on the animals that Frank had been so adamant about—adamant in that we couldn't have any. We had Matrix, but for some reason Frank believed me when I told him he would be staying down the street with friends. "You didn't bring home one of those dogs Reuben!" I protested. I stomped my right foot, slammed down the dish towel in my hands, which I had been using to dry dishes before picking up Patrick Roberts' *Todd* cartoon. Reu was

13

suppose to have washed hours ago. "You did not bring home a puppy just because she had too many. Oh my gosh Reuben, it was only two weeks ago! You can't bring a two-week old puppy here and expect it to live, its mother has to feed it, it doesn't even have its eyes open I'm sure." I continued protesting. I know I did, and there he was, smiling. While he wouldn't stop showing off those dimples, he reached into the folds of his football jersey, pulling out the fuzziest, yellowest, cutest little pointed-earred puppy I had ever seen . . . . without front legs. This was going to take a little faith!

PART ONE

Family

Chapter One

It wasn't as if I woke up one sunny day and decided to divorce my husband, go back to school, lose my job, and raise a two-legged dog. I'm quite aware of how it may seem to some as they read this book that this is what must have happened; however, I assure you I was one of those people who believed in staying married even if the guy I was married to wound up being the biggest jerk on the face of the planet. I had actually divorced him twice because my morality was such that I felt that I simply had to give him every chance possible. OK . . . having done that, and having been paid back in ways that will not only confuse and dumbfound you, the reader, I begin this story by backing up from the main topic of the book long enough to establish what it is that our family went through, and why the dog we call "Faith" is so endearing to us. It isn't simply because she is perhaps the most unique and unusual animal I have ever met, it is also because our family had been through so much before she came along; her coming to us at the moment in our lives when we most needed her was nothing short of a miracle.

I love my kids. I really love my kids. If I had to do the kid thing all over again, I would no doubt let my friend Denzel raise them. They would have turned out so very differently, and probably for the better. Denzel has a kinder, more intellectual view of the world. He would know just exactly where to place my children in his garden of life. I call my son Reuben the joy of my heart because he never ceases to surprise me. At every turn in my life he finds a way to jump start me into sheer terror, enthusiasm, surrealism, or some other emotion which causes my face to stretch into endless facial contractions; he can be such a loving and giving child, while at the very same time, he can be so brutally honest it leaves me dropping my jaw in embarrassment as he makes an announcement to the world which could very well have been kept private. At the age of two he bent himself over, pulled down his pants exposing his bum, only to tell the crowded auditorium at the Governor's Christmas party that he had wiped himself by himself . . . so proud! At ten he hit a baseball so hard it slammed into the chest of the pitcher on the other team, knocking the boy to the ground immediately. Because Reuben is so "Reuben", he never ran to first base; instead he ran directly to the kid laying on the mound, lifted him up into his arms, rocking him and trying to bring him back to consciousness. Naturally, he was thrown out at first base. I couldn't have been more impressed of my son than I was at that moment. It was Reuben who actually held me in his arms at the age of fifteen when the District Court Judge made a monumental error during a custody battle revoking my rights as the custodial parent. The error was obvious to anyone who had actually taken the time to read the case file; yet the judge refused to be corrected publicly. I fell hard to the ground in what must have been one of my few completely uncontrolled moments. I can never forget the day, or the moment when my future and the future of my two daughters was suspended without reason. I had gone to court with evidence which would show not only a preponderance of guilt on the part of my former spouse, but physical evidence that his wife had physically hurt my daughter Laura. I had left medical and taped evidence with my attorney, what could have gone wrong?

Once the hearing began I wasn't allowed to speak. My attorney had not surrendered the evidence on time, my own counsel had not taken the time to do his job, which in turn gave the Judge the impression that I was negligent in fulfilling my obligations as a parent. What was worse, if I'm not mistaken, was that the Judge had believed that it was I who had left bruises and contusions on my daughter's arm. She believed it was me who had held my daughter to the ground and spat on her. No, it wasn't me. I couldn't comprehend what was going on right in front of me. My voice was silenced, my evidence unannounced. In a moment I was hearing the Judge's announcement that I was being banished from my daughters and that I would have my visitation rights suspended unless they were supervised. This wasn't suppose to happen. I was the one saving them from the monsters they were being hurt by. Nothing made sense, and my county paid counsel wasn't making it make any sense to the Judge. I later found out that he had not even brought the correct file to court. This was not the first time an attorney had misplaced my file and I was the one punished for their mistake. For over three years this battle of sole custody had raged and my former spouse, their father, had managed to evade the court's true and correct ruling. Whatever trick he had played, whatever false document he had managed to file or have his attorney file, it was working.

Everything went blank, the room felt black, swirling with confusion and upheaval as my attorney tried to reckon with the Judge over his mistake. He wasn't willing to take the blame for not being prepared, but he did at least state that the evidence he would have brought would have proved our point. I heard the words and I realized that my girls were forever banned from me. I hit the ground, I hit the ground hard. The next thing I remember as I lay feeling nothing at all, seeing dust under the benches in the crowded court room was my son Reuben as he carefully reached down literally picking me up, rocking me in his arms. He held me so tightly, and he sweetly told me "It's going to be OK, Mom, it's going to be OK." This is my son; he is the joy of my heart. Today, Reuben is an adult by standards of the state. He can go to war, buy cigarettes, rent dirty movies, and pay his own taxes. I don't see him buying cigarettes, but you can bet he'll be taking advantage of the movie rentals. When Faith appeared in a controversial magazine containing nudity, violence, and other forms of questionable substance, it was my darling baby-boy Reuben who couldn't be pulled away from the pages long enough to understand that his mother had just been fired from her job for the event! "That's stupid!" He announced as he continued pouring over the scantily dressed girls with pouting lips. "Sue the bastards!" he proclaimed while turning the book's pages slowly, staring at the third-world pictures exposing terrorism, violent scenes of massacre, public flogging, and a river of blood created by the death and destruction of thousands of dolphins illegally. I took his advice.

Every family needs a Laura Ashleigh. I have one. Laura is the older of my two Irish-twin daughters. She is 14 months older than my daughter Caity. Laura is forever and a day different from her sister in so many ways. She actually believes she was placed on Earth in order to control not only her own destiny but also that of every single person who comes into contact with her. For the most part she is fully capable of this responsibility, however, most of the time people resent being told what to do, when to do it, how to do it, and why they should be doing it. Luckily for me I am in desperate need of having someone exactly like my Laura Cakes to tell me what to do. Considering her sister Caity actually knows absolutely everything, it makes my life that much easier. All I have to do is wake up, think about living my own life, and put forth the slightest effort to do so. As soon as it has been detected that I am doing something so damning, Laura will come to my unwitting rescue with a daily agenda full of impossible tasks which carry more weight and critical need than I would have ever imagined. If for some reason I am unable to fulfill her every desire, need, want, or care, her sister Caity is quick to fill me in as to why she would never consider my actions wise. If these two girls didn't exist I might actually be forced to make a decision for myself. I would be left to the wolves when it came to planning my daily activities. I would never have the knowledge I do of Linkin Park lyrics, which member of Chemical Romance or Good Charlotte is going to be my new son-in-law, or how to do my makeup using predominantly dark circles around my already line-ridden eyes. Laura can care for a dozen, no, two dozen animals at one time, break horses that have never been ridden, sing songs which she has heard one time, correctly assemble a Sauder entertainment cabinet within an hour, but she can't make up her bed or remember to do the dishes. Amazingly, she has her little sister to scream at her from the back of the house—this is usually as effective as setting off lead balloons in the park, as you can imagine.

My last child, my youngest, is called many things, however I have taken to calling her Caity-Baby Baby-Caity ("CBBC") because she won't answer me if I were to call out her Christian given name of Caitlyn. There are some children (adults too) who do what they are going to do; I believe Dr. James Dobson had my precious CBBC in mind when he began his historical journey into the "Strong Willed Child". Where Caity may be only 15 years old, this powerhouse has lived the lives of many old women and then some. She has the knowledge and capabilities to not only be the smartest person ever, she is not the least bit shy about telling you that she will be Queen of America someday and that for this reason alone you should be careful when dealing with her. When God decided to make Caity He must have looked around Heaven, and noticed that one of the demons from Hell had been hiding out in the clouds where she could not be found easily. He must have gently disguised her as a tender, sweet cherub of a baby, making it virtually impossible to reject her. He couldn't decide which of his mischievous followers were deserving of her presence until the day he realized that I had never quite asked for full forgiveness for my own deeds as a child. Caity is quite literally the manifestation of the curse my mother placed on me when I was six years old; asking God and His Holy angels to grant me the privilege of raising a child exactly like myself. Not only do I love my baby Caity, I have to grin just a little when she thinks she has gotten away with yet another devious act. At times, I want to assist her in her paths knowing that I have already walked in her shoes . . . but alas, I let her fall, stumble, jump, and leap into her own world of experience; holding on tightly because of any and every consequence to follow. Would I give this child away? Some days yes, some days no, but if so, only to my mother, to remind her of what it could have been like if I had a twin!

It was Caity who had decided that a computer would be the answer to all of our problems, I think she was in the second grade when she made this proclamation. She convinced me to get a computer that would be capable of hooking up to the internet. At seven she had become capable of installing programs, running them, and even detecting if there were problems on the system. She wasn't savvy enough to understand the true manipulations of the machine before her, however, she was capable of logging on sites she wasn't suppose to be viewing. After a year or so of constant companionship with the keyboard she had successfully tapped into a few files belonging to United States Government agencies. It wasn't long before our doorbell rang and a man wearing dark glasses asked me for identification. He was serious when he asked to see my computer, and quite surprised when I explained that I really didn't know how to click out of one site to find another, let alone be able to hack my way into the Pentagon! While he stood in my living room staring at my complete inaptness, my mind was turning cartwheels over Caity. There she sat, on the floor watching Cartoon Network, oblivious to what mess she had created for her mom.

To be honest, I tell a little story which after it is told, anyone can understand the vast differences between my three children and their personalities. All families have this situation, it is nothing new, however, the clarification is often appreciated when it becomes necessary to clear Laura's name for something Caity has done by stealth, or that Reuben has blatantly blundered into. To compare Reuben to a Saint Bernard puppy makes more sense. He can be the biggest, sloppy-handed playmate, capable of leaping from the ground to the hood of the car in one bound; however, if that bound is misstepped he can be the 220 pound paper weight landing on your left arm, crushing it to pieces, which is exactly what he has done to me. "Hey Mom, watch this!" These words have trained me. I move immediately when I hear them, and usually behind a wall or some place safely out of his reach. To explain the differences of these three beautiful and most adored children, walk with me down a little parable.

It would seem that there is a barn in the middle of an open field. The barn is not in use, it hasn't been occupied for quite some time, but nevertheless, because the barn is not mine I am not inclined to do anything about it. My son Reuben comes to me in a state of excitement. He's all but leaping into the air because he has discovered a perfect 120-yard football field in which he can play. The only problem is, there is a barn sitting on top of the fifty-yard line. He wants to know where I keep the matches so that he can set the barn on fire and burn it to the ground. He offers no plan of operation really, just the plan of taking out the barn. There is no discussion of method, no explanation of consequence, my son has a one-track mind, and it works on one incredible event at a time. From time to time he is capable of miracles . . . but not today. "No Reu, you can't have the matches, burning barns that don't belong to us is wrong, and besides that, you could hurt yourself, your sisters, or someone else if the fire got out of hand." To my surprise, this answer is actually accepted and he walks away just as suddenly as he had entered the room. His mind racing on yet another plan all together different from the finding of a football field.

Within a few hours my peace is interrupted again. This time it is my daughter Laura. She has brought me lunch. She has created crackers with peanut butter, carrots, pieces of apples, and a freshly brewed cup of coffee just the way I like it, with a little creamer and a little sugar as well. She sits beside me and is actually about to feed me because Laura has it in her head that she is the nurturing member of the family. I thank her for her generosity but know there must be an explanation for the special treatment. Never one to lie, Laura takes a deep breath and pulls out a little fat notebook with reasons listed. She begins her request with a prelude of reasons why I should be listening to her completely. "Don't say anything Mommy, until I have finished. I know how you sometimes jump to the end, but this time just listen and hear what I have to ask." She continues her list of reasons why the barn in the middle of the field is a health hazard. She begins with the events that could possibly have happened to the people who either built the barn in the first place, or who had lived in the area when it was new. For a few minutes she has created the picture of horror that she believes will be impressive to me, as she brings me up to date with more current events, which could somehow take place if the barn were actually destroyed, and "carefully" removed. She is even quick to add that she has already called the various contractors of the area, and she has estimates of the cost. (I wondered who the men were out in the field this morning.) When she has finished she tells me that she is finished. She sits up pretty in her best smile and awaits my answer. Knowing that there is absolutely no way to be kind about it, I simply explain to her the governing practices of land leases, ownership, adverse possession under the state laws of Oklahoma, and how it could effect me as a bread-winner for the family if I give into her wishes. The last part about adverse possession intrigues her, and she is satisfied. It was merely a question in the first place, she explains. She goes to the door and yells out to her brother who is waiting on the field with a magnifying glass and shredded paper that she tried. Off she goes to align her horse collection in her room.

Before the night falls, I am welcomed by a smiling-faced little girl without front teeth. She seems docile, and yet the skin missing from her two knees would testify that she has been landing rather abruptly onto a hard surface. "You skinned your knees." I say to her as she climbs onto the cabinet and reaches to the top of the refrigerator for cookies I have placed out of her reach on purpose. Thump! Landing this time on her feet she makes a completely unintelligent statement regarding her injury. Swallowing her cookie somewhat she states clearly that it didn't hurt. The phone rings and it is just as I pick up the receiver that I am able to make out the silhouette of smoke, flames, fire fighters and trucks at the end of the field just outside my house. "Hello", I say rather sheepishly into the phone. "Ma'am, do you have a little girl without front teeth? Is she wearing a blue t-shirt and a pair of green plaid shorts?" Someone is asking me. The caller ID identifies the call coming from the city police. "Someone saw her on top of the barn just before it went into its inferno. Seems she may have 'borrowed' a can of gasoline from a man down the way." I tell the kind officer that I have a daughter named Laura, she has been with me all day, in fact, she is not one to climb onto barns, and that I have a large boy named Reuben. He could have climbed onto the barn, yes, but if it was a little girl with missing teeth that he was looking for I couldn't possibly help him. As I hang up the phone I stop just short of picking up a long-handled axe from the closet door when I hear the sweetest little prayer coming from the girls' room. "Dear Jesus, Caity didn't mean to burn the barn. She wanted to make Reuben a football field for his birthday. She said she was sorry, and that tomorrow she'll get around to telling Mommy. Please let me do it God. I know how she is." With that, Laura's prayer for her baby sister ended and my ulcers began.

Where the story is not a true one, it clearly shows the vast differences between my three brats . . . kids, and it perhaps sets up the stories that are my life's treasure.

Chapter Two

Family. Erma Bombeck said they are the ties that bind . . . and gag. What truth lies in that statement. I wouldn't take another kid like any one of my own, and I wouldn't take a million dollars for any one of them either. Dealing with family is never easy, dealing with family requires having a faith in something, sometimes in everything. We've all heard it, it takes a village to raise a child. Well, it does. The church is a big part of that village, as is the school, teachers, neighbors, people on the street running away from my house, people calling me to inform me that they're missing a tool, a bike, a snake. I consider myself blessed and lucky to have been raised in a household where the faith we practiced was in Christ. It certainly couldn't have been Buddha that ruled over my brood, his beliefs don't allow fighting, clawing the eyes out of your siblings, standing on top of the chairs to get away from a flinging water balloon in the house, or ear-piercing screaming coming from the bathroom at the sight of wet bath towels draped over my open makeup which has been tipped over and is running freely onto the freshly mopped floor, and that's me! You should see how my kids live. Christ is all about forgiveness, Buddha never had my children; he never took a bath with a guinea pig or had to drive his daughter five miles to a toilet because she can't squat in the stables where she boards her horses, but she can go to school smelling like she's slept with them.

Where was Buddha when I found the catfish rotting in the back of my trunk that July afternoon? I didn't find him lurking in my closet the night I discovered my son's mushroom collection. He claimed it was a science project, but the black and purple painted hoods on the plants led me to believe he was up to something. The nicest thing about Reuben's insane mind is that when you ask him for a reason he doesn't always have one. He is completely satisfied with a helpless "I don't know why, it just looked good." If I tried to figure the boy out every time I ran across one of his imagination's feats I would spend a lifetime with a psychoanalyst. He simply can't be bothered with reason. Christ is big enough, strong enough, and wise enough for me to believe in Him. Every time I need something He has been there to at least provide strength to pull me through. I remember a specific incident during *one* of the ongoing custody battles that followed my divorce. I was sitting in the living room of a very small one bedroom apartment that I was renting. I had full custody of Reuben as he had been physically abused by my ex husband and had previously been awarded to me for this reason. The doorbell rang at 9:00 p.m. it was my daughter Laura. Always polite, she didn't know if it would be proper to simply walk into my apartment without asking. "Hello, come in. Did you walk?" I asked her. "Yes, Daddy said that if I wanted to see you I had to walk." The walk was about a mile, and even though it had not been incredibly dark at nine o'clock, I was devastated that he would have allowed an eight year old to make the trek. These are the moments when Christ has been most helpful. Laura needed $2.00 to go skating the next day at school. She told me she was the only one not going skating and that her dad was not going to give her the money because she had been a bad girl. When I asked her what she had done to make him feel that she was undeserving of the money or the privilege to go skating, her answer was a surprising "I told his wife that he had another girlfriend. I was only telling the truth Mom, it wasn't a lie and he knows it." I couldn't believe my ears. I couldn't believe what I was hearing.

Could it be true that this tiny figure of a girl had walked a mile to my house searching for the fare to skate the next day, and that she wasn't being given that opportunity by her father who wouldn't, or couldn't face up to the fact that he was hurting his own child by placing a greater value on his own philandering than he was in raising his daughter? Why would she, at eight, even know about the affair? This hurt. I went to my purse, but as I did, I remembered that I had literally spent the last dollar I had on gasoline so that I could get to work the next day and be paid. If I didn't come up with the skating money Laura would never have blamed me, however, I knew it would be a sting in her heart if she were left behind while the rest of the class had fun. With a little faith in my heart, and 4 cans of Green Giant green beans in my cupboard, I took Laura down the road to the Wal-Mart store to exchange the cans for a couple of dollars. We entered the store just at the time that the customer service department was closing down. I looked at the hours of operation and realized that if something didn't happen now it would be too late for my daughter's situation. Walking up to the counter I asked Laura to sit on the bench provided for patrons that was just outside the ear range of the clerk named Maria that I needed to speak to. Explaining my situation to her was simple enough. I didn't expect the tears in her Hispanic brown eyes, but nevertheless, I welcomed them as I gave my daughter her skating money and used Wal-Mart's telephone to call her father to let him know she would not be going to his house that night. Maria took my hand and whispered into my ear that she had a good mother as well. She actually kissed my cheek and crossed herself. Being born a Baptist has never stopped me from accepting the faith of others if they are willing to pray for me. I considered this blessing a gift.

I think I hung up the phone before Laura's father could complain too much about the situation. More often than not he would be more upset about the fact that I found a way to appease the situation rather than to worry as to where his children are sleeping safely. Despite the manner of man her father is today, having been changed somewhat by time, at this particular time in my daughters' lives, he was not willing to sacrifice anything for them, nor was he willing to work with me with regards to making their lives any easier. I told him on the phone that I would appreciate it if he would bring Caity by my apartment, or allow me to pick her up, as the girls routinely slept in the same bed. It would be hard on Caity to be without her sister, and I couldn't bear to think of her crying herself to sleep. Naturally I was told no. I was told that I was not only *kidnapping* Laura, but that he would be calling the police to be sure they understood that I was refusing to return her. If I had pressed the issues the fight would have continued as it always did with him ranting about incompatible issues which had nothing to do with the situation whatsoever. He would finish his tantrum by threatening to physically harm Caity to prove that I was the one that was at fault. His methods of brutality would soon be shown in a court of law, but that day wasn't for several weeks away; or so I thought. I couldn't gamble with his insensitive mind. I had to let it go this time.

Sometime between dream one and dream two, as I held my tiny daughter in my arms, I could hear her snoring her way to a peaceful oblivion. Laura may be the most polite little girl in the world when she is awake, but that little red-headed can wake the dead at night with her audibles. My only concern as I drifted back to sleep was for her sister. As I often do, I prayed quietly to God because I know He hears me. A simple "Be with Caity Baby" prayer was sufficient to ease my mind, as I know that God is fully in control, but nothing I could say or do at this minute could ease my heart. Mothers don't really sleep when their children aren't sleeping. Let me restate that; good mothers never sleep when their children aren't able to sleep.

Upon waking the next day I felt the unmistakable shock of being kicked in the head by the jerking foot of my youngest. I suppose sneaking out of her father's house, walking a mile in the middle of the night, using her key to enter the apartment and crawling into my bed without announcing herself, is just another way for her to let me know that no matter the circumstance Caity is fully capable of handling it. When things get hard for the rest of us Caity has an uncanny way of flipping the Devil off and going about things her own way. I swear sometimes I wonder if she doesn't have a brigade of battle-dressed angels hovering about her just in case she actually does step outside of bounds . . . again.

Faith in Christ is probably the only thing that has pulled me through the horrors that followed my divorce. The court records of Oklahoma county hold within their ancient walls the five inch folder numbered *FD97-4953; Stringfellow v. Stickley.* These are not the files from the first time I divorced Dale Stickley. However, they are the records of the final and most assuredly, the last time I divorced him. Prior to our divorce in 1997, Dale and I had decided that divorce would be the best solution for whatever one could call our relationship. I could stand here and place all the blame on his infidelity, his ranting, immature tyrant behavior, and gambling problems, but I'm sure there are more than enough books written about the trials and travails of a marriage united without good reason. I had problems too. I wouldn't allow his affairs. I refused to babysit his lover's kids, and that upset him.

Suffice it to say that because of what I deemed to be Christian morals, I decided to forgive his short comings and to marry him a second time following the very emotional event of the Oklahoma City Bombing. For Oklahomans, and for me in particular, having been downtown at the time of the bombing, making my way to the Alfred P. Murrah building when it exploded; I was living in a mental and emotional state of shock at that time, following the immediate event. I don't know what I was thinking, but it wasn't clear. Could this be a deeper sign from God that the divorce I was granted just six days ago was wrong? Perhaps I should be more forgiving, more understanding, or maybe I should have considered the fact that Reuben had already lost his biological father, and I was now taking him away from the man he had loved and trusted as a father for over nine years. Dale had been Reuben's baseball coach, his football coach, and his basketball coach at home. He had trained Reuben in martial arts and prayed with him at his bedside in 1993, when I had left the two of them alone in Texas while looking for a new home in Oklahoma.

Was I being selfish in not giving my marriage another try? Faith in God is one thing, letting emotions get in the way of making good judgments is entirely something else. Nearly every decision I have ever made about Dale was the wrong decision. I can't tell you why, but I know this: Heads and hearts do not come to the same conclusion, and where love is concerned, it would be best to listen to the head not the heart. The decision to remarry him was indeed the wrong decision. Within days of the Oklahoma City Bombing we were together again. Six days of being divorced had caused me to make an appointment with the Social Security office downtown to have my name changed on my Social Security card. The judge in that case had given me back my maiden name, even though in reality I had never wanted to change it to Stickley in the first place. One thing led to the other and I was forced to change my name when we purchased property together. Every time someone actually called me Jude Stickley I nearly cringed. It wasn't because I have an adverse reaction to Slavic surnames, it was basically because I had come to despise the last name of my husband when it was revealed to me that he wasn't even a Stickley. Talk about your Jerry Springer Shows, here's one for you. (Disclaimer: The details of this story vary depending on which member of Dale's family you talk to.) Dale's mother was born on the bayou of Mississippi, I don't think I was ever told much about her upbringing, only that she was out on her own making her own way by the age of twelve or thirteen. I do know that she met and married a man much older than she was, and that she gave birth to the first of her ten children by the time she was just over fourteen.

Whether she remained married to this man is a mystery, but what is known is that she continued "working" and "making her own way" for several more years. I was told by one of Dale's sisters that she married every father of every child, I find this fact hard to believe considering she herself couldn't tell me who Dale's father was, or who the father of her son that was born just before Dale was. She claimed this boy's father drove a taxi, and that Dale's father was a "shipyard dog". Her words were haunting of course, but fell on deaf ears when I tried to gather any truth from them by asking his sisters and brothers exactly what she meant by them. I was told that she was eight months pregnant with Dale when she married Mr. Stickley. Under Mississippi law, I was told, she had no other choice but to give Dale the last name when he was born.

Years into our marriage I became curious as to who Dale's father might actually be. With a little money and a private detective I discovered that his father's name was Bob Wilson, that he was a fisherman in Pascagoola, Mississippi, and that he wouldn't be interested in meeting his son or his two granddaughters. The cause was dropped, however not by every member of Dale's family. I continued to be harassed by his sisters, brothers, sisters-in-law, and others about the reasoning behind my investigation. I suppose I would have to admit that the knowledge of who my husband's real family was could be beneficial to my daughters if they were ever to engage in a study of genealogy, however, I was actually more driven by the fact that his mother's choice of men to raise her family and to take care of her was less than desirable. When Dale's youngest sister was only twelve years old Dale began petitioning me to help him gain legal guardianship of her, claiming that every other sister had been physically abused. Dale claimed also that he had been assaulted by his father when he was around the age of nine, having denied these claims since our divorce; nevertheless, we engaged in an open attempt at trying to get full and legal custody of his sister. Their 'father', it turns out was an adopted child himself. He is not truly a born Stickley. The name had absolutely no worth to me as Dale's wife, and I could think of no better name to claim than that which was given to me at my birth, the name of my own father, Stringfellow. Stringfellow is the name I returned to my son, and to Laura as well. Caity remains a Stickley.

It's never easy going through the files that collect dust at the court house and forever remind you of the great mistakes you have made throughout the years, but having changed my name back to Stringfellow was something I never regretted. The change would not come as easily as I had hoped the day I parked my car at the Myriad Convention Center and walked up Robinson toward the Murrah building. When the explosion came I was knocked to the ground forcibly with the strangest sensation I could ever imagine. It was as if my ears were turned off, and my eyes were somehow positioned all over my head. I saw paper flying, smoke rising, blood on the concrete beneath my knees, and people running. I can't remember standing up and I certainly don't remember talking to anyone. I remember thinking that a gas main had exploded and for whatever reason I believed it was on Robinson. I crossed the street at Dean McGee and ran easterly to the next main street, it was called Broadway. The Myriad Convention Center was at the end of the street and I clearly remember not being able to run quickly to my car. It was as if I was dreaming that I was running and my legs were stone. They wouldn't move. I had to push them with my hands and make them go. When I reached the car I was being helped by a man in a business suit that wanted to know what had happened. I don't know, I told him. I don't know. I was driving my father's little truck downtown that day because I had a couple of interviews with the Medallion Hotel. One of my appointments was for 10:00 a.m. and one was for 3:00 p.m.

I couldn't start my truck without keys and I couldn't find my keys. My hands wouldn't lift themselves up to help me, and I remember staring at my purse where I'm sure the keys were laying at the bottom waiting to be engaged. It must have only been a few minutes, but for that time I felt no time at all. My ears were still ringing from what must have been the enormous blast. Finally, with my keys in place and my truck pulling out I reached for the radio to hear a little music. Perhaps that would help somehow. I could get out of downtown, call the hotel to let them know I would not be coming to the interview, when the thought occurred to me that the gas main could be taking out the hotel as I driving past it. The Medallion was also on Robinson. I remember going an entirely different way home than what I am used to in order to avoid the downtown area. It wasn't for several minutes that I realized that the truck I was driving didn't have a radio. The noises I was hearing and the sounds of the day weren't music being played at all. Sirens, multiple sirens were echoing off of one another. Hundreds of police, EMT, fire truck sirens, rescue squads, and bells from everywhere were mixing in the air into a crescendo of noise making it virtually impossible to think of anything other than disaster. I do remember driving away and looking into the sky just above the area that the Murrah building would have been located; thick heavy smoke raced into the air, but with it I could see a white line of what appeared to be a streamer, or a cutting edge going through the smoke. Months later I read where people had claimed to have seen angels directly above the building. I wish now that this would have been my vision, but I can honestly say that I didn't sense any peace at that moment. I knew in my heart that God was aware of what had happened, yes, but this comfort was because of faith, not the application of that belief. Not at that minute.

Immediately following the bombing I drove my father's truck back to his house. No one was home. I sat in my parents' living room out in the country on a little farm located about 25 miles northeast of the blasted area from downtown. The time it took to drive to their house was enough time for news coverage to begin explaining what would turn out to be the nation's worst terrorist act on American soil until the events of 9/11. Until April 19, 1995, no Americans had been killed by terrorist on American soil. The immediate response to the day's happenings were somewhat predictable. Terrorists from the Middle East were being blamed for what had taken place. My name change would be the least of my concerns as I began attempting to contact my three children who were in school and daycare at the time. Phone lines were jammed. Hours would pass before my parents came home, and even more hours would pass before I was able to drive to pick up my children from school, as the schools were not allowing children to be released until more information could be given to them. With little else to do I decided to go to the local hospitals to see if I could help. This was a mistake as they were inundated with people who were professionally trained to assist. I thought about giving blood and would have except I was actually losing it from my knees and elbows. I wondered if anyone would take mine—it would be the first time in my life that I had ever volunteered to give my own blood.

When people ask me why I married my husband after I had divorced him in 1995, I usually come back with the standard, boring answer of "I felt it was my Christian obligation to forgive him for his infidelity. He said he was sorry, and we needed to be married for the children." The real reason is much more simple. I was incredibly stupid. If I have one regret it would be remarrying a man I knew I couldn't trust. Forgiving him for sleeping around on me didn't mean I had to give him another shot at me. I literally put myself and my family back into a bad situation, a berth of events for many more years to come because I couldn't get over myself. If I had the least bit of Christian education at the time I was reconciling with my ex, I would have realized that the angels flapping their wings in front of me were warning signs, not applause! Leave it to me to think the best thing to do to patch up a bad marriage is to give it another chance with the same two idiots in the starring roles. It didn't take long before we weren't going to church again, we weren't paying bills again, and we weren't living in a nice house again. Again, after the bombing and just before the next time we moved, we were living with my parents, an event that seemed to be taking place on the average of once a year since 1988, when I married the man in the first place. I can count the times I moved on two hands, but unfortunately I can also count the years that passed between these moves on one. My son had attended three first grade classes in three different schools in two different states, because my husband's job had moved us around. My mother took to writing my addresses and phone numbers in pencil, and my friends stopped asking if they could help me move. They knew I would be taking them up on it. I don't think my best friend Jeannie, who I have known since my first day in high school has even seen seven of the houses I lived in from the day I was married to the day I divorced . . . the first time.

To his credit, (and I don't say that often) my ex husband wasn't completely to blame for the moves. He worked for American Airlines for a while, and for several different loan companies which were up and coming in the early nineties. They moved us back and forth from Oklahoma City to Tulsa on several occasions. At one point we weren't even sure which storage center held our furniture. Our move from the only permanent house we actually owned had nothing to do with Dale, and everything to do with Caity Baby becoming so sick from asthma and what the doctors thought could have been cystic fibrosis. On the night of April 1, 1993, Caity became so ill that I could hardly get her to the emergency room in time. Of course, there were no doctors on call at the hour of the night that I brought the baby into the hospital, and just like you see now on television, I was screaming as I went through doors of the emergency rooms calling out for help. When a doctor was called and a nurse was summoned to start the ventilator I finally realized that Caity was turning blue from lack of oxygen. She would breathe. I don't know if it was instinct or a mother's mechanics, but I thumped the kid in the back with a considerable amount of force. The blow either upset her to the point that she wanted to wail at me, or it was exactly what she needed. Caity began breathing, and took the next twelve minutes of her life to shriek into my ear, alternating the oxygen mask between breaths, tears flying out of her two eyes, hands pulling out my hair, and legs kicking me in the privates as she thought about what she was being subjected to. It was the most wonderful moment as I realized my baby wasn't blue anymore, she was fully capable of perpetrating extreme pain to my groin, all the while puncturing my eardrums with her tantrums. I had to thank God, I had to praise Him right then and there for her nasty little I-will-not-die-you-can't-make-me attitude. It wasn't a week later that our house was sold, and we were moving to Midland, Texas so that my baby girl could have a fighting chance at gaining weight, size and the true ability to breathe on her own. I swear to God (and yes, I do that a lot) if He had given asthma to Laura instead of Caity I would have been interrupted in my sleep with a simple little wheeze and an apology. "Mother, I'm sorry . . . I'm such a . . . bother. I don't . . . . mean . . . . to . . . . die, but could . . . . you take . . . . me . . . . to the . . . . doctor.? Please . . . . and thank . . . you."

Not that Laura hasn't had her emergency room adventures. Wow . . . now that I'm writing this I realize that my children have nearly died more than a dozen times or more from whatever events take place in these uncertain times. Looking back at the memories that come to mind I think of the day I caught Laura and Caity doing cartwheels on a 4" beam-type railing that my dad had constructed around his house in the country. The house is actually a trailer that he has built any number of decks and porches around. At some points the decks are nine feet off the ground, at others they are only 4 feet from Terra Firma. You don't have to guess which end of the house the girls were turning flips on. It's rather like the day my dog realized he couldn't run along the top of the fence as he chased the birds and found himself on the other side of the fence facing the neighbor's rottweiler. I would have given anything to have recorded his facial expression at that encounter. But I digress.

Back to the emergency room adventure with Laura. We were living in Moore, Oklahoma, a sleepy little community nestled between Oklahoma City and the University of Oklahoma in Norman. Being a working mom, I had the responsibilities of picking up the kids, getting the groceries, paying the bills, making dinner, and cleaning the house before the kids were put to bed. Dale worked nights and was unable to do much of the daily chores which somehow were pushed onto me even though I worked as a legal secretary and had a part time job selling insurance. It was sometime in February, I know there was snow on the ground, as I pushed the garage door opener, drove my 1992 White Mazda Protégé into the garage and told the kids to sit still while I unloaded the groceries. I would only be a minute, I put Reuben in charge. That wasn't the most intelligent decision, as he was not quite six at the time. Nevertheless, both the girls were in their car seats in the back of the car, the groceries were in the trunk, and as was my habit, I had left the garage door leading to the house open so the cat could do her business in the cat box located in the garage. If things had gone to plan I would have been back in 30 seconds, the groceries set on the counter or in the frig in the sacks, where I could deal with them later . . . that didn't happen.

Laura, who couldn't bear to be without her mother for more than 10 seconds began climbing out of her car seat. She was only two and a half years old, but fully aware of the mechanical workings of the buckle strapped across her chest. With the front door of my car open so that I could make easy access back to my family, Laura crawled out of the back seat, over the front seat, fell out of the car completely, and raised her tiny head off the ground where she had smacked it. The front door design of the 1992 Mazda Protégé, I soon realized, were made in such a way that the door comes to a severe point. This severe point met my daughter's forehead as she lifted her tearful, screaming face off the garage floor. My son left the car shouting at me, trying to tell me that Laura got out of her car seat. I couldn't see her because she was literally on the ground in a dark garage, with her head completely attached to the bottom of the door of my car. When I did manage to find her I was immediately struck with the impossible task of getting her head unstuck. They don't teach you these things in college . . . . there is no manual wherein you can look up this sort of need in a section marked *"Troubleshooting when your child's head must be removed from the edge of your car door"*. Without blinking, I placed my right foot on top of Laura's head and pushed her head off the car door. In one swift move I picked Laura up, opened the passenger door, and swung her back into her car seat. I called out to Reuben, telling him to go next door to get the neighbor to watch him and Caity. Reuben was already getting Caity out of her car seat. I remember driving off with the back of the trunk open because I had not closed it after getting my groceries out.

This was during the days of big, fat, heavy, car phones. The neighbor I asked Reuben to run to wasn't home. I could see this as I drove past her house to the nearest hospital. I called another neighbor whose number was on speed dial. I quickly explained my situation to her, and like an angel Lori Weeks came to my rescue. She lived next door and was so down to earth and sweet I knew she would be able to handle the children in a crisis. Just as before, there were no doctors on call at the little hospital, and I found myself calling out for help the second I came into the emergency room. Laura, unlike my blue baby Caity, was not quiet. The Republic of China could have heard her crying and calling out "No, No!" as I fought time and what I assumed death, to find someone with a medical degree. Within a few minutes I had convinced the E.R. assistant that I was not about to take time to answer her questions at this time. I would answer them as my child received medical attention, yes, I did have insurance, I would be giving her the card just as soon as I could, but that if she didn't do something at this very second, I would be bringing down the Health Department, my attorney, and every professional I could find to close the hospital down immediately for putting my child in further danger. I think she believed my tyrant behavior. It was either that, or the look in my crazed eyes as I demanded attention for my baby. It has never ceased to amaze me how a small town hospital with a limited staff can assume that there will not be an emergency on any given day at any given minute. When life and death swing in the balance, please people, hire the staff necessary to perform whatever is necessary. I realize our health insurance capabilities in this country could be better, but to under staff intentionally is begging for law suits.

Laura's head had not bled. This was not a good sign to the doctor. He realized that the wound had to be deep if I were telling him the truth about how I had managed to get her off the edge of the front door of my car. He looked at me, asked me to hold her tightly, as he took a long pair of a tweezer looking instrument and gently pulled the inverted flap of baby skin on my daughter's forehead, just above her right eyebrow. Upon doing this, an immediate gush of red blood spurted forth out of her head, causing she and I both to scream with fright. I screamed because it hit me in the face, she screamed from either the pain, or the shock of seeing that much blood coming out her own face. Though they tell us that head injuries bleed worse, and that most of the time these sort of injuries look worse than what they are, Laura and I were both rather put into shock from the blood flowing all over the emergency room floor. The nurse assigned to help the doctor was not only equipped at handling the noise coming from my child, she managed to give me clear directions as to how to hold Laura for the suturing procedure. Six tiny stitches were required on the outside of the wound, eight on the inside. I couldn't believe the way her tiny chest expanded and released during each knot. It was as if she was telling the world that she was being killed and I was helping the people hold her down to do it. I cried like I had never cried before, but even through this moment of pain, hurt, torture, and healing, I remember whispering to Jesus for help. I remember whispering to Jesus to be with the doctor, to be with the baby, to be with me . . . . I cried again as the nurse reached past my body, which was literally laying on Laura to hold her in place, as she stated out loud that *Jesus* was a welcomed name in the E.R. I left the hospital feeling the power of God, and knowing that even though bad things happen to good people, I am absolutely never alone. I don't have to think I am, I don't have to fear that I will ever be left out in the cold without a way to escape hard times. Having just a *little faith* is better than having a great deal of hope.

Sometimes having a family can be challenging in other ways. I don't know how it happens, or why it happens, but my children and I never have been on the same time table. When they're born they wake up when they want to, forcing me to feed them. People told me to put them on my schedule . . . right! You do it. You come over to my house, and you tell this wiggling, screaming, take-no-prisoners brat to shut up, go to sleep and get over himself. You come over to my house at 2:43 a.m. on a Tuesday, when I have to get out of bed at 6:00 a.m., and you tell the little tyke that she will be given a bottle when it's time to give her one. Diapers can wait, feedings can wait, train the kid to do what he or she is suppose to do, that way you can rest and the entire parenting experience can be a rewarding one. Let me know the success rate on that one. Maybe I can get a grant to study the likelihood of that happening any time soon.

Chapter Three

It's time to introduce my other family, the one I started out with. Stone Mountain, Georgia. Dad, Mom, two sisters, a brother and me, 1972.

Journal entry: (revised)

"We left Grandpa with the animals, he can handle it, what was he by now? 81? If I was born when he was 71, and I'm 10 now . . . then yes, he must be yes, 81. Wow . . . he's getting old. It was just last year that he was only 80 and getting into the lake with me. He only has one leg, the doctor took off the other one and he has a big heavy wooden leg with his shoe attached to it. We went swimming and he just stood there. Then he got out of the water, but when he did he fell into it and his leg popped off. It's not like it hurt or anything, he was laughing, but his leg was floating out to the buoy. (I think you spell it that way). I had to go get it and since it had a strap on it, I just put it in my mouth and paddled back. That was hard. There was a lady with her kid on the beach laughing at me but that's OK, Grandpa needed to laugh after that. I think it's funny because on Sunday I saw him dusting his foot off. It was just something that struck me as being funny that's all. We left him with the animals; Rover, and Lady Wayne, our dogs, and he can feed them and make sure the mail gets brought in. Our mail box is too small for three days worth of stuff. I think about that and I don't know why. We're going camping again, but this time we're going to Stone Mountain, Georgia, all the way to the other side of the country. I'm in the back again, but I don't care. I'll sleep."

Three weeks of camping and the thing is, we didn't realize that our 14 foot Shasta trailer was in stark contrast to everyone else's nice big trailers. I guess Mom realized it, but we kids didn't know. We knew we had to walk the block to the bathhouse to use the toilets and showers, and we knew that Dad and my brother Mike had to sleep in the back of the truck because there were only three beds in the trailer and 4 girls. We knew that we had to use a cooler instead of a real refrigerator, but that thing was always full to the hilt with orange and grape *CRUSH*. There's no way we cared about silly things like bigger and better living facilities. What do kids know? We swam in the lake and laid on the white beach, totally ignoring the fact that a chain gang wearing striped pajamas and who were shackled to one another were literally building that beach truck load by truck load. The authorities told us to stay away from the prisoners, they told us that they couldn't talk to us, but these men were really very friendly. One even told me I was pretty and that I reminded him of his own little girl Lily. Lily, that's a pretty name. I didn't tell him my name, and it was partly because I wasn't sure of it. I was just then at that time in my life beginning to play with the name I wanted to be called. My dad had always called me JUDE and my mother called me JUDY. My brother called me Boot, which came out of a name game of Judy Booty. My teachers called me other things when they thought I wasn't listening, but I was always listening. Just because I didn't show up to school and sit in their class didn't mean I wasn't there! I usually could be found. I liked my little hiding places around Apollo Elementary. I was in the fourth grade and fourth graders hide a lot.

It was about the same time, maybe a year before, that I had decided not to match my socks anymore, and this particular summer was a perfect time to make sure on my promise to my mother who told me that if I wasn't going to actually match my socks and put them in the drawers where they belonged, she had better never see me wearing them matched ever again. FINE! I wouldn't match my socks and she couldn't make me. I would unmatch them in fact. I didn't know my name necessarily, and I liked it better when my Grandpa called me Pumpkin anyway. Sometimes I thought about the mail box being too small to hold a pumpkin and sometimes I thought about putting socks in it just to surprise my mom. I liked 1972, the music was awesome. I remember being in love with so many different singers and bands. My favorite of course, was (and still is) the Bee Gees. I had a few of their records and even an album called Cucumber Castle, but one of the Brothers Gibb, Robin, wasn't on it. It didn't matter, Maurice was, and he was really the cutest anyway. He had to be a little shorter than Barry was, but he looked much better in tights. He had a dog too, in the pictures, and there was even a song about dogs on the album. I loved dogs. I loved Maurice, I loved the Beatles, I loved Elvis. I think mostly I loved looking in the fan magazines and seeing more boys than I even knew could be singers. Neil Young was good too, my sister had his records, but he wasn't cute.

My sister Linda was in love with Bobby Sherman and David Cassidy. She told me I couldn't love them so I didn't. It didn't matter because I was going to marry Maurice. He was English. That was until 1977, when I decided I was going to marry Derek Longmuir of the Bay City Rollers. He was blond too, and he played the drums. He was Scottish, so I decided that my last name was Scottish. I told everyone it was, but in the real world I knew it was English.

My friend Robin (not the member of the Bee Gees) was my age and we used to walk our dogs together. We had been really close bestest friends since before kindergarten because my dad worked with her mom and my mom watched her. She didn't need babysitting because she wasn't a baby. She told me so, and I believed her. I was the same age and I didn't need a babysitter either. Robin loved Derek too and we were both going to marry him. I told her she could have him half the week and I could have him the other half. This didn't seem to bother her so the deal was struck. Besides being in love with the same musicians Robin was a musician herself. She could play the piano and she didn't even need sheet music in front of her. I used to sit on the stairs in her house and pretend to be in a mansion. Her house, a ranch style two story house, was a mansion compared to mine, but nevertheless, I used to sit on the stairs and pretend that I was in the moors of England in my mansion and Derek didn't mind being in England instead of Scotland because he had been living in Scotland all of his life. We could live happily anywhere and Robin liked England too. This fantasy was a good one.

In 1978, just a mere 18 months from the time I had decided to marry Derek and share him with my bestest friend, I had become much more mature about relationships. I was no longer going to marry the drummer of the Bay City Rollers because I was in love with a real guy who lived in the same city that I did. I was going to marry him instead. He went to my school and he was tall, blond, and played football. Football, it would seem, took up more of my time than anything else at this point. I found myself sitting on the bleacher seats outside during practice. It didn't matter if it was raining, snowing, hot as hell, or just perfect enough to fly a kite. I watched the boys play ball. I wanted to understand the game completely so that I could impress my new conquest. He and I would have football babies and we'd go off into the world together with or without Robin. In fact, it was going to have to be without Robin, or as she also had changed the spelling of her name, and was now being called Robyn, because her circles had not included me for quite some time. My new best friend was Jeannie Larwig, two grades higher than me in school, but she didn't have any problem with me wanting to graduate a year early, or with my new obsession with "Blondie" or football. She even came over to watch it on television with me from time to time. Jeannie couldn't make up her mind which of the Bay City Rollers she liked but she was dead set on being in love with Barry Gibb. Barry was the oldest Gibb of the Bee Gees and that was fine with me since I was still secretly in love with Maurice. I did find his marriage to Yvonne somewhat annoying, but after all, he hadn't met me before he proposed marriage to her, so I suppose all is fair when something like that happens. That, and the fact that he was nearly 12 years older than me, a famous rock star, and that we had never met.

Jeannie had a real stereo and it even had an 8-track cassette player, something my one armed record player didn't. By this time I had acquired quite a few 8-tracks including the Bee Gees' Mr. Natural, which had another song about dogs on it, and Jeannie liked dogs as much as I did. Jeannie, like Robin, had been born into a family with just a tad more money than my own. I lie of course, she was the daughter of a very affluent family on both her mother and her father's side, but to look at how she dressed, carried on, and even talked, you wouldn't have known she was anything other than normal . . . poor like me. We hit it off the first minute we saw each other because we had so many things in common; boys, football, and the Bee Gees. And doughnuts.

It was Jeannie who went to the Bee Gees concert with me in 1979, when I saw and met Maurice for the first time. Infact, it was Jeannie, and still is Jeannie, who I call my best friend. She and I have been to many concerts and events together, but the highlight of our years as friends had to be the August 4, 1979 Bee Gee concert in Oklahoma City. Neither she nor I can remember what led up to the moment really, but both remember the second the two of us spotted one another in the hotel lobby or foyer. Strangely, I recall the first glance as if it was happening still. I hadn't been such a fan that I was going out of my way to go up to their room; however we were staying in the same hotel on the floor below the Bee Gees and their people. As I was coming back from checking a message at the front desk Jeannie called my attention to the fact that the Bee Gees, or at least Robin and Maurice, were walking through the lobby on their way to the elevator. She called out my name and Maurice answered her. He said "What?" as if she had called him instead. For a second we stood about four feet from one another and stared at each other without a single word. Robin was trying to get Maurice's attention because the elevator (the lift as he called it) had arrived. Robin had not wanted to ride the elevator, saying he preferred the stairs, but they were staying on the 10th floor. No one really paid the least bit of attention to what Robin was saying except for Jeannie, who related the one-sided conversation to me later. Robin ended up taking the elevator up, not waiting on Maurice, who had been so distracted that he hadn't moved. I couldn't explain the feeling exactly, and I can't tell you now what it was that was happening, but it has been a source of reoccurring peace in my mind every time I think about it. We both sort of half smiled and he said to no one in particular, "Oh, I'm sorry, I thought you were talking to me." Jeannie nodded toward me as if to say, No, I was talking to my best friend. Putting out my right hand I shook Maurice's, and without talking we just stood there. No one else was there. Nothing was around us, it was as if the air was missing as well, but I didn't care. He couldn't stop looking at me, and I was not about to stop staring back at him. "I know you." He said.

"I know. I know you too." I replied

"No," he continued, "I mean, I think I know you. We've met before. A very long time before now. I don't know when." He questioned himself.

"I know, it was before—" and I stopped suddenly. I couldn't believe the words were about to come out of my mouth. I wasn't necessarily into the metaphysical in 1979.

"Are you coming to the concert?" he asked.

"Yes, we've got floor seats. We're staying on the 9th floor by the way. Room 906."

"Come to my side of the stage when the show starts. I'll tell Steve to let you stand there. I have to go." And with that, he was leaving.

"Jude. My name is Jude."

"I know. I don't know how I know that, but I know." His elevator returned and he never stopped smiling and as the doors shut he was shaking his head as if to clear a cobweb.

Those words took me to the moon instantly. Nothing sexual. Nothing out of the extreme, just a meeting of someone who thought perhaps we had been friends in another time. I wasn't into that sort of thinking at the time. Today I know more about when we met for the first time and Maurice had been right. It was many years before that concert encounter. My faith at the time of our meeting was embedded in what I call the Baptist Box. It is a safety net really, a place where I had been trained, conditioned, and held in complete harmlessness. The only problem with the Baptist Box is that it would not allow outside thinking. My heart was hurting, pounding in fact, my head trying to reach beyond that which I was accustomed to, but to no avail. I couldn't release the seams of that box. I didn't realize it at the time, but over time I would have to squeeze out of the box entirely if I had any hope of living by faith. I read a quote recently by Robin Gibb, Maurice's fabulous twin brother. He stated that he didn't see why he couldn't pretend, or think of Maurice as being alive still in this world, if people were saying that people existed in other worlds after they had passed away. Like Robin, I can't see or think of Maurice as being dead. He isn't dead. He did die, but only for a second or two really. After his passing, he came right back to us. To anyone that is who is willing to let him in. I don't pretend that Mo is alive, he is alive. What are the options? No, really, what would the options be if we didn't have faith? Why would preachers, priests, those we love, and family or friends SAY that someone is in another place if they didn't think it true? This faith is different from what we're taught in Sunday School, I understand that, but in the past few years since his passing, I have seen, felt, heard, sang with, danced with, loved, and been loved by Maurice Ernest Gibb in a very sweet and kind manner. I can't say why, how, or much more about it, but the smile on my face is real, and the pain in my heart gone. He is alive. Robin . . . he is alive, and he is here. I love your faith, and it helps. It really helps to know that faith is universal, deep, different, shared, and accepted in so many forms.

It wouldn't be right to not mention an incredible legacy left by Mo through his beautiful daughter Samantha and her band MEG. MEG, of course stands for *Maurice Ernest Gibb*, and has been performing for quite a few years under a couple of names in Miami. MEG has recently released their first major CD titled simply *MEG the Samantha Gibb Project*. You have to listen to it; Sam's voice creates a medley of field and flowers against a backdrop of youth and experiences that only the daughter of a very talented music man can produce. I think of Amy Lee from *Evanessence*. Maurice's son Adam also provides additional lyrics, some written with Lazaro Rodriguez, Samantha's longtime boyfriend and the band's technical and guitar lead. Maurice actually produced most of the songs on the CD, perhaps the best way in my opinion to keep his heart alive. MEG consists of Nik Sallons on Bass, Brando Garcia on guitar, Kris Morro on drums and the silent man, sound genius simply known on the *www.megmusic.net* website as "Gabe". You guys are awesome! Keep the music burning!

Chapter Four

Flash forward—30 years. Family: for me it is myself, my son, a football playing, football eating, football breathing, football pooping boy with nothing on his mind other than the strategies, tasks, challenges, statistics and schedules of the game. Where Reuben is not the son of the boy I was in love with in High School, he certainly could have been when you consider the vast connection he has to the gridiron. There is Laura, my docile, sweet-natured daughter who takes in every stray animal she finds, even if she must convince it to follow her home in order to become an official stray, and there is my younger daughter Caity, who, as before mentioned, is a demon posing as a little girl. Wouldn't you have loved to have seen the look on Satan's face the day Caity took Christ into her heart? Not that any of us ever doubted that it would happen in the first place, but to be quite honest, she has been what some would call an unorthodox Christian. For Caity there was never the restraint of the Baptist Box. She had managed to live within the confines of an invisible boundary which simulated the Box, but thank goodness, it was *"more or less a guideline"*; to steal a phrase from Captain Barbosa! Even her baptism was somewhat of a fluke. We happened to be at a creek one day in the early spring of 1999, when Caity announced that she was ready to be baptized. The only suitable person handy was my friend Nancy Henry, who's credentials included being a Christian, a flower-child, and the daughter of a Baptist preacher. Her father had passed away, but she was sure he would be able to guide her through the event. Cold as the water was, my little girl got into it, stood freezing her butt off as she was completely immersed and as she was *"raised to walk in forgiveness of Christ"* by my good friend, the clouds began to break and God gave us a little smile through a ray of sun. It was official. Family: I'll keep mine. Usually people would say that I don't find it the least bit difficult to talk about myself. Perhaps writing for prosperity may prove to be a different experience for me. I can tell you that I am a well educated woman, this much cannot change from one person's opinion of me to the other. I hold a PhD in

Administration, and a Masters degree in Literature from Oklahoma City University, a private college in the heart of the capital city where tuition can run as much as ten times higher than the state colleges, however, due to its proximity to my office at the time I was attending college, Oklahoma City University was an easy choice to make. I could literally run to work a few minutes late having completed a class, go on my lunch hour for another class three days a week, and pick up a night class as well. Oklahoma City University doesn't offer any doctorate programs other than Law, and where I was fully capable of attending, the judge in my family court case made it perfectly clear to me that if I were to pursue a degree in Law I would be doing so without my children. Before you go off thinking that the judge doesn't have that much power, I need to remind you that I not only agree with you, I made my point in court, which cost me several months of custodial rights as well as my standing with the good judge. It wasn't until I was able to hire the junkyard dog of an attorney that I ended up with, that I was able to make the slightest bit of sense of the laws as they were interpreted by the judge in my case. It seemed to me as if she made up the rules as she went along, and while she was doing that, she decided that I wasn't necessarily important enough to be in the courtroom when she handed down her judgments against me. Obviously, truth was completely out of the question, it all boiled down to what my attorney knew that my ex's attorney didn't know, what my attorney could use as leverage over the judge, and how far she was willing to use her wisdom of the laws in court without blackballing herself for any future cases. I just knew that at any given moment the two red-headed bitches, my attorney and the judge, would be going at each other with case law flying, decisions being challenged, and compromises being reached, all without my knowledge of what I was agreeing to; without Anita Sanders standing in as counsel, I can say now that I would not only have lost custody permanently, I would probably have been hauled away to the pokey for suggesting that the judge in my case actually go by the big, fat, statutory law books upstairs from her office located in the Law Library of the courthouse. I was quite sure I could have found at the very least three or so laws she had arbitrarily decided needed her personal touch before administrating them to me and to my family.

As I was saying, Oklahoma City University didn't offer a doctorate program, and I know enough to know that if I wanted to teach at the college level full time I would need at least one post graduate degree in whatever discipline it was that I wanted to teach. On line universities seemed to be the only option left, with a PhD In Administration, I remain to this day, an educator. That is not to say that I am paid well, in Oklahoma the words *"Education"* and *"Money"* seldom go hand in hand. More appropriately, the words *"Education"* and *"Adjunct"* go well, or *"Education"* and *"Unemployed"* go steady quite often as well.

Admittedly, I am a self-proclaimed arguer. It's not necessarily that I think the entire world would be better off if I were in charge, it's just that I think it would be a great idea to at least let me give it a good try at some level. I'm quite capable on paper to run a university or community college. According to my resume I've taught at, written for, researched, and been employed by several colleges and/or universities. Adjunct here, adjunct there, here an adjunct, there an adjunct, everywhere an adjunct. Do I seem bitter to you? I drove 86 miles a day to work three days a week, and 44 miles a day two days a week, for longer than I care to remember. Working for three separate colleges, teaching three entirely different types of students every semester, keeping my books, bags, papers, and supplies in the back of my already overcrowded trunk, trying to convince the administrations of each facility to hire me full time. It was always the same answer, no money in the budget. No money this semester, no money in the future, not unless we get another endowment. It was unlikely that any of the crusty old dogs on campus were going to die any time soon. Students had been secretly praying for that miracle without me even suggesting it. Chapel at one of the colleges I worked at could certainly be a lively event when the students decided to actually wake up and be counted. I remember a girl praying that she got her period! Needless to say, she was asked not to return the following semester. I was asked to fail her if I could. Such is the way of life at a private Christian based university in the Bible Belt of America. Being a Christian myself didn't eliminate me from the claws of the traditionally minded gargoyles sitting in their oak chairs above the mossy walls of the old rigid school. I made the mistake of wearing a Viking helmet on October 31, declaring the day to be a wonderful day to study pagan rituals as a means of understanding the differences in the various religions students would be faced with once they graduated and left the hallowed grounds of the sacred campus. Needless to say, I was not asked to return the next semester! Such is the way of life at a private Christian based university in the Bible Belt of America.

If my faith wasn't tested during my failing marriage, as I tried to struggle with the questions of whether or not to forgive my husband's philandering, it was certainly tested as I applied for jobs in the state of Oklahoma under the impression that an education and experience were all that is necessary to be hired full time at a state or private university in the capacity of an English Professor. How wrong I was; how could I have known that being able to work 18 hours rather than the national average of 12 is required. How could I possibly compete with candidates who are married to staff members, administrators, legislative members, and those who are employed by the state of Oklahoma? If the world was somehow suppose to be fair in its dealing I wasn't made aware of it. Semester after semester I drove from one far reaching county to the next, adjunct teaching and teaching two or three classes a day for less than what could be considered decent pay, without benefits, and without the respect given to full time faculty. Certainly I deserve to be hired, if experience and education mean anything. Until then, I'll write.

Chapter Five

Faith is a strange and unique choice we make, something we intentionally intend to do. It isn't fate or what may happen. It is, if you can understand it, the actual force behind the reason we believe something will or must happen. I use the word choice because it isn't an emotion. It isn't something that you take lightly, use without consideration, or put up on a shelf to take down during the ravages of a storm or tornado. That would be the word *"prayer."* According to the author of Hebrews (who is that anyway?) Faith is the substance of things hoped for, the evidence of things unseen. Faith completes my prayer life as I conclude with the words "In Jesus' name", without the evoking of the name itself there is no hope for an answer to whatever the petition may be. *Faith* is the reason we look for the sun to come up in the morning, not hope. We already know there is a promise given that there will be another tomorrow. Believing it, living your life as if you know it will happen, that's faith. By faith I was able to face the judge over and over again, even though in times past she had continuously made monumental statutory errors in her rulings. There was always something inside of me that said "She can't do that, you can get another attorney, you can prove to her and to everyone else willing to listen that she's not legally allowed to take these actions against you. Keep the faith, keep the faith, keep the faith." I remember the day my wicked and wretched judge leaned up out of her chair when I had corrected her, this was before I had proper representation, but at a time when it was obviously clear that the law was on my side. She leaned up out of her chair on the platform, shook her face and hand at me and demanded of me as to whether or not I was an attorney! She repeated herself twice, and I was hoping to find her threats being recorded, only to find out that her clerk was not required to record everything that happened in her courtroom; only those things during which time the judge was controlling what was being recorded. My answer to her was not a timid one. I did not back away from her frightening expression as I remarked to her that I was not an attorney, but that the plaque on her desk clearly read that she was a JUDGE, and that by definition she knew what she was legally capable of doing, it was not up to me to make the decisions which were already made for all of us having been set in case law many years before. (Did I mention that my mouth has gotten me into more trouble than most?) I told you being honest about myself may prove to be a difficult task. Faith in the justice system, faith in the statutes, faith in the fact that I knew she had to be controlled by someone, led me to answer her in the manner that I in fact answered her. The results of my answer, faithful as they may have been, were devastating. I lost my kids temporarily, I was held in contempt for my outburst, and it took two more years and three lawyers later, to force the hand of the judge to do what the laws said she must do. Faith is likened to food for me, it's something I have to have, but it doesn't always satisfy at the time that I want it to be satisfying. I have to wait just like everyone else.

If I were to be completely honest about it, I would have to admit to you that I never wanted to teach a single student, not ever. I wasn't going to be a teacher. Teachers were underpaid, never thanked, and hardly ever respected beyond the 16th week of the semester. I knew I hated a few of the teachers I had growing up. I couldn't wait to blow out of their classes, and away from their tyrannical rule! Teachers represented to me those who had grudges to bear, students to flunk, and people in subordinate positions to chew on just long enough to make themselves feel that much better in the first place for having chosen a career without a path. I was never going to be a teacher, I was going to be a lawyer. Thank you judge, thank you. Through her unlawful misuse of the laws of the state of Oklahoma, she was able to force me to give up a dream, only to dive into a whirl of light. I can't tell you now, how many times I have believed in someone more than they have believed in themselves—to work with them, show them the various ways and methods of success . . . and then, when the light bulb glows just above their heads . . . . miracles happen. I may not ever stand in a court room and defend an innocent mother of three, but I can say without regret that I have taught more than a couple of hundred of these women, and in the classroom I have far more say, far more ability to make an impact on the lives of their children and their children's children if I can guide them down the road of success through learning and applying the strict rules of grammar, literature, writing, and research. I am a teacher.

Chapter Six

Even writing this book is a test in faith. I really did not have a good time of it. When I think about it, it is as if someone didn't want me to start the book, let alone to finish it. My first thought of course, was to wake up in the mornings and sit at my home computer, write a few lines every day, get the book started, maybe get a few ideas from the novels and great books I have sitting perfectly still on my bookshelves. I would want to read a few of them first, and get a feel from the various successful authors how to write, what to do with styles, you know, steal a few ideas. I sat up the desktop, put a new screw in the chair because I had remembered that it would flop around on me when I sat up straight; all the things you do just to prepare yourself to work a little. When I turned my computer on it would literally take about 11 minutes for it to boot up and I couldn't force it to run faster when I yelled at it. I don't know about you, but I use hand gestures, dancing moves, facial expressions and even deep-throated threats when I want my personal home computer to obey my verbal and keyboard commands. It absolutely refused. Sat there as if it had the right to mock me. I showed it, I called my guru student, the one I caught skating through English the entire semester; however, he was able to rebuild every computer in our lab class, downloading free ware, taking off unnecessary materials and files. He was constantly tapping away at the keys and seemed lost inside his little world . . . I nearly cried when I had to stop him long enough to go home to his beautiful wife. "Hey, John, remember, class is only three hours once a week . . . . you actually have a life. Oh, and you have an essay due next week too, it's on Blackbeard." I won't tell you what John deserved on his essay. I gave him an A. He worked it over and over and rewrote it, finding ways to improve himself on his language skills. My home computer, following the semester, became a breathing monster when he was finished with it. I swear it could bake cookies if I asked it to. So why wasn't it working now? In a word . . . . Caity.

"John, she did it again. She found a way to hack into your password and she's downloaded Spyware, SWAT this and SWAT that, and every other means of tracking down government agency information on criminal types . . . like herself!"

"Don't worry Professor, I'll be right over." John was such a great student, he had paid someone to finish his essay on Blackbeard in record time; just so he could help me! What a guy! "John, when you come bring that movie you downloaded last week, the one my kids said was too gross for me. I'll make the decision."

"It is too gross for you Professor." he added

"Fine, get me another one, they can't have all the fun."

"How about 'Finding Nemo'?" he asked

"Sure."

While John decided my computer was fried and needed his undivided attention for a few days, I couldn't wait. I needed a computer now. Reuben had one. I could use it, or so I thought. It took a little faith on my part to go into my son's apartment to even use his computer. Most of the time boys are a little messy, and from time to time they even leave things about their apartments that they wouldn't want their moms to find. My son fits the bill when it comes to the mess; clothes on the bathroom floor, cards thrown on the table, pizza boxes everywhere. I used to think he used Little Caesars as a decor theme, until I realized that he was simply avoiding having to take the oversized boxes three city blocks to the nearest dumpster. Why can't apartment managers understand the need for more big blues? It only makes sense, put a few more dumpsters on the premises and there would likely be less cockroaches, less mice, less mess . . . maybe I can get a grant to study this theory. They give government grants out for everything else. I'll have Caity hack into the Pentagon again and find out. She owes me.

Reuben plays a game with me. I told him I would be using his computer so he set up his apartment to be "mom-ready" as he called it. When I walked in the door there was big wooden sign pointing to his room, on the sign he had hung a paper message it read: "Don't look in the box on the left side of my closet." Another paper message was on the refrigerator, it read: "Don't ask whose beer is in here. You don't like her." I opened the door of the refrigerator, I knew my baby boy hated the taste of beer. Why would he allow someone I didn't like to bring over her beer, and if he did, why would he tell me I didn't like her. Why couldn't he let me think he was keeping the beer for a friend, or for that matter, maybe I wanted one. I looked inside, and all I found was another note: "Made you look! You know I wouldn't do that!" I didn't look in the box in his closet. I thought maybe he'd have stacks of books in the box. Proving to me that he was actually reading. If that ever happened I don't know what I would do. I like thinking to myself that I actually know my son. The day he reads for pleasure may be the day my heart gives out for the last time. I left the box alone and said a little prayer for my son, or rather for his future. "Dear God, give him hell. Make him the father of twins exactly like himself . . . no, make them eat more if that's physically possible, and God, when they visit Grandma, make them pick up their clothes and pizza boxes. Why should I have to go through this again?"

Reuben's computer was in his room, crammed between the wall and his king size bed. That's when it hit me; why did he have a king sized bed in a 12 x 11 room? Why did he have a king sized bed when I only had a full? Why did he have a king size bed? Who gave my son a king sized bed? Note to myself, ask Reuben about the bed and find out why he has a better computer too, he doesn't even know John. I sat at the desk, pushing the chair back as far as the edge of the bed, and realized that my stomach was literally touching the cabinet that held the computer. How in the world was this going to work? I'm not that big of a woman, but I was squashed between the bed and the cabinet, trying to get the computer to turn on, boot up, and obey my every command. My arms could wave, at least I had that. What did he have downloaded on this machine that took it forever to start up? I can go to CONTROL PANEL, I can look up what is to be added or removed, but I don't have a clue as to what the files are, or what importance they carry in terms of whether or not I'd fry the machine if I took them off. I decided to sit on the edge of the bed and simply lean over to type. Extending my arms, squinting to see the monitor, I realized that this simply wasn't going to work How in the world did this boy do anything on the computer? Every time I would try to type something on his keyboard little pieces of pepperoni or what was left of one popped out of it. Maybe he thought he was suppose to feed the electronic mouse or something. The screen went blank after a while, and it was obvious to me that he had placed a password on the machine just in case his friends wanted to do a little porn searching. The password screen wouldn't disappear. I tried everything I could think of: FOOTBALL, TACKLE, PLAYBOOK, PIRATES, his number, #63, nothing. I went the route of the only other interest in this boy's life: PIZZA, BURGER, FOOD, TACO, I knew he didn't know how to spell LASAGNA. Note to self: Get Reuben a twin sized bed. Second note to self: Laugh! Where would he put the other half of his king-sized body? I suppose as time surrenders itself to the rest of the world, and I am cognitive enough to notice the thirty-five cent increase in bread at Wal-Mart, I hadn't really paid that much attention to the fact that my baby boy was actually big enough to play linebacker for the state Championship football team . . . . oh wait, that's exactly what he was! Yes, third note to self: Thank God for little boys. Password? What was it? I tried the only thing I could think of at this point . . . PASSWORD. Bam! I was in, but to no avail. The boy didn't have Word or any other sort of writing software. At least I knew he had a relatively safe home to live in, he was eating, sleeping well, and wouldn't be able to write nasty notes to me online!

My quest to write continued and I found a friend with a nifty little lap top, but not until after I had driven about 300 miles inside the city limits tracking down a few of them that were reported in the newspaper, or from what I was told when I called every electronic store in the book. "Yes, we have laptops for under $200.00, they sell rather quickly, but you can see them if you . . . . oh, I'm sorry, we just sold out. You can try our competitor." I did that. I called every competitor in the area. My favorite was a guy in a little house on the south side. He was a bit spooky. I thought I liked him because he spoke with a little accent, he was always looking from one side to the other, and when he invited me into his tiny little entry way he asked me to remove my shoes. I didn't of course, pleading it as against my religion to put myself in the clutches of a would be murderer . . . he thought I was funny too. I walked past a graveyard for keyboards, an arsenal of mice, (do you call them mice if there are more than one?) It wasn't long before his pit bull "Blue" came out to see what I was doing. I realized Blue was all business and I stood perfectly still. "Did you go somewhere that I should be concerned about?" I called out to the little man. A voice rang out from under the house, perhaps a basement. "No, I'm in the cellar. I have a laptop somewhere down here. Don't pet the dog. He's really not very friendly." I believed him. Blue believed that I believed him. I prayed. I do that. I pray a lot. "Dear God, you remember Blue. You made him when you made all those other demons that you cast out of your Heavens that sultry afternoon way back when. Could you please tell him the story of Daniel in the lion's den, and how you will get around to feeding him later. I'm not really . . . ."

"Nope, couldn't find it. Must have sold it." Nothing more. He didn't offer any names of his competitors, he didn't ask me to call again, he didn't say a word. I stood there for about a time span of 20 seconds wondering if it was my turn to speak, or if he was going to ask me something. Finally, I spoke. "Well, thank you for looking." He reached his hand out and took Blue by the collar. I backed away. I drove away, I finished my prayer . . . "Thank you God! P.S. Don't ever let me be that stupid again. Amen."

Niki and Eric have been married about 17 or 18 years. They have kids like mine, all too smart, too pretty, and too busy to be bothered with parenting. I step in from time to time to remind one or the other of them that they actually do have to listen to their mom or dad. When I do they think it's strange, but not one of them has ever been rude or disrespectful. I would hope that if my children were saying things or doing things inappropriate (God forbid . . . .

hahahaha) that either Niki or Eric would step forward to pop one on the side of the head. That would be more of Eric's style, Niki, I'm afraid would try to reason. Why do people with her intelligence even think it's the correct method? I love Niki! Educated, beautiful, thin, (not skinny, she hates being called skinny) and a talented marathon runner. My feet hurt just looking at her. Eric, on the other hand looks like the Gorton Fisherman! Big-bellied, brawny, gruff, and bearded. I'm convinced these two met at a Halloween costume party. She thought he was . . . the Gorton Fisherman, and he thought she was an Angel. He was right. She married the king of the wharf, and they moved to Oklahoma to be close to me. I know they did. Somewhere in the back of their minds they hated living in Boston, hated the seven years they lived in Greece too, they were thinking out loud I'm sure "Somewhere out there is a land of beauty, grace, treasure untold, and there must be a talented and creative friend just waiting to be found." (Leave me alone, let me have my fantasy!)

They moved to Oklahoma because it was cheap and I lived here already. Besides, I am talented and creative, they do love me, and they loaned me their laptop! About two days into the writing process I noticed the computer had a software problem that I couldn't fix, and I had to give it back. If it wasn't one thing it was another. I couldn't get the time or the computer to write this book. Everytime I turned around I was being forced to give up a laptop, my own machine was incapacitated, my son's was impossible to figure out how to use, and I was losing the two weeks I had set aside to write. Two weeks. Can you imagine? Thinking about it I have to laugh. Authors of any success at all will write how the books they are working on take them years to write. I didn't have that luxury, I'm one of the poor American citizens. In fact, at the time of this writing I was not only an Educator in a poor state, making very little money, I had been fired from my position because my dog Faith had appeared in a nudey magazine. I'll write more about that in a subsequent chapter, but to tell you the situation I was in, I was unemployed, without enough money to feed my family really, looking for work, typing on broken or unusable machines, trying to afford a laptop I couldn't locate, and all the while saying to myself that this is a great book. It really is a great idea. If I can just get it out of my head and onto the screen. What screen? The problem was that I didn't have a computer. Where am I going to get this screen and will it work when I get it? Faith people. Faith. You gotta have it. If you don't look to a higher power to help you, you truly are on your own, and in my case it wasn't a good bet. I wouldn't bet on me. The last time I tried to do anything extraordinary I found myself standing in the unemployment line again. I have these really great ideas when I teach, its just that sometimes they don't work out. Like the time I thought I would get to work early so that I could get a few things done. Thinking back I remember now that my boss had told me to come a little after noon, I remember that now, but at the time I walked in on him doing a bit of cocaine! Fired. Right there, I was asked to leave. I don't think I was even allowed to get my things. He threw a few at me, but to say that I was given the opportunity to gather them would have been overstatement. Yes, I called the police, I made a report. I was still unemployed and I was still standing in line thinking to myself "Don't go to work early, don't go to work early." Things happen to me that never happen to anyone else, and for the life of me I can't tell you why. I can tell you this . . . it has made it impossible *not* to have faith. Faith is the proof of the fact that I do actually believe that no matter what happens to me I'm going to be OK. I believe that now because I've been OK for so long. Somehow I always wind up living and usually intact. There is something to this belief thing. Faith is good. Faith is very very good to me. Like Toby Keith says "Get ya some!" I think he was talking about babies, but still, it works with faith as well.

Niki and Eric encouraged me to try again with the stores in the area, and I found one. This one. I've taken it back a few times to have the keyboard replaced, Word needed to be installed, it needed to be given a new battery and floppy drive, but other than that it's a fine little machine. I had faith, and at times that requires an enormous amount of work as well, but nevertheless, I am writing, and the book is being written. Finally. I hope you like it.

Chapter Seven

I wanted to talk about some of the things that my family and I went through before we were given our dog Faith. I want you to understand that we're a normal, typical family, that things happen to us, and that because we have faith, things work out. It isn't always easy, in fact, it never is easy. Where is that guy who told us that the world was fair? Where is he? I want to pop him in the mouth for lying. We were kids when we learned to play fairly. We were told that we should be fair, that it was the right way to be. Where this is true, I also tell my kids that it won't usually be given back to you. You play fairly, and you are to be as fair as you can be with others, but to expect less from them. I'm not a pessimist. If anything I am an opportunist . . . I believe we can take the experiences given to us and find a better way. My favorite boss in the whole wide world, even better than when James Garner was my boss, is Mr. Moler. Mr. Moler, an attorney for the City of Nichols Hills, told me not to look for justice in the courthouse. He said it wasn't there, he said we make it. If we wanted justice we had to be willing to be the one that creates it for others in our lives. He couldn't have been more correct. Without fail every trip to the courthouse proved so opposing, so out of the ballpark when it came to fairness, that I often wondered why we have a judicial system in place at all if the judges are not going to be forced to use case law as precedent. If indeed they can arbitrarily decide for themselves what they will hear and what they will not hear in terms of the guts of a situation.

Having faith is a difficult and essential part of being a parent facing an uncaring, biased, unwilling judges of this world, real or in position, who have been assigned the duty to listen to people lie as they explain their reasons for having drug the one person they swore to love into the courtroom, now accusing them of immoral perpetude or worse. The job itself has to be damning, it's no wonder we don't have more of a suicide rate among our bench warmers, then again, perhaps they get their revenge by creating as much havoc from their vantage point onto the lower classes who dare to interrupt their lives with trivial matters such as accusations of child abuse, endangerment, lack of child support, broken promises, and worse, kidnapping. Mustering up the faith it takes to face the days in court is in and of itself a feat. One that takes more than what I personally am able to do on my own. Faith in my friends was important at this point. Faith isn't just about trusting and hoping in God, you've got to put your faith in others as well. You have to believe that they were sent here, put here, to help and that they have the abilities to help when you can't. I remember once I had a friend in court, a man I had never met. I was crying, the judge was displeased that I showed my emotions in her court, I was taking up her time. He came over to me, held my hand, looked at the judge and asked her to be patient, to wait just a minute, that a mother's heart was breaking before her, and that it needed some time. I never saw this man again, I probably never will again, but he was exactly what I needed when I faced the opposition.

In my personal case, my ex husband had been ordered to restrain his current wife from physically beating and hurting my daughters. He had been ordered not to use corporal punishment on the girls, and I had been ordered, (yes, ordered) by the court, not to call the police again when I suspected that my daughters had been beaten, abused, or neglected. How a judge in any state, for any reason, can think that he or she has the right to tell me I can't call the police is beyond me, but it is of record, that is exactly what she ordered. I was told that I was not to call the police again because I had called too often. With every call I had placed to the Oklahoma City Police Department I had been given a number, an assignment number, proving that the officers who had responded to the call had actually completed their task. Problems arose when one police officer merely said he had made the stop by the house on Rambling Road to see if the children were safe. I had called after a neighbor had called me to say that their father's wife was pulling Caity into the house by her ponytail, and that she had been kicking her in the legs while she was pulling her inside. I called the police and according to the report he filed, he had spoken with my daughter and nothing of the sort had taken place. I had not seen the event, but upon later conversations with my daughter the event was true, all except the part about the police officer questioning her. This became a concern of mine and I reported it to the correct authorities. The next thing I knew, I was being ordered not to call them if there was another problem. The logical conclusion is that the officer realized his mistakes but was unwilling to fess up to them. Instead, I was the bad guy. I was calling unnecessarily, I was overreacting as far as they were concerned. To tell the truth, I had called the police a great many times to see if my children were well and being taken care of because my children were calling me telling me that they were being left alone without food, that they were being hit by their father in the face, or on the legs with the buckle end of a belt for not doing the dishes. They reported that his wife had kicked one of my girls in the stomach for yelling at her son when he poured grape juice on the dog. Not having custody was not an option for me. I sought it at every cost, order or no order, I called the police when my daughter Laura called me screaming into the phone that this woman was again kicking Caity in the head out in the backyard. No neighbors came to her assistance when she screamed at them over the fence, however, one of the neighbors called the police anonymously, saying their father's wife was always doing these sort of things. Dale, for his part, quickly loaded the kids into his van after the police spoke with him, and drove away so as not to have to deal with the situation. The police responded to my next call because of his behavior, but I have to believe they did so under the influence of my neighbor's call, not mine.

It may be best to explain how things could have gotten so far out of hand. Dale and his new wife Bella lived in a house on Rambling Road. The house we had purchased after we had remarried. This was the house we were suppose to have started our lives over in. That didn't happen. In the original divorce decree he wanted the house, and it was understood that we would have *joint* custody of the children. Because I was returning to school, a mere freshmen, knowing it would take a few years to become established on my own, I allowed him to have *physical* custody, but not *controlling* custody. We were to make every decision about our daughters together. It was never a question as to whether he would be free to marry, or date, he had promised me, the girls, and even my parents that he was not going to disrupt the girls' lives with dating or marriage because they had been through too much. That lie lasted about as long as it takes a butterfly to breathe and die. Within sixty days of our divorce in 1997, Dale had met, dated, shacked up with, and married his new wife, a married woman who was pregnant with a third person's kid. Dale, a man who had at least claimed to be against abortions not only paid for her to have an abortion, he used money he had withheld from me to do it. He had owed me a couple of thousand dollars for the down payment on the house, or rather he had owed it to my parents. With this woman now living in the house, given her past of being married at least two other times, and of having been kicked out of at least two places for non payment, having been fired for alleged embezzlement, and knowing that she was under a doctor's care for extreme depression, and even a bipolar personality, I wondered what Dale must be thinking. It had been myself who had called Dale to let him know that she was married to a man in another county. Dale didn't want to use his own money to investigate the woman he was about to marry, and he knew I would do so without a problem because he intended on keeping her in his house. This was literally less than two months after we had divorced.

"She's married to a Tommy Beldner. It is registered in Stephen's County."

"Did she divorce him? She said she divorced him." he wanted to know.

"Her petition is filed, but it hasn't been finalized." I added

"Why not?" What's the hold up?", he asked

"She's being accused of infidelity, if you can believe that Dale, seems Tommy thinks Bella is sleeping around on him, what do you think?"

"Shut up! I just asked you to see if she was married. I don't need your preaching."

"Did you know she was married to a J.D. Skymaker before Tommy? Did you know her high school principal said she was married to someone else when she was a junior? Did you know she was fired from a financial company because she allegedly embezzled from them? Did you know she took drugs for being bipolar?"

"Shut up! I don't give a damn", he continued, "She does what you won't do, and you left me, remember?"

"I left you", I declared, "because you did things I wouldn't do! You had an affair, no, you had a lot of affairs! I was just nice enough to forgive the ones I knew about before we got married again."

"Fuck you!", he exclaimed

"Not now, not ever again. Thank you. You're married to a married woman!"

Having a little faith was not enough. At some point I had to take more action than was allowed by the law, and finally, after a beating, a kidnapping, finding another attorney, being ran over by a van, and finding Dale and Bella in contempt of at least 20 rulings, I had my day in court. MY day! This of course didn't happen all in one day, but that would have been nice. I wouldn't have had to live through the months of hell had it been limited to a 24 hour period of time.

Chapter Eight

March 4, 2001, Bella's birthday. Dale "allowed" me to have the children, as if he thought he had a choice, it was my weekend. I wasn't "allowed" to pick them up until he said so, and when he made the arrangements for me to pick them up they weren't ready, and I was forced to wait outside in my car for over an hour. I took the girls home, we had dinner, we talked and watched a movie, and the next day I took them to church. Dale wanted them back before 3:00 p.m. as the judge had ordered that I could only have them for a limited time following an error of my legal counsel from a previous fiasco. Even though it was proved in court that the error was made, I was having to obey rules which were not only damaging to the girls, they were out of line legally. My time with the girls had been shortened and it had not been reassigned when the opportunity arose. This to me was a blatant attempt on the part of the judge to prove she was indeed in control as she knew there were laws she had to obey, but she could certainly control my life as it pertained to the girls, that is until someone stopped her. It would be up to me, up to faith to find that person.

When I had kissed the girls and loaded them up to take them home Caity crawled into the car with a grimace on her face. "What is it" I asked. She raised up her pant leg and showed me a big bruise just under her left knee cap. "What the heck is that!" I asked. "Bella kicked me because I wouldn't get out of her chair." I was furious! I knew I couldn't call the police, but I also couldn't continue down the road that would lead to me dropping my children off with that monster. I handed Caity the cell phone. "Call 9-1-1", I directed her. "Ask for the Will Rogers Station, and tell them we're on our way to the make a report of child abuse. Do it now." Caity made the call. Of record, she even stated to the 9-1-1 operator her name, where we were driving at the time, and that her mom wasn't allowed to call the police because the judge told her not to. When we arrived at the police station we were met by a man whose concern about me having been ordered by the judge not to contact the police was evident. "You mean to tell me that a judge told you never to call us again?"

"That's correct. I was told that I had called you too often. Now look!" I told him as I pointed to Caity's knee.

"I'll take care of this one personally." He promised.

He and another officer took Caity behind the thick glassed entry and into an interview room where he photographed the bruise and took her story. He told me that under no circumstances was I to take the child home, that I was to go to the emergency room of the Children's Hospital, and that she was to be seen by a physician immediately. I did what he commanded. I allowed Caity to call her father to let him know that she and Laura were not coming home that evening. As I suspected, he called my cell a number of times. Seeing his phone number appear on the calling ID I did not respond nor did the girls respond. It was the first time that Laura had actively chosen not to talk to her father. She wasn't used to disobedient behavior, even if it was for the best.

We arrived at the emergency room doors of the hospital and met with a triage nurse. She asked us if we could possibly come back early in the morning, as she was sure the wait would be several hours. They were backed up, and a bruise was important, but not important enough to move ahead in the line. I was immediately reminded of the times I had taken my children to the E.R. when they were understaffed and I was screaming for help. I understood her situation completely, and decided to come back in the morning.

Before I went back to the emergency room of Children's Hospital on March 5, 2001, I called my legal counsel. The same mad man that had made the critical error in court just months before which had led to this new beating being possible. He happened to be downtown and he made an effort to come to my office to speak with me. For a man weighing over 300 pounds he managed to dress himself quite professionally. When I had first met him he seemed caring, interested in my case, and willing to help. In subsequent months and even years since the custody issues were being heard, he became too involved with his personal work on issues not dealing with Legal Aid. He had made comments about being underpaid. I wondered if he wanted me to make payments to him personally. I never made any, but I wondered if I were able to if he would be more likely to help.

He rode the elevator to the 28th floor and looked out of breath. He acted as if being my lawyer was an inconvenience, that Caity being injured did not fit with his daily schedule. He was acting rather strangely. In fact, he was acting as if he wasn't wanting to be my counsel at all. Where he was appointed by Legal Aid, I felt that he had obligations to me, obligations he obviously was not interested in upholding. He asked the girls to wait inside an inner office. He wanted to speak with me. He read me the riot act on having contacted the police about Caity's leg. I reminded him that child abuse was still illegal in the state of Oklahoma. He was not interested in helping me, but knew he had some obligation to inform me that he would be asking to be releaved of his duties because I failed to comply with court orders. I knew something was up. When the elevator bell rang I ran down the hall and held the door open. He asked me to step aside. I asked my children to get aboard. He demanded that I wait for another elevator, I demanded that we all ride together. The man was furious. Caity looked him in the eyes and lifted up her pant leg exposing the injured knee. "See it!" she demanded. "See what she did to me." This was all the law required. He now knew first hand what had taken place, and he couldn't resign, not until the matter had been resolved. "Damn you!" he whispered at me. "Not today!" I whispered back.

When the emergency doctors took Caity into their examining room they found more bruises than the ones we saw with the naked eye. She was literally covered in micro bruising from her head to her legs, bruises of various sizes, shapes, age and distinction. The doctors asked about a specific set of bruises to her arm, how did she come to have them. Caity explained that a few days prior to being picked up from her dad's house, she had been screaming names at Bella, and that her dad had twisted her right arm behind her. He had then shoved her into a corner with force. This bit of information warranted a closer look of her face, where more bruises were found under the skin, visible by alternative lighting. These marks were consistent with having been hit in the face, or having one's face hit the corners of two walls joining each other. There were bruises on her left cheek and her little nose. Considering the house for a second I asked Caity if she had been shoved into the corner of the foyer by the laundry room. She said she had. This was enough for the doctors and a report was made. Unfortunately, I was unable to get a writ of emergency from my underpaid and overworked legal counsel. He instructed me to return the girls to Dale or he would have reason to pull out of the case. What choice did I really have? At least I had the DHS involved, and I had proof of violent behavior. I knew I had to get another attorney, a real attorney, and that thought consumed me. I made less than $22,000 a year, how was I going to afford someone that would actually be able to do more for my girls? Through faith. This one would be up to God.

I returned the girls to Dale on March 5, 2001, after work. I remember giving them both names and numbers of their guardian ad litem, Glenda Tucker, and made them recite the number back to me. I was certain that Dale would not allow them to call me again, and I didn't know how long it would be before he decided to obey the order of the court and not hurt the girls. What I was certain of is that he would be very angry when he was made aware of the fact that the girls were the ones wanting the investigations. They had given interviews freely to the DHS workers, the hospital nurses, doctors, people who were sitting next to us at the emergency room, and virtually anyone who would listen to them tell their stories. When I think about it I am compelled to recall Pat Benetar's song *Hell is for Children,* a song about child abuse and how parents train and teach their children to tell little lies to cover up the mess they have created. "Tell Grandma you fell off the swing." My girls weren't shy at all, perhaps Laura continued to apologize for her father's behavior, saying that he didn't mean to hurt them, or that he didn't know Bella was hurting them, as she explained how they were being hit, kicked, pinched, spat at, and being called names that no one should endure. Names a father should certainly never use and names he should never allow his wife to use with regard to his own little dolls. These things did not matter to him or to his wife. What they did next was criminal and inexcusable. Faith was hard to come by on March 6, 2001.

By faith Moses put forth his staff and God parted the waters. By faith John the Baptist shoved locust into his mouth and God made them tasty. By faith Robert E. Lee signed a declaration which in a nutshell, ended the war between the states but it cost him more than he could possibly have imagined. What was gained of course, was a treaty of peace, the ending of bloodshed across a nation whose morals, ethics, and beliefs were strongly supported on both sides of the Mason-Dixon line. By faith I called out to God asking him to find my children and to keep them safe when it was reported to me by one of Laura's little friends that she had not been to school all week long.

Spring Break 2001 wasn't for another couple of weeks. For Laura not to be present at school meant that she was sick. Her father refused to answer my calls, he had caller ID as well, and try as I might, I was unable to get the interest of my attorney. When my daughters hadn't called me from the house of one of their friends, which had become a habit I appreciated, I decided to contact the schools. Laura was attending a middle school where my son was attending. He was an eighth grader, she a sixth. The principal knew me, and was well aware of the current situation in Laura's life, as the strangest stories and scenarios were being told not only by myself to her teachers, the principal, the nurse, and to her counselor, but they were being repeated by her friends as well. Several of Laura's concerned friends went into the principal's office, or the counselor's office to report that Laura's father had thrown away her home work, or that he had snatched her out of their house when she was given permission by him just an hour beforehand to play. They were concerned not only for her safety, but also because she was telling them that she wanted to live with her mother. She was afraid her father might physically hurt Caity. Laura rarely mentioned that her father might try and hurt her. She was always and forever concerned for her baby sister. Ironically, it was Caity that fought back with each attack, heaving loose bricks at her perpetrators, scratching and clawing her way out of a ponytail hold; and even flushing diamond rings down the toilet when her more aggressive behavior was not appreciated.

On the morning of March 13th I walked into the office of Cooper Middle School to speak with Dr. Ronald Green, a man I have always admired, not only for his ability to remain calm in just about every situation, but because he was wise enough to listen to the children in these cases, rather than making decisions based on the tales he heard from either side of the parenting camps. Naturally, as the principal at their school, it would be difficult to make a judgment call based solely on one side of the story. Every story has two sides, and in this case, the stories I told had multiple and unusual endings. We absolutely never knew what to expect out of Dale Stickley. He was literally capable of such grand scale destruction that to even guess at his irrational behavior was an exercise in futility. He would say the same thing about me in court, he would produce documents which were falsified, not certified, and the police would trust him because he was so calm. I was afraid the principals of my children would believe him as well. After months of observation by a court ordered therapist and a very expensive psychiatrist, it was deemed in court that I was sound, that I had more traditional parenting skills, and a more stable lifestyle than that of their father. To be fair to Dale, it also showed that he had decent parenting skills, but that he lacked judgment concerning who he left the children with. The reports showed me to be argumentative, defensive, combative, and ambitious . . . OK, so what? I am, these were my kids!

The problem with the report was that the judge was unwilling to reverse her order for custody because it would mean that she had acted inappropriately. Even through the psychiatrist had also found Dale to be a liar, a pathological liar, and that he tried to manipulate the test several times, she wanted to wait until something extraordinary happened, or until the kids reached the magically age of 14 and the courts had no other option but to listen to them. This was 2001, and Laura was only 11 and Caity was only 10. Dr. Green met me with a concerned look upon his face. He was a father, a married-to-the-same-woman-forever type of father, and he was personally unable to feel empathy for me in this particular area. He knew that Laura had been missing from school, but he was bound by the state laws of Oklahoma to lean toward the custodial parent in these situations, which at this time was Dale. However, he also knew that as Reuben's mother I was completely aware of where my child was at all times, that he was encouraged to do his homework, that he was supported dogmatically at every school activity, and that I was very concerned with his progress. Dr. Green also knew from Reuben's reports that the girls had been taken and that they had not been allowed to contact me or anyone else because of the abuse Caity had sustained. Reuben had told his counselor about the hospital, about the reports of abuse, he assured the woman that the DHS was involved, and that the police reports were real. After the counselor spoke with Dr. Green, his answer to my question about Laura's whereabouts was simply that he did not have any idea where she could be, but that as soon as he found out he would contact the DHS and ask them to contact me. I also knew that he would find a way to let Reuben know where his sisters were as well.

Caity attended Northhaven Elementary, a school all of my children had attended before the final divorce. The principal at Northhaven was a belittling man, a man with an ego the size of Kilimanjaro, and in my opinion, one of the worst principals to walk into the Putnam City district. He and I did not get along as he was surrendered to believing even insane but calm word out of Dale's mouth. It was true that he was a better actor than I am. I was unable to hide my emotions, I was unable to put on the face of pity, which Dale often did, claiming I was a victim of incest, that my history with drugs and alcohol was such that the children were taken out of my custody. Tsk, tsk, he would tell the principal, it is a grave shame that she was asked to leave the children and to never speak with them, she has had severe mental breakdowns and she simply isn't stable to be trusted with them. All this without a single report of proof. Where I was seen in the eyes of the highest ranking officer at the school as being a complete danger to my child, the only saving grace I had was the fact that Caity's counselor knew me from an acquaintance. She was Mr. Moler's friend, and she had taken the time to ask specific questions about me and my personality. Convincing the principal that Dale was not only lying about my person, but that he was indeed the culprit behind the missing homework, the bruises, and now the disappearing of my child, was another matter. Mr. Pansy, the principal, literally asked me to my face where my child was when I went to Northhaven to ask him the same question. I felt perhaps a friend of Caity's had been contacted. I had a police officer waiting in a car outside to help me if I needed it. He was an off duty cop that I had asked to be there in case I needed support. Mr. Pansy leaned over the counter and told me that he was ashamed to say he knew me. He didn't have a clue as to the depths of my character and I needed a court order to be on the premises in the first place. When I asked him to produce anything, anything at all with that sort of restriction, he came back with "The children's real parent has told me what you have done to these children." I think Mr. Pansy needed the cop outside the door, because I was just about to kill him with my bear hands. bare

I had other dealings with the teachers and administrators of Northhaven Elementary following one of Dale's little visits. It seems he was successful in hiring Laura's fifth grade teacher Mrs. Laya Wilcox to do a little tutoring for Laura during the summer. Interestingly enough, I had custody of the girls during the time he had promised Wilcox the tutoring gig, and considering she had previously lied on stand in court about Laura's whereabouts the year before, having believed Dale without evidence, I chose not to allow her to tutor Laura. By this time I had graduated with an education in Liberal Arts. I knew more about teaching my daughters than this young, limited experienced teacher with her general education, and I told her when she called seeking the employment check that I would be canceling the order. I had not given permission to Dale to make these arrangements, and as far as I could tell, Laura had not learned anything remarkable during her fifth grade. She was now in the summer of her sixth grade, going into seventh grade, and without the least bit of knowledge of standard grammar, literature, social studies, math, or history, things that Laya Wilcox was commissioned to teach her. Of course, Mrs. Wilcox's rebuttal was that Laura would not pay attention in class, that she had many tearful breakdowns, and that she was simply unable to be a participant in class. She had recommended that Laura be held back. Nearly every one of the girls' teachers from the time they were in the 2nd and 3rd grades respectively, had wanted to hold the girls back because they refused to participate. I knew my girls. I knew what they were and were not capable of performing. The performing part was the problem. Do you blame them? Who could ask a kid that was being thrown around at one house, protected by the law and a forbearing mother at the other, to become a willing participant in school. I'm amazed they have survived at all, and when I look back on the days they were kidnapped, or shall we say "taken without permission", by their father in 2001, I am sure it was their own faith that brought them through the days and nights of being abandoned by their father to stay with friends who were given strict instructions, withheld from their mother. Can you imagine?

Chapter Nine

No parent should fear that walking into their child's school will be a situation where a police officer will be called to escort them out immediately. No parent should be shunned by teachers and administration on the word of a man who had no evidence to support his outlandish remarks and comments. Nevertheless, I was not given free speech at Northhaven elementary until after the girls were returned from what has been called by them the kidnapping. On March 26th, 2001, I received a call from Caity, she was at school. She had walked into the office and demanded to use the phone. When the principal wouldn't let her use the phone to call me she immediately began to scream out loud that she had been kidnapped by her father, that she had been held in a house without a phone or internet to contact me. That she had been left with people she did not trust, and that she was going to call her attorney Glenda Tucker. Caity has never been one for subtlety. I don't know what Dale was thinking when he brought them back. He had intentionally kept them from me over Spring Break, which was my custodial time, he had kept them from me over two weekends which were my custodial periods, he had not been with the girls even for a day. He had left them in the care of his friend Byron Barker, a man he had personal knowledge of being a wife-beater. The wife Byron was married to in 2001 was not the woman he had physically assaulted in 1997, but Dale had been his friend, coworker and even his boss in Tulsa since before 1995. He was the man who stood beside me when I remarried Dale, he knew of my love for my children, and yet Byron believed Dale. Whatever Dale told him, however he managed to convince Byron not to allow the girls to contact me, was successful. What was Dale thinking when he dropped Caity off at Northhaven 19 days after having kept her captive? Did he for one minute believe she would be quiet, or did he believe she would not try to call me? He obviously miscalculated his youngest.

I had already anticipated that he would be brining the children back this particular day. I felt in my heart that he understood that I was not playing games with him any longer. On March 23rd, when I had not heard from my daughters I walked into the courthouse and onto the 4th floor with a writ in my hand that I had typed and was about to file. It was an explanation of my perspective of the kidnapping. I had taken Victoria Reddling, my personal spiritual counselor, and a church friend with me on the previous weekend and had contacted the Oklahoma County Sheriff's department to be an escort for me as I attempted to rescue my daughters. Victoria was well aware of all of the things I had been going through since my divorce. I had joined the singles group of the Metropolitan Baptist Church, a church just up the road from where I lived. Victoria and her roommate Katherine Martin had been strongholds for me since the very beginning of my custody woes. Both women had prayed for me and had come to the courthouse on several occasions to be with me during my appearances. In fact, the day I lost custody due to the error of the court, was December 5, Victoria's birthday. She is certain that this would be the worst birthday she would ever have. I hope she's right. I hope she never has another bad birthday as long as she lives. Both women have been pillars of strength for me and for my family. I think of my entire church family when I remember the old saying that it takes a village to raise a child. Katherine, small, petite, stern, and intellectual, can be juxtaposed in her countenance by the fact that she loves to speed around town in her sexy little convertible, her long brunette mane flying in the wind. Were it not for Katherine's keen mind and quick wit, I would never have found the faith to continue my fight. She refused to allow me to stop. She knew the hearts of my girls and where they needed to be.

It was believed on March 23, that the girls were in Stephen's County with Bella's parents even though this claim was denied by Bella, her parents and her ex-husband, who I had become acquainted with since I had given a written testimony for his case against her for the custody of their son. Of record, an Oklahoma County Sheriff, Officer Abernathy, contacted Dale using his cell phone. He demanded that Dale bring the girls back to the house on Rambling Road, he demanded that Dale surrender himself to the County on charges of kidnapping. Dale told the officer that he could "fuck himself" and that the "girls would never see their mother again". This was enough for Sgt. Abernathy to file a report which was later used against Dale, and was instrumental in reversing the order in Judge Cauldron's courtroom a little under four months later.

Faith. This is the stuff it is made of. I had to sit there in the driveway of the house I was suppose to be living in raising my children, and I had to put up with a man who not only abused our relationship, but I had to sit there and listen to the officer tell me that he could only file a report. Of course, I knew I could not force the Sheriff's deputy to conjure my girls from thin air, but I had to remain calm, not only because it was the civil thing to do, but also I knew that faith was worked by God, and believed by me. Faith is something we have to have when we absolutely can't change the situation. We can't force life to happen the way it is suppose to happen, but we can have faith that God is in control, that He can change things, that no matter what is happening He will be the one to fix it and to make it tolerable again. There's a really cool verse in 2 Chronicles 20:12b and it says "We don't know what we are doing, but our eyes are on you Lord."

What was Dale thinking when he dropped Caity off at the school? God had made a little me when He created my last spawn! She was never going to allow him to get away with kidnapping her. She was never going to allow him to take her away from the internet. This child lived to hack her way into the world of the unknown. She was fully capable of grappling with Bella by this age, and this is the one reason she was hoisted away. Dale was going to be going out of the state and he could not take the chance of Bella or her new baby Morgan getting hurt by my darling devil-of-a-kid Caity. She literally stood in the foyer of the school screaming until someone took her aside and let her call me. To think, all Mr. Pansy had to do was to do what Dr. Green always did . . . . listen to the kid!

Friday, March 23rd, before the scene in the foyer of the Northhaven Elementary school, I was making my own scene on the fourth floor of the courthouse. The place was packed with suits. I was wearing a pair of Rider jeans and a pull over I'm sure, as I usually never dressed up on Fridays at Mr. Moler's office. Actually, I never dressed up at all when I worked for Mr. Moler, except on the days after he and I had engaged in a little disagreement. At times like that I wanted him to think that I perhaps had a lunch time interview. There I stood at the clerk's desk with writ in hand, and it occurred to me that the best way to get a great lawyer was to ask for one when 100 or more of the species was standing around me. Did you wonder where Caity got it? I asked loudly "Does anyone know a damn good lawyer. I need one now! My ex husband has kidnapped my children, and is extreme contempt of court, can anyone suggest a name?" A man from the left side, about to file a motion for continuance in his own case said out loud and very pointedly "Anita Sanders!" About that time a mumble was heard throughout the room. This room is a long and deep room. Mumble turned to rumble, and I wrote the name Anita Sanders down. "Would you like for me to call her for you?" came another voice from behind me. "She's kicked my butt a few times in the courtroom." Then another voice chimed in, and another, it seemed this Anita Sanders was something of a legend. I was ecstatic, until I realized that if I couldn't afford her I would be wasting her time. "I don't have any money." I said to the last man who had offered to place the call. "I don't know that she takes money." He said. This was the most surprising news I had ever heard in my life. He continued to say that part of the thrill for Anita was the fact that she really enjoyed beating the daylights out of attorneys who represent people they should not be representing. He said that Anita was well known for her bartering and that if I had something of value to offer her that she might very well listen to me, and at the least, she could do it for the kids. I let him place the call.

Anita F. Sanders didn't look like a monster, when my friend Joseph Hamilton and I visited her on the morning of Saturday, March 24, 2001. In fact, Anita stood about my height, she was considerably smaller by weight than I, and her *fangs* weren't showing, her claws must have been retracted, and when I took a quick look around her office I didn't see any ball collections, at least not the kind that were proclaimed as being her favorite. To me Anita seemed quite pleasant. She offered John and I something to drink, even a bit of pasta salad she was so proud of herself for having been able to concoct alone without help. She mentioned that her maid had taken leave and I wondered if I could use this bit of information for bartering purposes; at least the thought occurred to me. I was willing to beg. Anita's game plan was simple, she wanted me to write down everything that had happened from the day Dale and I broke up for the last time until the very day I walked into her office. Simple yes, but impossible. I explained to her that the highlights alone would fill a volume or two of the worst rot you could ever imagine reading— albeit true! She wanted most of the highlights, with a special emphasis on what was going on this very minute with the kidnapping. I held in my hand the report from Officer Abernathy, which Anita found not only amazingly stupid on the part of my ex-husband, but incredibly detailed. She stated that she had never heard of an officer taking the time to actually fill out the report so well, this man must have found Dale particularly upsetting as well. I suppose it was a good thing that my ex could be so terrible to more people than just myself, in the end it was his undoing.

Our court plans were simple as well, Anita was prepared to file an Emergency Order on March 26, 2001, asking for an immediate reversal of the last Order, and giving me permanent and full custody of the girls based on the facts surrounding the kidnapping. How could it be jeopardized, what could possibly happen to stop the action . . . a van, that's what. The morning of March 26, 2001, found Caity being dropped off at the school just about the same time Anita and I were walking to the courthouse. Dale was expected to show of course, given the gravity of the situation, his attorney was contacted, however, since there wasn't a 24 hour notice given his attorney expressed Dale's decision not to be present. However, a separate Order and court date was scheduled for the same case in the same court room on the same date. He didn't have a choice in showing up or not. He was expected to be in the courtroom. As Anita and I walked across the street to go to the courthouse we were physically struck head on by a moving van. The van it turns out was rolling at about 20 miles an hour. It was the same color, make, model, and year van as that of my ex-husband. Naturally I screamed when it hit me somewhere around the knees. Thoughts racing in my mind of being killed by the idiot rather than him facing the inevitable, people do worse you know. I was dumbfounded! Neither Anita nor I were knocked to the ground, but we were pushed against each other, beaten a little and bruised by the van. I remember my brief case hitting me in the upper arm somehow, and from the mark it left you would have thought I was punched by George Foreman. Immediately Anita informed the driver to stop. He wanted to drive on. He was driving without a license, his left arm was broken and in a purple cast, while his right hand was busy holding a cell phone! The man was rounding a corner and had no intention of stopping. Though he wasn't my ex-husband, the shock of the van being so close to the same type of van Dale drove, it took quite a while for me to get over the vivid imagines that my mind was trying to conjure.

When the EMTs arrived Anita and I begged off going to the doctor because we weren't hurt too badly, however, in time my arms really began hurting, as well as my back and upper thighs. Our case was postponed of course, and the only thing that was ordered without my presence was against Dale, he was ordered to never leave the girls with anyone besides me. Though he was not present to hear this, a copy of the order was sent to his attorney. Not that he obeyed the order, he was always one to believe and behave as if he believed that he was above the law in these matters. To him the judge was useless unless she was ruling in his favor. Wouldn't that be grand? I wouldn't have had to run to the bathroom every 10 minutes I was inside the courthouse if I felt that the judge would be ruling for me on every issue. As it was, I couldn't be too far from the stalls. It was incredibly annoying to me that I would be able to take kidney stones, three natural births, and so many other events in my life, but standing in the stale musty courthouse while waiting on a ruling that should be in my favor, but was often not, made me sick to my stomach . . . often.

Journal Entry:

May 1, 2001

"This day made me sick. I don't know how much more of this I can take. Judge Cauldron knows that Dale left the state. She ordered him to leave the girls with me if he did that again. Why can't this just end. He's such a liar.

Here we had an emergency order because he left the state again and let Bella watch the girls. Caity called me to say she was getting hit again. I called Anita. We had the order in place before the judge and then she doesn't show up! We got a new judge, he wanted to give Dale a chance to get back from Virginia to testify. Hello, he wasn't suppose to leave again without giving me the girls. This is so simple. He can't leave the state without giving the girls to me. He did it again. Put his butt in jail for contempt . . . again!!!"

Giving up my faith was never an option. Falling flat on my face praying for answers was the best option I had. I couldn't possibly think of asking for help from any one else but God. To even think there is no God would be impossible. If there was no God there was no hope. If there was no hope there was no reason to do what it was that I was doing, which was trying to get my little girls back home. Prayer was not enough, faith had to be present. Without the faith, the active work which comes with faith, and the active works of others who carried the same burden of faith for me as I did for myself, the girls would not have had a chance to be free. The girls needed me, they begged for me to take them away; no one listened to them or to their cries; of course, they weren't allowed to listen. I wasn't alone in this sorted mess. Everytime I went to court I heard the same stories in the corridors. Everywhere you turned someone was screwing someone they used to love and cherish over. Someone wasn't paying child support, someone else wasn't following orders. Why? Why can't people do what they're told to do, and why can't the law be enough to make someone do what they're suppose to do? Under the laws of the state of Oklahoma, the girls were given a guardian ad litem, someone to represent them in court. This doesn't mean that Glenda actually listened to the girls either, in fact, Glenda was their second GAL. She was better than the first one they were given, that woman, Carrie, had been asked to leave the case when my first counsel was fired. If I could have fired the GAL I would have, but it was made perfectly clear to me that the only way to make sure I was given a different GAL would have been to drop the case in its entirety. This was before Legal Aid was involved, and had I realized that the lawyer I was dealing with was as inexperienced at this type of law as I was, I may have been wise enough to file a protest. Surely there had to be another way to have a GAL assigned to the case. It was 1997 when I first realized I would need to seek custody of the girls, and the first GAL was appointed. She was white, thin, middle aged, a smoker, a liar, and I suppose worst of all, she was uncaring and if the case wasn't going the way she anticipated she would intentionally leave a file in her office forcing the judge to reschedule the court date. This was her way of making sure she made it to her nail appointment! That may sound bitter on my part, like something I would simply say because things weren't working out for me, however, I was extremely new at this game, so I followed her. I followed her all the way to the salon downtown and I watched her. I heard her making the comment to the beautician that she would have been there earlier but she had a case to "deal with". She stated that she had left the case file in her office, and how the judge had rescheduled the hearing. I wanted to expose her, instead I asked my attorney how I could have her reassigned. Her answer was to release her as my attorney, and to reopen the case, asking my judge for a second GAL. She was at least kind enough to mention that the judge would probably say no, but that I was to insist on grounds of the first GAL's contempt for the law. Like that would work, but I thought I would try anyway.

When you're as green as I was about the matters of divorce and subsequent divorce issues as I was in 1997, you really don't consider the thoughts racing in and through the judge's mind. She wasn't happy to hear that I had fired my attorney. She wasn't happy to see that I had reopened the case the next day, and she certainly wasn't pleased with my explanation; that I had been directed by my attorney to do so because the GAL was incompetent. "Are you stupid Ms. Stringfellow?" asked the judge. "Are you so completely stupid that you would believe your attorney would have anything to do with reassigning the guardian ad litem? She has nothing to do with assigning and reassigning these people. You are either incredibly stupid, or incredibly gullible, and either way I'm inclined to believe that you are incapable of raising children properly." This to me sounded as if the good judge had already chosen to give my daughters to my ex-husband based on the fact that he was able to pay for a better, more experienced attorney, and because he never once argued with her. Why should he have argued with her, she was ruling in his favor, and believing the lies he was able to get by with. Her ruling to have us all examined by a psychiatrist should have been enough for me to realize that her idea of getting rid of the Stringfellow case was to see to it that I spend more money than I could possibly come up with. She darn near succeeded too, and she would have except for one thing—faith. My church was behind me. There were prayers and prayer meetings. There were literally meetings where the people in my singles department did nothing else but gather at my friend Joseph Hamilton's house to lay hands on me and to pray over the situation. These people knew me. They knew I was not always the most quiet and calm of the two parties involved in the case, but they certainly knew I was the one telling the raw truth. Perhaps the fact that it was so raw was the problem. Judges and lawyers alike don't relish having to listen to details as sensational as to say that this man had actually beaten his children on the sides of their legs, their backs, and on their faces with the buckle end of a belt in their own beds while they slept. They didn't want to hear how he had left a 6 and 7 year old more than a mile away from home and told them to walk home because they had seen their mother at the store and wanted to be with her. If no one was willing to listen to the children, there would be no hope. Glenda Tucker was the best Cauldron could do for the girls. She is a middle aged, shorter than I am, African American woman with a soft and steady voice She was not a smoker, and she seemed more or less dedicated to children and their causes. She may not have been friendly to me at first, it was her job to be impartial when it came to the parents, and I know I annoyed her more often than not by insisting that she listen to the girls. She met with the girls, and after the initial meeting Glenda accused me of manipulating them because I asked the girls to make lists of things they wanted to talk to Glenda about. In her world children talked freely about issues or nothing was wrong in the first place. This not being the case with Laura, I asked both the girls to come up with lists to provide Glenda a more precise picture of what was going on.

"Ms. Stringfellow, are you telling the girls what to write, they are telling me that you told them what to say."

"No, I asked them to make lists, and I helped them create their lists, in that I helped them to write 1, 2, 3, and to list out what it was they wanted to talk about."

"Did you correct their spelling?"

"Yes, I did correct their spelling. Is that a problem?"

"Yes, it is a problem, it looks as if you are telling them what to write."

"Well, I'm sorry, I didn't want them making spelling mistakes."

"Next time Ms. Stringfellow, let the girls decide what they want to tell me."

She acted as if I were sitting the girls down and instructing them on what to tell her. I told them to tell her about the spankings, yes, but I left it to them to describe when and how they were spanked. If these guardian ad litems truly believe that every child will speak freely about details, they haven't been around children enough to know that the first thing a child will do in these cases, no matter how badly they have been hurt, is to protect the parent who is doing the damage. My girls were unwilling to tell stories that could put their father in jail, but at the same time, they also realized that the stories would not be heard if they were not told. They realized that they could not live with me if they did not tell Glenda the truth. I think at first it was Caity that told the more gory of details. She was somewhat closer to the situation than Laura. Laura, for whatever reason was still under the impression and hope that her father and I might reconcile. It was her duty to try her best to see to it that Bella was blamed, leaving the doors wide open for her father and I to be together again. My poor baby, she should never have had to be placed in that situation. Glenda told me over and over again that Laura simply couldn't tell on her father. To me this was evidence that there was more to tell, to

Glenda it was a brick wall she simply couldn't get past. She was inclined not to do anything to help the girls if Laura was unwilling to help herself. It was time for more drastic measures and DHS was called in to do what Glenda either couldn't or wouldn't do.

Chapter Ten

Like Glenda, our DHS worker Ellen was not in the Jude-camp immediately. Looking back on her decision to be impartial makes much more sense now, but at the time I couldn't even imagine how anyone could want to give Dale a chance to explain himself, knowing what I knew about him. Then again, it was usually only my word against his word, as the girls were either not being listened to, or when they were being listened to they wouldn't tell the secrets deeply embedded in their hearts, as they didn't want to see their father getting in trouble. Faith is a funny thing, it actually requires a person to do something, and doing nothing doesn't always mean a person doesn't have that faith, it simply means that person isn't willing to help themselves. Sometimes you just have to let go and get it done. This is exactly what Laura was doing, she was doing nothing to help herself, therefore, it was hurting the cause; nevertheless, God wasn't finished with the case or the cause. Through Laura's non communication about the matter He was able to show Ellen the depths of the damage being done. The only problem, as it always is a problem, is that the process took a great deal more time. This time allowed Dale and Bella the opportunity to do even more damage.

One of the first things Laura was willing to discuss with Ellen, Glenda, and even Dr. Champlin our court ordered therapist, is that her pets continued to be given away. This is such a major issue that I simply can't let it go without saying that with each new pet she would receive she would end up having it taken away, given away, thrown away, or dumped on the side of the road for absolutely no reason other than her father was tired of its animal behavior. If the dog or cat pooped on the carpet, Heaven forbid, it was given away or the gate was left open intentionally to allow its escape. This action was nearly always done while the girls were in class at school. They would come home only to find their beloved dog or cat missing. A search was made of course, Dale tried to look and act concerned, but when the time came for Laura to discuss these events in her life with the proper authorities her guard for her father was finally severed. He could beat her, yell at her, take her toys, sell her clothes and dolls in a garage sale without allowing her to retrieve them with her own money. He could cuss at her friends, he could take her food away from her, or force her to eat things he knew very well that she hated; but take her animals away and Laura refused to protect him any longer. With great detail she showed Ellen a final list. This list was not created in any way by me. This particular list was a creation of Laura and Laura alone. It contained the names of over forty animals that Dale and Bella had given to her and Caity over the course of a couple of years, only to have them given away, thrown out the door of the car in front of the girls, taken to a dump site, or let out. The list was simply names, names without faces, fur, or stories if the list was merely read. As Laura held the list in her hands she became angry, upset, and eventually she became straight-faced, looking into the eyes of the DHS worker hoping for justice, wanting to put an end to something that was causing her so much pain. "Doc, Diamond, Lady, Wishbone, Jasmine, Jade, Sadie, Max . . ." and the list rolled on. "This one we had about three days until Dad decided it was ugly. This one bit Morgan on the hand when he pulled it by the tail. This one didn't do anything at all, but Caity got a D on her spelling test and dog begins with D. I guess if she had gotten a C the cat would be gone." I couldn't do a thing to help my daughters. Every week with my visitation, if I was granted the privilege, I was told about another animal, another story. I began telling the girls to not become attached, not to go through it again and again. They couldn't help themselves, they were little girls and the animals were always small, furry, cute, and so playful. Dalmatians, German Shepherds, a Collie, a Beagle, a Jack Russell Terrier. Next they'd come home to find one missing and another to replace it, it developed into a stressful, wishy-washy wondering game of what to expect in the house or the backyard with each new day. "Trouble, Coco, Patch, Gus, Lucky . . ." and the list goes on, "Dakota, Bear, Caesar, Simon . . ." Ellen had heard enough. This time it was going to be over. This time I had the weight of the law, as well as the height, breadth, depth, and long arms of it on my side. She couldn't do much more than make a recommendation, but due to the extreme mental and emotional stress Dale was imposing on the girls by taking away their animals, and replacing them so often, something could be done. A pattern of neglect and abuse was established. Lists can be a good thing, too, Glenda; lists can save the world.

Faith, or the act of faith, isn't always associated with bad events. We can't think of faith as being the saving tool that comes to our rescue when we're depressed, sad, or hurt. If faith was apparent only during troubling times we would only be expected to use and have faith when we were going through some sort of trial or tribulation. With faith I find there is a constant need to renew communication with God. Why talk to Him only when you need something desperately. I wouldn't want my own children to ring me up on the phone only to beg me for something, or to blame me for what was going on in their lives. I find that faith, or having faith is something so ingrained in our souls that we do it, have it, use it, whatever you want to call it, on a continued basis. Take for instance the time that Caity was doing cartwheels on the four inch beams surrounding my parents' house. It wasn't that I believed she would fall, I had faith that she was going to be OK. I didn't believe she would fall, I remember thinking that I would fall if I had tried to do something like that, but I remembered being six and climbing over a very large fence with a large yellow sign hanging tightly to its webbed encasement. The sign read (but I couldn't read at the time) RESTRICTED AREA, DO NOT TRESPASS, FEDERAL PROPERTY. Wow, big words. I knew I could climb over the fence, I had a mission to accomplish. There were bones under the ground and I wanted to find a few more to show my friend Willie D. He didn't believe me when I told him that the bones were in there, just sticking out of the ground and everything. How could he not believe me? Wasn't I his best friend? Wasn't I with him when we found the great big crawdads in the creek and I was the one that ate the head off of one to prove I wouldn't die? That was me, he had to believe me when I told him I had found a real live dead bone of an Indian! Faith. I would get over the fence, I would get to the wooden house about a city block into the field, and I would dig up another bone to show Willie D. He was the one too scared to go this way, he had to go around the creek, over the cliff and around the park. Man, that took forever, and you had to ask permission of the lady who lived in the blue house to use her backyard to get to the field. Sometimes she said no if her husband was home. I wasn't about to take that chance. Up and over. Fast like, no one looking, and thank God for that handy-dandy sign I could put my foot on to hoist myself over anyway! Faith in one's self can be very liberating! You don't always have to have faith only in God or in things not of this Earth . . . heck, I had faith in the people I wrote to asking for help to publish this book. I needed the money, I asked, and I believed it would happen . . . you're reading the book aren't you?

My first grade teacher was another strong faithful influence. I don't want to get her in trouble or anything, but she wasn't exactly orthodox. She didn't exactly go by the rules, not unless the rules included carrying your shot gun to school and keeping the bullets in your pocket. She let me hold the gun once but it was too heavy and I dropped it on my foot. It wasn't loaded, she had already used the final shell on a rabbit we had come across on our way to the school. Mrs. Adelaide Earp lived just across the street from me. She was at least sixty-five years old when she started walking me to school in 1967. Earp was one of those pioneer women you see and read about in books so old the pages have all turned yellow. She was short but I was too. She was stout, about as strong as the oak trees in her back yard that she used to climb into the get the acorns to make whistles out of. She had those hose that hung around the base of her thick trunk-like legs which where shoved into the black clog boots that had hooks instead of ties. My hair was long I thought, but I had no idea how long hair could get until the day I saw my first grade teacher pull the hairnet off her round, tall bun. Down to the ground her hair fell in dark and gray strands in the most amazing demonstration of hair-letting that I had ever seen. Country music fans remember Crystal Gale's hair and the way it hung behind her when she posed for pictures, or stood on stage, literally having to flip it behind her to even see where she was walking. Adelaide Earp used six strong hair pins made of tortoise bones and shell to hold her mass up on top of her head. I can't imagine the weight she would release each evening, but I saw it often when I snuck up to her bedroom window at night and watched her comb through the long train. It was yet another thing I couldn't convince my best friend of. He didn't have Mrs. Earp as a teacher, and living three doors down from her made him nervous in the first place. She never did take to walking over to his place to drag him to school by the hand. I was the only kid in the entire school who had that privilege. Why me? I couldn't tell you except I know she had been my three siblings' teacher and maybe they had told her stories about me. That was the only thing I could think of. It certainly couldn't be the way I crawled under the street through the sewer traps, or how I rode my bike at neck-break speed past the red eight-sided signs reading STOP . . . whatever that meant! Five and I couldn't read yet. By six she saw to it that I did. What stopped me from crashing into the side of an on-coming car or bus? Probably my mother's faith because I didn't have any at the time. I just have dumb luck to hold onto.

The book of Hebrews goes on and on about the faithful in the stories of the Bible, how they did this or that with faith and to be honest I wondered when I was little how the author of the book even knew about some of the stories that he was writing about. There weren't books, television, movies or even newspapers relating these stories. Maybe he was in Mrs. Earp's first grade class because she talked about Abraham, Isaac, Jacob, Joseph and Moses all the time. Abraham, at least in my opinion, had the most faith. Joseph sat in a well waiting to be rescued, but when he was he was taken care of. Jacob had to raise twelve sons but in order to get them he had married the wrong woman once (how do you do that after being in love with someone seven years? I'm thinking Leah and Rachel's dad was the best confidence man ever!) Jacob raised twelve sons, and he had two wives and two concubines to help, nevertheless, raising twelve boys couldn't be easy . . . however, he wasn't asked of God to literally sacrifice his one and only baby boy. Abraham was. I've thought about it, I couldn't be an Abraham. I did notice, and I often notice, that when God requires the blood of a child he never asks the mother to do it. He asked Abraham, not Sara. Can you imagine what Sara would have said to Him if He had asked her to take the life of her only son? I can tell you now that she had absolutely no idea where Abraham was taking her baby boy that sunny afternoon when they found themselves at the top of the mountain preparing to obey God's will to the fullest. God is the Father of Jesus, Mary is His mother. God did not ask Mary to give up her first born. God knows all too well the hearts of the women He has created. I can think of one or two women who could give up their children and to this day I abhor them, creating in my mind the deepest pit in Hell for any of them who could say or do anything to harm their own children; so why does God expect us to be able to follow a command that could actually cost us the lives of our children? Some questions simply have no answers? St. Augustine asked a great many boundary questions in his confessional journals and I suppose I do as well, however, I know that the best answer I can give you is that God has never required this sort of faith from me, and probably because He knows my answer. I would rather die myself. Whether this is wrong or right, I can't tell, but without the mentioning of my faith's limitations I would wonder about such limitations. Where does my faith end? Where does any faith end? For that matter when does it begin? I remember being two years old and being in the hospital under big plastic curtains. At the time I had no idea that I was dying of double pneumonia, but I do know that I didn't worry about that part of it. The beans were fun to pop in my nose. The doctors and nurses came quickly into the room every time I did it. They held me, kissed me and kept me happy when my parents couldn't. Beans aren't exactly an ordinary tool of faith, but I knew how to make them work. Faith? The angels must have been signing the petitions against me, asking God to find another soul to protect! Something tells me there really is something to penance and angels probably have to pay it as well. Any angel falling short of his or her angelic duties has to watch the two year old babies of the Earth! It's a rule! That could very well be why the angels smile so often in the pictures I see of them. "Thank you God for not putting me in the nursery! Sing Hallelujah!!"

Faith at 6 weeks standing in the snow.

Caity: Poet, Author, kid.

Faith and Ean playing at 3 months.

Anchor Linda Cavanugh broke the story on June 23, 2003, on
KFOR-TV Oklahoma City, OK.

Reuben: Faith's original rescuer.

Maurice Ernest Gibb, the man I wanted to marry at the age of 6.

Laura: Actress, singer, sister.

Rocker and Poet.

Looking forward to the future.

Chapter Eleven

In time faith prevailed. In time even the great Dale Stickley had outstayed his welcome in the courtroom of Cauldron. With the various contempts adding up through kidnappings, missed visitation, horrible actions and reactions to orders, an Emergency Order was filed in the case. With Anita, Ellen, Glenda, and the report of Dr. Lora Champlin, our therapist, in the file, I was given full and permanent custody of the girls on Caity's 11th birthday, July 25, 2001. Ironically, Cauldron had yet another lapse of good judgment when she ordered that Dale had a couple of days to gather the materials and goods for the girls to be delivered to my attorney's office on July 27. Rather than demanding that the girls be turned over immediately, she allowed him 48 hours to say good bye, and to prepare them for this permanent readjustment. Caity was at home with friends that morning, and with Bella. She had woken up to a bright stark sunny sky, and the faith that she would be holding me soon. When Bella asked her what she wanted for her birthday, Caity answered "God is giving me my Mom today, just like He gave me to her eleven years ago." The comment caused Bella to hit Caity on the shoulder with a cooking spatula. It didn't matter any more, Caity and Bella both knew that they would forever be free of each other in just a few days. That didn't stop Dale or Bella from creating as much havoc or damage as they possibly could for the remainder of two days. Every shirt, skirt, pair of pants, undergarment, toy, pillow, or belonging owned by the girls was stuffed into black plastic bags.

If the girls believed they were being taken to my attorney's office they were wrong. Dale delivered less than ten percent of what belonged to the girls to Anita's office. Instead he took their things to the nearest Good Will store, leaving them outside because the doors were locked. Had I known what he was doing I could have driven by and retrieved the gifts my sisters, mother, friends and family had given to my little girls. When Laura and Caity realized that they were without clothes, toys, china dolls, and jewelry given to them they cried, but it could not dislodge the joy in their hearts as they danced up and down the courthouse halls, literally shouting "Mom got us back! No more Bella! No more!"

It was actually a little unraveling to tell the truth, it felt both good and bad to hear them feel so relieved to be away from the man who had been in their lives since the beginning, but there are times when I would have died to give them this freedom. Faith prevailed. There's a woman we call Grandma, (her real name being Martha Washington) works in a little Italian restaurant called Ricolettos downtown. No one really knows how old Grandma is. She's ageless, she's dynamic, and if nothing else could be said about this African beauty wearing sparkling berets, one thing can certainly be said. She is a woman of faith. I found myself going to Ricolettos for more than the inexpensive pizza on days I simply couldn't take the stress of missing my children. Grandma would come out from behind the counter and she would hold me. She would raise her hands into the air and proclaim through uninhibited faith that the Lord would deliver to me my babies. She called them the "Blessed Babies". "Lord, bring the blessed babies to this woman! Lord, I cry to you, YOU, YOU GOD, are the only one able to deliver us, you are the one God, you are the lone and the only, through our faith, through our prayers you hear us. Lord today bring your peace! Lord, be with these children, these blessed babies. You know where they are today! Bring these babies to their mother!", and as I cried and I prayed along with her, I secretly wished I was black. I wanted the freedom that wasn't taught to me in my white Baptist upbringing. I wanted to throw up my hands and wail. I wanted to let God know that I believed He could do this! Thank God for faith, loud faith and quiet faith. It's all good. I love you Grandma Washington.

July 27, 2001 found my daughters in my arms again. Reuben was even happy to see his sisters which wasn't always the case. Even Reuben knew what it meant to have the girls back, certainly it meant he would have to share me and my affection, but he knew the torturing would end. Reuben had been eleven when Dale had spanked him for crying when the Green Bay Packers lost the Super Bowl to the Denver Broncos. John Elway received a gold and diamond ring, Reuben was placed in a hope chest at the house on Rambling Road when he wouldn't stop crying. Dale sat on the box, a wooden chest that my own father had made my son, until the crying stopped. My son, my baby boy was unconscious in a wooden box, and I think I was at a restaurant having cheese fries with my best friend because it wasn't my weekend to have the children. This event led to the three year battle for permanent custody of the girls. As soon as the event was reported to the police Reuben was removed immediately. For the life of me I can't understand why all three of the kids weren't removed from the house on Rambling Road after that day. Reuben knew all too well what it meant to have his sisters home again.

END OF PART ONE

PART TWO

FAITH, a Little Dog

Chapter Twelve

I woke up this morning with my legs and feet trapped under the blanket and under the weight of a yellow dog draped ever-so-lazily over the back of my calves. Since Faith has been in our family I have learned to lay flat on my belly when I go to sleep and I stay that way, unmoving, no rolling over, no turning whatsoever. We have a code in our family. We simply can't disturb the dog (any dog) once he or she has settled and given up that lingering sigh which tells us that the dog is ready to relax. I don't know how the code began, but it has been an endless source of laughter for us. I can literally call out to one of the kids and have them utterly interrupted to ask them for a cup of coffee, to turn down the stereo in my room, or to give me the book at the base of my bed because I can't possibly disturb the dog. Sometimes they give me face about it. I can be annoying when I take the code to the extreme. Why it doesn't work with the cat is usually because the cat won't stay in my lap long if I bellow out to the kids for assistance. Dogs don't care. Dogs in my family know better than to look the least bit rattled. Laying in one spot after scratching the blankets to make them just right is the beginning of the signally of the code. "Dog in the lap!" I call it out just to let them know. This gives Laura the initial clue that I am about to call her to get my coffee, a book, or to anything else I might need. Disturbing the dog is never an option! Mornings can be an exception to the rule, the dog has rested.

Each morning, just like this one, I get up in a stupor and ask the dogs to get off of me. When I say that I ask the dogs, I'm really more or less demanding them to get off of me. Faith lays on top of the covers and between my legs, pinning me to the bed, while Matrix lays beside me under the covers, his long, fat, black dachshund/beagle body stretching from my head to my knees, and my face is usually at the wrong end of the dog. Often times I don't even require an alarm time, a fart from Matrix is signal enough for me to get out of the bed and take the dogs to the backyard. Why do we indulge our animals? Why do we put such an emphasis on the loving of these mangy, half breed creatures who have been spoiled beyond any degree of sanity? Because in my house the list of animals is much shorter, and to give one away would be virtually an impossibility. Matrix has his own miracle story, one that begins during the time that the girls were in Dale's house on Rambling Road. I had decided to lease a little house just around the corner from the girls so that it would be easier to keep track of them. Their friends began walking to my house to be with the girls on my weekends. Some weekends when it wasn't my weekend to have my own daughters I had three or four other *daughters* who couldn't resist the smell of chocolate chip cookies. I usually ended up with Helen Stakker and Ashley Tubble for at least one or two nights a week with or without Laura and Caity to play with them.

Matrix, Faith's adoptive brother, was found at *Pets and People*, a wonderful no-kill shelter in Yukon, Oklahoma with dedicated volunteers and workers who have it in their heads to find good and permanent homes for dogs and cats who are either abandoned, strays, or about to be killed at the city shelters. Pets and People have a very rigid record keeping system, and they keep pictures of each of the hundreds and thousands of animals that make their way through their doors. Matrix was officially called *Lambert*, and he was considered too sick to be sold with any guarantee. When he came to the shelter he had worms, ringworms, and other puppy problems. He wasn't over six weeks at the time, and therefore he wasn't for sale. Why is it that whenever I write that down, he wasn't for sale, that in the very next sentence I'm telling you how I talked the shelter's keepers into giving him to our family. We pleaded, we begged, we even promised not to worry about the guarantee. We wanted a dachshund. "He's only part dachshund." They countered. "He's enough dachshund" I offered. "He's sick", "I have experience with sick dogs. I can medicate him. I'll let you medicate him, I'll take him to whatever vet you want me to take him to." In secret I knew I was going to be leaving Pets and People with a dog that day and I really wanted another weenie dog. They have always been my favorite. "Fine, take him to Dr. Diane Delbridge. She's here in Yukon, and we'll know if you don't go to her. I'll personally come to your house and get Lambert back if you don't do everything she says to do."

I made the promised agreements and I took my little sick tri-colored, mostly black, mixed breed dachshund with me. There was no way I was going to call him Lambert. I thought about the latest most up to date names, and not one of them struck me as being cool or good enough for my little dog. He was awesome. He was going to make it, he was going against the odds, but then again, he was in my family, that was a normal and every day thing. He would have to get used to it, and he would have to be above reality. That's when it hit me. I'd call him Neo for the character Keanu Reeves played in the Matrix. He wore mostly black, he was sleek, fast, a great fighter. He had to believe he could win, he had to believe he could make it through the toughest of tough times. That was it, I was going to call him Neo. My children decided Matrix was better, and therefore he was renamed, but from time to time when no one else is paying the least bit of attention, I whisper in Neo's ear and I tell him how great of a dog he truly is.

Matrix wasn't exactly accepted by our two cats Sting and Tigger. Cats are cats, you can't argue with them, they always win because they decide before the argument begins that you're wrong and they simply walk away. I threatened to withhold food once to make my point, however, I realized that my leg could actually be considered a choice of nutrition to a cat whose food had been withheld. Matrix wasn't like that. He would be mine, he would listen to me, he would obey my every command, and he would love me no matter what happened. Cats are cats and they don't have to follow rules. Why do I have cats? I can't remember the reasons behind the first one I brought home, nor can I figure out the reason I keep one. Wait. I've never had just one. I've always had more than one of everything when it came to animals, cats were no exception. Tigger, the gray tuxedo older brother of Sting (Tuxedo Black) made the first sweep around the kitchen to examine the new invader. His decision would satisfy Sting who actually never left his perch from inside the cabinets to investigate. Leave that to Tigger, thought Sting. If he doesn't like the dog we'll kill it, it will be over in day or so. Matrix must have said or done something right because he lived. He did however, make the terribly stupid mistake of trying to eat out of the cat bowl, which brought about the hardened swipe of a clawless foot across his face. I could see the eyes of my loathsome gray cat as he looked at me in utter disgust! "I could have used my claws at this moment, thank you!" Still, with or without claws the point was made, and the docile pup took his rightful place in line which was right behind the backside of the younger brother Sting, a fatter, darker version of the king, Tigger.

I can imagine the conversation between the three went something like this:

Tigger: Eat out of our bowl and you will die.
Sting: Tigger, don't you think he has to eat? Perhaps after we eat would be appropriate.
Tigger: The woman may not leave enough.
Sting: She seems intelligent enough, she knows she must feed him as well.
Tigger: HE isn't even a cat!
Matrix: May I interrupt? What exactly is a cat?
Tigger: Kill him. Kill him now.
Sting: Let him be. We can train him. He can be . . . he can be our pet!
Tigger: Pet? Are you suggesting that we pay attention to it?

Sting: Him, he's a him. I looked. He can be our slave actually. Would that make you happy brother?

Matrix: What exactly would I be doing as this . . . . slave, is it?

Tigger: Did we speak to you?

Matrix: Well . . . no, but . . .

Tigger: Shut up!

Matrix: Of course.

Sting: See! He's learning already. Good dog. Very good dog.

Matrix: Are cats really dogs?

Tigger: Kill him . . . . kill him now.

Sting: You amuse me Matrix, you amuse me. Come and sit.

From day one the dog was trained. I never had to tell him twice not to eat all of the food in the bowl they shared. Why it never occurred to me to get two bowls for the different species I don't know. I had a big bag of cat food and he could eat that for a while until pay day anyway. He learned quickly to wait until he was given the right to eat, and he learned even more quickly to hide behind the considerably larger butt of String if he wanted to avoid another face swiping from Tigger as well. Sting found it quite interesting to tease his older brother by walking between him and Matrix. Dr. Delbridge was another story!

"You know you can't feed the puppy cat food. I found cat food in his stool." They always know don't they? You can't get anything past them. "You need to start the dog out with Iams and keep him on it. I'm going to insist." I nodded my head. I agreed to do this until the keepers of the shelter were completely satisfied that my more than thirty-five years of pet owning were enough to satisfy them. They were quite diligent in their follow up routine with this little mutt. Weekly visits were required as well as progress reports. Matrix was given injections, pills, lotions and creams to rid him of the ringworms. If Pets and People had any idea that I had owned devil-cats they would never have allowed me to take the dog in the first place. Cats can be the source of ringworm and with his extreme condition, it would have caused quite a problem. They never asked, I never volunteered. I suppose I could have answered an ad in the local paper for a dachshund, but I didn't have the $300 plus to shell out on a dog at the time. Besides I wanted a mutt. I don't really trust purebreds they can turn on you! (laughs)

The house on 88th, just around the corner from the girls, was owned by a small, blond, foreign woman from Poland. She, among other difficulties, could not speak English well enough to understand that the house was in need of repair. My rent, as a matter of fact, was suppose to be going toward the lease/ purchase of the house; however, repairs such as were needed were never introduced into the bargain. When I refused to pay rent until the drains were fixed, the water heater replaced, the chimney repaired, and the foundation cracks sealed, the owner of the house did the unthinkable; she sold the house out from under me. It was amazing! I came home from church and a process server was at my door. He handed me a summons which stated I was required to appear in court. I fully understood her reasons for taking me to court for the repayment of rent, and it would give me the opportunity to speak with a judge who not only understood the laws, but could understand the English language which the contract had been written in. As is par for the course, they sided with the owner of the house because in his opinion, her lack of the grasp of the English language exonerated her from anything binding. I couldn't believe it, I was being asked to leave a house I had poured money into, had intended on purchasing and had a contract stating that these facts were real and immediate. This new disturbance was critical to the lives of my pets of course, as the only credit I had was bad credit thanks to having no money after paying three attorneys to get my girls, and there was absolutely no way of gaining any additional credit to purchase another house in the area. I was forced to move to an apartment and with that move, I was forced to find homes for my pets as well.

It wasn't that day, or the next day, but soon after the court hearing we were packing and moving to a small two bedroom apartment with hardly enough room for our furniture, let alone the hopes of what it would mean if and when I won custody of the girls. Between the divorce issues, school work, working full time, and trying to find homes for my animals, I believe the word "stress" was used on a routine basis. Not to worry I told myself, I always land on my feet. I always seem to be OK no matter what happens to me and this was just one more thing. But it wasn't just one more thing; it was the giving away of more pets. There were no dishes needing to be done, no homework missed, not a single reason to say good bye to something we loved except a nasty woman who won the flip of the coin in a court room which in my opinion should have seen that she knew enough about the language to draw the contract up in the first place; it should have upheld for me. In time the woman lost her war. The people who leased the house after me took her to court and used my contract as proof that she did in deed know more about the laws and rules of the language in order to submit a subsequent contract to them. They won the ruling, and in turn, because the owner was so negligent, they now reside in the house that should have been mine. Nice I could help.

The basic plan was easy enough, though the weather wasn't cooperating, we decided to place an ad in the paper for all of the animals and to interview the prospective callers. When we finally found the couple who were more than willing to meet us half way, over 15 miles, to adopt our now 8 month old puppy, we were happy to see that the woman was pregnant. It meant that they truly wanted our doggy for the family and that he would be loved and cared for. I explained to her husband that Matrix was a rather spoiled dog, and that it wasn't his fault all together. We were the culprits, having allowed him to live in the house, and we slept with him. I slept with him for the most part, but from time to time he would leave the bed sometime in near the early dawn hours and crawl under the covers of the girls if they were staying with me over the weekend. They completely understood. That's why I was taken completely by surprise a few months later when I received a call from a man claiming to have found Matrix in the parking lot of Tinker Air Force Base, a military base about 20 miles from my house, but in the opposite direction of where we had taken Matrix to live. Spring months had melted the snow and ice which had become such an obstacle in finding him a new home in the first place, perhaps now that the weather was better, and the baby born, the family had decided they couldn't take care of him any longer. We'll never know why this seemingly loving couple lost Matrix to the base parking lot. The man turned out to be a Captain in the Air Force, he said that he would be willing to keep Matrix, that he in fact had been a dachshund owner as a kid, and that Matrix was more than welcome to share the little house he kept on the base. Great! My little dog was now going to be a fly-boy, and I could rest again that he was being cared for; although it did bother me to think that in the several months that had passed between the January deliverance to the lovely couple, they had not seen fit to get him a new tag—I had explained that his rabies shot was due in April. The only way the Captain could have reached us was to contact the vet, and she must have given him our number as we had continued using Dr. Delbridge after we had prayed Matrix to health and had what we felt was a successful adoption of him. Thank God again, the good Captain was going to be more careful with out bundle of love. Or maybe not.

Another few months passed and the custody battles raged. This was the time of the kidnapping, the beatings, the belting, the bruising, and the bullying of Bella. Matrix was far from my concerns as I had found homes for the brother cats the day I had found his first home. The cats, being brothers, and being tuxedo in costume, were no problem at all to find homes for. Both brothers were cared for immediately, kept fat and happy in the arms and hearts of a family living right outside of Oklahoma City with a 13 year old son who had cancer and needed more than one kitty to love. As I cried I handed the box of furry feet and tails to Penny Makington, prayerfully asking her to be careful driving through the blizzard conditions; Tigger was prone to car sickness. We surrendered a couple of nice bath towels for the cause, just in case. After a few initial calls to tell us the boys were doing fine, we lost contact. From time to time I think about Tigger, more so than I think of Sting. Sting had become Reuben's cat, more or less, and Tigger was the one to bother me more often with his insistence that I had made the worst mistake of my life for bringing the mongrel into his life. I wondered what the good Captain was doing with my most precious boy now. That was some time in the Spring of 2001.

July 27, 2001. Custody was finally mine, and the girls couldn't be happier. We hadn't had a chance to celebrate Caity's 11th birthday and in doing so I allowed them to pick whatever place they most wanted to go. I didn't care if it had been Disneyland! I would have found a way to do it. Lucky for me they wanted to go to the unusual choice of Yukon's Pets and People. An odd choice, since they knew we lived in a tower apartment and would never be allowed to keep even fish! Rules were rules in this place, and they were forever checking to be sure no one was breaking them. Pets and People it was! We could scoop poop to their hearts' desire, we could walk dogs, help hold the dogs being bathed, and we could kiss on everything with four feet and fur. Sometimes strange things happen, and so it was that when we walked through the doors at Pets and People we were followed by fate.

We walked into the front door of Pets and People on the brightest of days in late July. I asked to see the manager and explained to her that my darling little girls, who I had just won complete, full and permanent custody of, wanted to celebrate by cleaning out cat boxes, walking dogs, and giving baths. She understood. To say that this sort of thing happens all of the time would be an overstatement, but there are times when kids can't help themselves. They have to pet a dog or two. This was one of those times. We were ecstatically happy, and the dogs deserved a bit of that joy. Let's walk 'em all. About thirty or forty minutes into the session one of those strange God-did-it moments happened. Matrix, our Matrix, came around the corner, pulling his collar off, letting loose of the keeper whose job it had been to gather him from the bathing room and to deliver him to his kennel cage. "MATRIX!" I heard my daughter Laura shout. "LAURA!" you could almost hear Matrix cry. If I had not been the believer that I had been I would personally never have believed this story if someone else had told me. What are the odds of the dog we had to give up over 6 months before would be standing in the very foyer of the one place we had found him in the first place? Hadn't he been adopted, dropped off, adopted again? Now he was back in our arms? The keepers explained that he had been brought to them just a few months before by the good Captain. Seems after he had told us he would be taking care of Matrix he received orders to go to Germany. He couldn't take the dog. We had changed our phone number, but had not given it to the vet, as we had not taken her any animals, we didn't have any animals to take. The Captain decided that Pets and People, though a good long drive from Tinker, would be the best place to drop off Matrix. He was surprised that he would not have to pay any drop off fee because Matrix had once been Lambert. The records from Dr. Delbridge's office had confirmed that Matrix was a Pets and People pup, and as is their ruling, they always take back one of their own. But that had been three or more months? Had poor Matrix lived in kennel cages and on hard tile floors since the early Spring? No. It seems that according to the records, Matrix, as he was officially being called now, had been unsuccessfully adopted three more times. With each adoption he was returned before the end of the week! "This dog barks if you don't let him in. We have neighbors and we can't have this." Then there was "This dog is a mess! He won't sleep in the yard, he won't sleep on the laundry in the laundry room, he actually expects to sleep in MY bed, and he wants under MY covers! I don't think so!" The last one was the kicker. This particular person had been counseled on all of Matrix's strange and spoiled ways. She adopted him, paying the standard $55.00 fee, and was told that for whatever reason, if she needed to bring him back, and that she more than likely would be, she would be refunded all of her money. By this time Pets and People had heard it all.

Susan Mario, the last "owner" of my darling doggy was the victim of the fart-in-the-face routine one too many times. She understood that he had his own particular schedule. She understood that he wanted to go out in the mornings, pretend he wanted to go out in the afternoon, fully expecting you to stand in the door waiting on him as he walked around the yard, scoping out the smells and dealings of the yard, but that he had no intention whatsoever to do any real business. She even understood that he only ate dry cat food, and that he was never going to sleep outside, in the garage, in the laundry room, or under the bed. It was going to be in her bed, next to her, and under her covers. That did not bother Ms. Mario in the least. She had been a dachshund slave before. What she could not bear were the morning fart fests. They start at about 7 a.m., and if one is wise they will simply turn their head, tuck the covers under the dog, or put him out, as it really is an indication that he needs to be relieved. Mario's answer was to harshly scold Matrix, and to threaten to return his tri-colored butt to the shelter. Ordinarily this would have been effective I suppose, to an animal who couldn't go on living without their owner, but Matrix, obviously, had other places to fart. He was in the hands of the only one that could know, and to know without doubt, that the two little girls in his life from the beginning were going to be given back to their mommy, and that this very day they would be returning to the one place they had met just a little while back. Faith doesn't always have to take the defensive—offensive works as well. We took our little dog home and home is where he has been ever since. On my lap, under my covers, wherever he wants to be, eating whatever he wants to eat, barking whenever he wants to bark, and no, because he doesn't have Tigger and Sting to contend with, Matrix is the king. And then, there was Faith.

I was sitting there, minding my own business on January 21, 2003, because that is what I always do, and my son came into the house with that "look" on his face. We had moved again because we had obtained full custody by this time, and we had managed to rent a little house without having to put up much of a deposit. Reuben knew the rules, we couldn't have pets. The fact that we had pets, notwithstanding, Reuben knew the rules. He was standing in front of me. He was smiling. He wasn't going to tell me why, but I knew that in the 17 years I had known him that there were very few reasons for this particular smile. Funny isn't it? I can tell which of my children has let gas in the closed car by the smell, it doesn't matter how well you've trained them, they all do it, and I find it a little disturbing that I can detect from my nostrils which of my kids to blame. I'm never wrong . . . this smile, this barely showing the teeth, but all the dimples being exposed for optimal cuteness. What was he about to do? What was I about to get myself into? In a flash my life changed. "It was true Mom, Princess had a bunch of puppies and she had some of them without legs and one died because it couldn't fight off the others. Another one died when it walked into the snow and she didn't go out and get it. I found it, I buried it." A tragic story yes, but he hadn't stopped the excessive smiling. That's when it hit me. No! He didn't! He knows we can't have a dog in this house! We already broke the rules with Matrix. Then he had to have that cat, and when one cat comes another one finds its way into my house. I was already being asked to pay more each month to cover the deposit on the animals that Frank the landlord had been so adamant about—adamant in that we couldn't have any. We had Matrix, but for some reason Frank believed me when I told him he would be staying down the street with friends. Idiot. "You didn't bring home one of those dogs Reuben!" I protested. I stomped my right foot, slammed down the dish drying towel in my hands, which I had been using to dry dishes he was suppose to have washed hours ago. "You did not bring home a puppy just because she had too many. Oh my gosh Reuben it was only two weeks ago! You can't bring a two-week old puppy here and expect it to live, its mother has to feed it, it doesn't even have its eyes open I'm sure." I continued protesting. I know I did, and there he was, smiling. While he wouldn't stop showing off those dimples, he reached into the folds of his football jersey, pulling out the fuzziest, yellowest, cutest little pointed-eared puppy I had ever seen . . . . without front legs. This was going to take a little faith!

Janet Rios (now, Martinez) is a beautiful woman, dark, Hispanic by heritage, with long, long, flowing dark hair which tends to be pulled up and bunched around her head most of the time. When she comes to my house the poor woman is subjected to torture because of her incredibly beautiful hair and pure, clean, skin. Laura and Caity have played with Janet since they were very small, perhaps as far back as their 1st and 2nd grades respectively. Janet has always tolerated them, letting them pull on her hair, making it into dozens of tiny ponytails, twisting it and braiding it. She has sat perfectly still for hours while they put makeup on her face, testing colors which probably look best on her eyebrows to be put on her lips, and vice versa. Janet is one heckuva babysitter and always has been. When the time came for Janet to graduate from high school she was honored by the vocational school she was attending when she wasn't attending Putnam City High School. Janet was the best in the State of Oklahoma in general masonry and had the mounted trowels and awards to prove it. Within a few months of her graduation Janet decided to go to college and I was her choice for an English teacher. I didn't know if she was trying to tell me that she wanted to learn something from me, or if she thought I owed her an easy A for the things my daughters have put her through all these years. Either way it was decided, I would be teaching Janet English. Toward the beginning of the Spring semester of 2003 Janet had completed her first English course and chose me again to teach her English II course, not a problem for me, but it seems to be one for her. She was making excuses the first week of school saying that she couldn't get the assignment completed because she had too much stress at home. I knew her family well, Janet and her brother Johnny had virtually lived at my house off and on since 1996, and this semester was no different. I didn't want to pry, but I explained to her that it wouldn't be fair to the other students in my class if she was excused from the first essay on Favorite Zoo Animals if they had to complete their essays on time. "I know" she complained, but it wasn't just her mother's illness, or her brother missing so much school, or her father's new girlfriend, (her parents had divorced just a few months before) and it wasn't just the fact that her sister in California wanted and needed her in that state to help with her growing family; it seems Janet had another altogether interesting problem, which if I had thought about it, I would have known about because I had not seen much of her during the Christmas break. I had heard a great deal about her since Johnny, her brother, was my son's best friend, and they had been best of friends since 1996, when the two of them were in the same fourth grade class.

Janet tried to look me in the eye when she told me, but she wasn't sure I would believe her. She tried several times without being able to talk about it, and when the tears came out of her eyes I had to concede that whatever the problem was, it was serious indeed, and it was going to cause me to become involved . . . again. Normally, these things were just a matter of money, time, a little effort, whatever it took, but this seemed different. She was genuinely concerned about something she didn't have control over.

"Remember a few weeks ago when I told you my dog had puppies?"

"Yes, you told me there were some without legs and I told you they wouldn't survive, I remember."

"You said I should maybe put them down, and I was kind of laughing because I wasn't actually holding any of them."

"Yes, I thought that was funny too", I said.

"Well, Princess had a few of them without legs and Johnny found one of them dead today." I was truly sorry to hear that, it was bitterly cold outside, and I could only imagine that the puppy had gotten away from its mother. She wouldn't have gone after it. Princess was not the mothering kind.

"Janet, what's going on? ", I asked.

"I have to feed the other dogs. Princess won't do it. She won't feed the puppies."

"You're feeding the dogs yourself? You're going outside to the back lot and feeding them, with what? An eye dropper?"

"Yes! I'm using the medicine dropper that I found in the cabinet to put milk and vitamins into them. They don't always take it and I think one of them is going to die; she won't let me pick her up and Princess keeps biting me when I try. I think Princess is going to kill the dog and it's my fault." She began to cry into the phone.

"Why is it your fault?" I asked, Janet had never been able to hurt anything.

"Because, she knows I'm trying to help it, and she won't let me. It's like she doesn't want me getting close to it, but she won't help it either."

I didn't know what to tell her. I couldn't really empathize because I didn't have anything in my life to compare it to. Her dog's motherless actions were alien to me, every time one of my dogs had given birth I was there, I was the midwife, she had let me help her in every way. Princess was repelling everyone and pulling the deformed puppies underneath her in a perverse manner. It was as if she was deciding the fate of the puppies for herself; it was really getting to Janet. She couldn't let the puppies die without trying to help them. When Reuben came home from school I asked him to go by Johnny's house to check out the situation, maybe he could do something to prevent the puppies from suffering. He was, after all, a stronger person than either Janet or I when it came to possibly having to deal with putting the puppies down humanely.

Excerpts from journals:

January 28, 2003

"The word sucker is clearly painted on my pointed head or somewhere on me because it never fails to happen. I'm always caught because I don't have any common sense. I can't say no. I don't know why. Johnny and Janet (Rios) have an old dog named Princess that was supposed to be spayed a long time ago. I think I paid for that, but she wasn't spayed and naturally she had puppies. She had them last month, and now I have one. Reuben brought her to me last week. This one is extremely small, and quite odd really. Her front paw and leg are dead and the other one (right) isn't there at all, there's a little nub and a claw. It won't ever develop and she's going to be lame forever. She's sandy colored, fuzzy, smooth haired and she has a little white spot on her face near her nose. She is only going to be 20-25 pounds probably I don't know who or what the father dog is. Princess is nearly all chow, black and hairy. I guess the daddy had to be yellow and smaller. We decided to name her Faith. We could have named her Miracle because Reuben said she didn't have a chance of surviving. Maybe he just told me that, but he said that Princess was crushing her and he had to drag the puppy out from under her. I think she's going to make it, we don't let dogs die in my house, but this is going to be an experience."

January 28, 2003, (later)

Faith is drinking well, she's eating off the floor, she can't scoot up over the rim of the bowl, but that's just today. She'll get much bigger and stronger and she'll be OK. We'll definitely have to watch her to be sure she doesn't put her head in the bowl of water, she may not be able to get it out. I don't need her drowning on me. She has to be taken care of, but that's not a problem at our house. Dang it!

January 29, 2003

Faith is a really cute puppy and I probably would have picked her out if I had seen the rest of them. I don't know if they were all this badly deformed. Reu said that some were and today Johnny said that some of the puppies had died. I don't know if he's just saying that or if it is true, but Princess is a really mean dog. She may be killing the deformed puppies. I just would have thought she would have done that a long time ago.

January 30, 2003

I really miss Maurice. I didn't think I would. I didn't realize when he died a couple of weeks ago that all these feelings were going to flood back. I only met him a few times. I mean, we were friendly but we weren't really friends. Maybe we were but we weren't good friends. Why is my heart hurting? I don't get it. Laura is sick today, she has tummy cramps but I think she just wants to be home with Faith. She has her in her arms and she's telling her how she's going to get her a new skate to roll around on. Can you imagine that? Yes, Mr.

Wal-Mart Man. I think his name is Barry. His son goes to school with my son. "Can we have a Barbie skate so we can cut it in half and then strap it onto our little two-legged dog? You see, she doesn't walk and she never will, her front legs are gone. (one anyway and the other useless) Faith scoots pretty good. She got under the bed and then up into her box again. Its great to see her in action really, she is determined. I'm hoping she won't even need wheels but I don't see how it would be unavoidable. I could get her a little set now and a professional one later. I have to try."

Chapter Thirteen

WHAT DID WE KNOW? We thought perhaps that Faith would have to be carted about because she didn't have any legs. It didn't dawn on us at that time that two legs in back have worked well enough for chimps in the past. Dogs aren't chimps, I know that, they aren't human either, but they do have one thing in common, well, two, they're all mammals, and they have the same Creator. I couldn't make it happen but He could. Prayer time!

Faith was going to have to get around and I was, after all, a professor at a real live college with a real live Engineering department. I can't even tell you the excitement she instilled in the hearts of the security officers when I stopped by their station first thing to let them see her, to register her as being a visitor on campus, and to let them see her scoot around. She actually left them a tiny little gift. Their reactions were precious. One of them asked me if he could frame it? I had to laugh. We used a new tissue and decided collectively not to keep it or to preserve it. Faith's ability to win hearts didn't end with me obviously, several dozens of administrators, students, teachers, and staff at Oklahoma City Community College were delighted to see her that first day we took her to find out if the students in the Mechanical Engineering classes could possibly come up with something that she could use. Anything had to be better than the half-baked Barbie skate idea, even if our little idea was created in love. I wish I had taken a picture of our poor puppy laying there on the floor trying to gnaw her way out of that contraption. To be perfectly honest, strapping Faith to the skate with velcro was not an easy task. I'm sure she wasn't wanting to be attached to it, and the skate seemed to be repelling her as well. It would roll away from us. It took two people to strap a little dog that weighed under six pounds to a Barbie skate that weighed about the same. Come to think of it, I'm glad I didn't take any early photographs of us torturing Faith, they could have been used against us in a court of law. "No your Honor, I wasn't trying to kill my dog. She's armless. Armless your Honor, Look!" Maybe I'd get off with an easy sentence.

Dr. Mansaroh was not available. His classes had started yes, and the syllabus was being followed. It was explained to me that the cause was great, but without permission from the Chair of the Department to change the syllabus guidelines, and in his case, the instructor would have to approve it as well; we would have to put the project off until the following semester. That wouldn't be until August! This was late January, and by that time the new semester rolled around my dog would be well established on her chest, or so I thought.

When I teach college students I ask them to keep a journal of everything they do from the time they come into the class to the time they leave. Their final exam is often an overview of everything as they have experienced it in class and/or at home or in their daily lives. It's no surprise to see that my journal entries during this time of my life would be helpful when recalling exactly what I was going through in terms of what I thought would be the future of this little yellow dog. Sometimes, when I have nothing else to do, I'll randomly pull out a journal, one of my hundred notebooks stashed around the house, and I'll read about a particular time in my life. Would I remember everything I wrote, would I be able to relive it if I had to? The thought occurred to me that I may have to surrender my journals for court someday . . . wow, then everyone would know exactly what I was really thinking about them. That could be interesting.

January 31, 2003

Reuben is gone. He moved out and it's sad because he's growing up but he did say that I have to feed him still. I guess the ties aren't completely cut off. He gets paid tomorrow, and I have to pay his electricity, get him groceries, and do a little with trying to get him his own phone. I'm sure I'll end up paying for that too. Wouldn't it be nice if I had a, oh, I don't know . . . a job! Oklahoma City Community College has 2 classes for me, but that's it. I lost Redlands and OBU to budget cuts. I'm not that upset about OBU, but it was money. Faith is actually pushing herself along from what I can tell. It looks like she is scooting faster, I'll say that, but she's going to have to learn to lift up that face. She bumps it to the ground with each bound and that has to hurt!

February 6, 2003

I'm an idiot. I call myself an idiot quite often, but this time I mean it. I was online and found that someone had been using my name and information for a matchmaker site. I did the unthinkable, I asked them to stop using my screen name. That set off a multitude of harassing e-mails and then it dawned on me that I'm not the only person in the world that uses that name. OK, so I guess I can mark that up to being a real dummy. Reu came by, he's not surprised I got chewed out online. He said he had a name online with several numbers behind it because there were over 400 people using the name he picked. There you go. It snowed today about 3 inches and I'm going to put Faith in it to see her reaction."

Faith not only liked the snow she dug her face into it over and over again wanting to burrow. I had to ask myself at that point if her father wasn't a yellow dachshund, but I knew better. It was nearly impossibly to get her tiny face out of the snow without forcibly picking her up and moving her. She liked the feel of it, or she did until I think it dawned on her that the snow was rather cold. Her tiny furry chest and chin were completely covered and she realized about four or five minutes into the snow fight going on behind her, that she was getting a little wet. Yelp! Yelp! I looked at her and she was trying to get my attention. The crying wasn't enough to make me really think she was in any trouble, so I watched, I waited to see what she was going to do for herself. I hadn't heard her cry before. She had been completely unable to bark or make any sound whatsoever before this moment. Naming her Faith was intentional after all. We knew that God could work His miracle, but it was going to take faith to walk . . . it always does. God opened the door of the prison and He sent His Angel to guide Peter, but He instructed Peter to put on his own shoes, and to WALK out of the building itself. Walking was going to take faith. Walking was going to be Faith's work, not mine. I watched her. YELLLLP! Finally! That's what I wanted to hear, that's what I wanted to see! There she was, no longer laying on her face and chest with her head buried in the snow, the puppy was up on her hunches, sitting. Just sitting and just crying out. Something she had not done before because her mother had laid too long on her voice box. These were the first cries we had heard from our little furry baby. It was time to do the dance.

Matrix wasn't exactly the best mate for Faith. He was after all fully grown, dominant, and well . . . he's half dachshund. Dachshund have a long standing reputation of being neurotic and my black mutt was no different. It was really funny to watch him when he spotted a squirrel in the yard. The beagle in him told him to stand and point, the dachshund in him told him to dig in with all four feet about 3 inches from the ground and tear off after it. The dog literally stutters in a run-stop motion across the first 15-20 feet of the pursuit, giving the animal a heads up! Don't be scared little guy, he wouldn't know what to do if he were to catch you, the cats trained him. He would no doubt meow, and bat you away with his front paw or something. Perhaps ignore you completely.

Journal Entry:

February 9, 2003

Happy Birthday Joseph Hamilton. What a grim day for weather. I guess if you're a duck this sort of thing is good. Today at 6:00 p.m. I saw an ad in the daily on the internet and I couldn't believe it. Corgi puppies, full blood for $150.00. I can't possibly do that. I know I don't have a job. I don't have permission from my landlord for the animals that I have, why on Earth did I drive to Newcastle, Oklahoma to pick up a little tri-colored dog? For Faith. Happy early Valentine's little girl. How many other dogs can say that they got their own best friend for Valentine's Day? Getting to the place was so scary. We drove through pea soup fog from Southwest 74th off the highway all the way into Newcastle, and people passed us as if they could! I was going the speed limit and I couldn't see two feet in front of me. These people had their high beams on, a big no-no in the first place, and driving more than 70 mph in those conditions, I was going 30 by the time I arrived in Newcastle. I got lost two times and there was a man and his dog Sam to help us. "Over that way in the trailer." That was good news. We were going to a trailer in the middle of a muddy lawn, we had to walk in 30 degree weather about two city blocks from the road, no, the deserted road, to find the little beaten up trailer. For a damn dog! Well, it was a Corgi, and he was really really cute. Caity named him Ean, you pronounce it Ine. Like Mine, without the M."

By her 10th week on Earth Faith was sitting up and just about hopping to me. She would certainly think about it. If nothing else, she was at least off of her face most of the time. I wasn't sure, but there was a time that I actually thought I caught her doing deep knee squats. Reuben was doing them in front of her, and she was either trying to imitate him, or she was trying to jump up to him, but over and over again, she was making the very motions he was. That had to have played a part in building up those legs. People see Faith and just after their initial shock when they realize she doesn't have front legs, they comment on her back ones. "Wow! What leg muscles!" I suppose it's been a while for me now, and to be honest I'm very used to seeing her walking around the house and yard. I don't even notice any longer, but yes, her leg muscles are quite defined. The beginning movements were of course recorded. We have still shots and motion video clips of her first hops. Parents dream of the moments their babies walk, and they take out the camcorders to capture their every movement. We were no different. I don't think I've seen video of other puppies taking their first hops and skips, but we have Faith on tape. She made her way around the house and over a spoon first. She was trying to lick the peanut butter off of it. We had first used this method in the snow that first night. We took a little plastic spoon with peanut butter and held it just before her nose. Hop. We did it again. Hop. The dog was definitely a dog. The practice was repeated over and over again until her mind took over and the matter of being legless was forgotten. Over and over she hopped to us, and we began to think that walking would not be a far fetched idea. Placing our hands under her and moving slowly backward . . . one hand under her and the other holding a peanut butter laden spoon . . . . faith! She walks. Soon she would be making her way into the hearts of not only disabled people, but people with disabled pets. Amazingly, we received letters from local people who had seen us walking around the block, going to the stores, the vet's, or just anywhere. They had to be a part of Faith's adventure, and we welcomed their cards and invitations of hope because it meant that we as a family had actually followed our hearts and made the right decision to keep our little fuzzy girl.

The camera became her constant admirer. She didn't quite understand why we would be so interested, after all, she had to get around some day right? Peanut butter, ham, olives, grapes, tomatoes, it didn't matter. Feed the puppy and she would follow you anywhere. I remember walking into the bedroom one night when she was about 12 weeks old and catching her climbing on top of Ean to get to the top of the bed because I had left a spoonful of peanut butter in the center of it on a plate. Could she find a way? Oh yes, she found a way, Ean suffered a little, but she was most grateful. Not grateful enough to share, mind you, but she was nevertheless on top of the world. We have pictures. One of the more desperate moments involving movements came early on in Faith's life when Reuben, Laura, and Caity decided that a skateboard would be really useful. Because Wal-Mart is the only store we shop at for these sorts of things the kids took Faith into the toy department of the newly opened Super Center on N.W. Expressway. Back to Barry at Wal-Mart. He was so excited to be a part of Faith's experiences with learning to get from point A to point B. He took the kids and Faith to the area where skateboards are sold and they decided that a mini board would be best. About six dollars later, they were on their way to training poor Faith to be a master at rolling. Flop! She would not stay positioned. She should have learned. Velcro wasn't going to be a part of this torture. Shoe strings hold more things in place than simply the sides of one's tennis shoes. If I were a sadist I would have taken pictures of these sort of inventions as well, the only pictures of Faith riding on a skateboard are ASACP approved. Not that the memories aren't vivid.

Journal Entry:

March 6, 2003

Faith looks so pathetic. She's being strapped down to the skateboard the kids bought at Wal-Mart. How did they think she was going to stay on? They put shoe strings around the board and tied her down in about 4 places. I swear, the poor dog is going to have nightmares of falling of a cliff strapped to a surfboard or something. AAAHHHGGGHH. Kids. She's going to have to walk, there's just no other way out of it. The dog's going to be killed with these contraptions."

I went on the internet and looked for sites using Google. I think my keywords were "wheels for dogs without legs" or something. I found a site at *www.wheelchairsfordogs.com* and for the next few days corresponded with them about Faith's needs. I needed to download a couple of pictures of her, take her measurements and be prepared for their responses, however, they never wrote back after I asked them to give me a price for a wheelchair or cart that Faith could use. Back to the internet and I found another site, this one was *www.dogswithdisabilities.com*. They were a bit more responsive. They told me they could not help me. I asked why of course, and without hesitation they returned my e-mail with the fact that they had never heard of a dog surviving without both of their front legs. One maybe, but the front legs, as it was explained to me, are used to push, not pull. A dog without his or her back legs can pull a cart around and get from one place to the other as long as the terrain is smooth. To expect a dog to push a cart would require strength in the entire body. The legs of course would have to be strong, the spine would be compromised, and the idea of building one unit for this one dog was simply not feasible. At least they wrote back. I thanked them. After about four weeks I received an e-mail from the people at Wheelchairs for Dogs. They had also contacted Dogs with Disabilities and were told the same thing. I suppose the idea must have created a stir in their minds, and the fact that they hadn't returned my e-mail was not to be taken negatively after all. People respond in different ways.

Faith's ability to stay put on a skateboard has not improved. She sees one now and noses it before she comes near it. She won't hop onto one, and if placed on one she runs away. Yes, runs. She developed a method of movement which far surpassed our imagination. Her ability to stand up and take off is not credited to any sort of contraption whatsoever. I recorded it diligently in my journal, and if I hadn't been there to see it for myself, I may not have believed it.

Journal Entry:

March 22, 2003

Happy Birthday Baby Boy! You got something today that you may never have realized would be a wonderful gift. Faith stood up and ran across the yard. She literally stood up and chased Ean clear across the yard when he bit her legs and then took her bone away from her. I thought she was going to kill him. I took pictures."

Ean did it! Viva la Valentines! The puppies were outside in the bright sun shinily day playing with their new rawhide bones and barking at one another. Ean, whomwe often call Corgus decided that it was time to test out those herding skills that are naturally inbred into his genetic makeup. He thought about it, then pounced on Faith, jumping from her left side to her right, forcing her to move from one point of the yard to the other. He had her in his control, and she wasn't the least bit happy about it. NO ONE takes the bone from this dog, or pushes her away from her food, NO ONE. Not even her own present.

Hard and fast Faith stood up completely on her back legs like a Tyrannosaurus Rex, running one foot in front of the other at a pace fast enough to be amazed at. She reached the thief and bit the head of the Corgi dog hard enough to shock the surprise right out of him. Gripping the bone in his mouth he took off and tried to escape her wrath. Nothing doing. Faith took one giant hop and then another, before long she was bounding like a kangaroo across the backyard in all her glory. This continued until the dogs met in a pile of flying fur. I think Ean was laughing at his friend, but I could hear Faith and it didn't sound very pleasant from where I was standing. Within a few seconds the little dog had given up his prize to the more dominant and certainly more bipedal animal in the backyard. Faith, the avenger! Bone retrieved, Faith laid down and continued her blissful pursuit of her rawhide. All the while Matrix, in his kingly way watched, never offering assistance to either of his subordinates.

From scooting to sitting, sitting to hopping, hopping to bounding, and finally a means of movement which still stuns and amazes everyone who sees her walking, Faith has developed into what we believe, is the ONLY upright walking biped canine in the world today. Again, as I walk her or see her rounding a corner in the house I am not impressed, I have no reaction of surprise on my face when I take her to Petsmart or to her vet's office. I'm used to seeing her walking and it is merely something that she does to get, as I mentioned, from point A to point B. She commands attention from nearly every other person and animal alive when she is noticed. To be honest, I am proud of her, and when I do see the attention she is receiving from her abilities to walk upright I am immediately reminded of her struggle, and of her self imposed determination to stand and walk. Faith comes in many ways, and certainly this dog's faith is not to be dismissed. No where is it written that animals cannot seek the Lord's will the same as we do. We may not understand their method of communication with Him but there is no reason for me to believe that He has limited His personal divine intervention to humans only. I won't ever believe that. When Faith came to us she was without the use of her arms and she was voiceless. It was an act of utter dependence on her part to be in our charge. We literally had to pick her up, put her places, help her, watch her, and make determinations for her because she could not let us know vocally that she needed out, wanted food, or simply that she wanted to be picked up. She used her eyes, her facial expressions, body language, and other methods to let us know.

It wasn't long after we took Faith into our hearts that I understood that God's love is really quite the same for us. On a larger scale of course, but when I was going through the custody battles, the divorce issues, and the financial troubles after I lost my jobs, I had felt armless in court. The long arms of the law were completely wrapped around the judge, and my voice was quieted a number of times as I stood before a seemingly heartless group of people telling me that I was unimportant, that my children were better off with people who I knew were hurting them. I was unable to make my points in that courtroom I was forced to cry, to show expression, to wait, and to depend on the only one that would forever be able to make the difference in our lives. I had to wait on God. Faith wasn't the easiest thing to have in those days and for our little dog, faith wasn't the easiest thing to demonstrate as she wound up sloshing in her own squalor when we weren't paying the best of attention.

The similarities between her physical condition and my emotional condition were parallel in so many ways. Her eyes were open as she would stare up at us and hope. My heart wanted to hear the words of peace, and I would stare, hoping that finally the judge would understand. Speaking, barking in her courtroom would only bring about disaster, as I had proved to myself over and over again. I really do have a thick head at times. If only I could be more like my son Reuben, who takes the answer he is given and walks away, thinking of another way to achieve his goals. Or maybe I could be more like my daughter Laura, who takes the answer she is given and analyzes it to the point of finally understanding it. She can justify just about anything and make her condition more acceptable. Not me, I'm exactly like Caity, what is mine is mine, if I'm right, I'm 100% right! I shouldn't be punished because someone else is too stupid to see things my way, and God help the person who dares to mess with me when I get my mind settled on something. These tactics don't really work in the courtroom and it took me just a little longer than most to figure that out. With faith came the patience I had to find, and once it was crammed down my throat by my all-to-fabulous attorney Anita F. Sanders, I was able to walk upright and run to my rawhide . . . well, to my children. And yes, I will admit, I stood upright like a Tyrannosaurus Rex and bit the heads of the people who had taken them from me. There were many parallels, including the joy on our faces when we realized that we actually can do what we think we can do if we just let go and let it happen in due time. His time, with a little faith.

Chapter Fourteen

Around the same time that Faith began to walk the United States had declared war on Iraq. I was working a temporary position at a downtown law office and I remember being in the lunch room/conference room, eating my grapes and cottage cheese, listening to the lawyers discussing the events of the day. When I put my two cents worth in I was asked to remain quiet. I couldn't believe the rudeness of these people, did they really think that because they held law degrees they had more to contribute to the conversation? Oh, wait, maybe it was because I wasn't one of them, I wasn't employed full time. I was a peon, a nobody, a . . . temporary. I was in the room before them, and it had in fact been me who had filled them in on all of the CNN and MSNBC updates. "You can go back to work now", stated a particularly egomaniac. "I'll go to work when my lunch is over," I retorted. Is it hard to see why I don't exactly keep jobs very long when working for someone else? Mr. Moler would never in a million years have been so arrogant. Within a few seconds of the eye-to-eye I-am-not-about-to-back-off standoff that was taking place in the little room, a former student of mine walked into the lunchroom. "Professor!" she cried out. "What are you doing here?" I was somewhat embarrassed to admit that because of budgetary cuts I had been released at Oklahoma Baptist University and I would not be returning until possibly in the fall. The word "professor" brought an all together different facial expression to the man sitting across the large mahogany table from me. "*Professor* Stringfellow? What do you profess?" He wanted to know.

"English for one, and Ethics, if you think you'd like to learn a little something." "Oh, funny, one would think an English teacher could be employed these days", he continued, eating his tuna salad, and smugly laughing that he had at least chosen the right path in life. I secretly wondered how his essays fared in his freshmen and sophomore years. I had somewhat of an ideas as it was my duty to clean up his letters and pleadings, at least on a temporary basis.

I had taken a few pictures of Faith with me to work that day and was actively showing them around when the arrogant lawyer from the lunch room sidled up to my desk. "Working hard?" he wanted to tease with a pointed edge. "I wouldn't have to work as hard as I do if you could spell, or use the English language in the manner that it was properly created." I came back magnificently, I thought. "You're fired! Go home immediately", was all he could come back with. In my mind I thought about using the word "twit", but chose rather to push a picture in his direction and state without being the least bit upset that the dog that I resided with would provide better company than the dog I was looking at now. One of the secretaries begged the idiot to let me stay. She was too accustomed to working out his horrid use of grammar, and knew I was the only one strong enough to stand up also to his sexually based innuendos. I don't put up with sexual harassment in the work place, how could I if I were to be successful at teaching Ethics the following semester to people I had hoped would be bright enough to listen? Her request fell on deaf ears; however, within the next few months the man was apologetic enough.

Riding on an airplane to New York City to film the Ricki Lake Show in October of 2003, I was actually given the seats across the aisle from Mr. Lunchroom Moron. His company had not seen fit to fly him First Class. We were in the bulkhead just behind First Class, where our real seats were, but we had given them up so that Faith could have more room. Faith preferred to ride in comfort, where she could lay down if necessary. Stunned and amazed to see that I told the truth about having a dog with only two back legs, the lawyer asked me to forgive his comments and for having fired me. Not a problem I said, but you know what, it was a problem. I didn't have any money coming in for several more weeks. We ate less, I paid bills late, and the war raged on, making it impossible for me to be hired. No one was interested in interviewing anyone, no one knew what was going to happen to the country. We didn't know who was going to be going to fight, we didn't know if we were to expect another 9/11, or if we were going to go in with both barrels leveled at Iraq. "That's OK, I found other work, I always do." I commented, looking down at Faith.

"Didn't she have another leg?" He asked

"Yes, it was removed in July, it had began to atrophy." I commented

"I read where you changed vets. Did the first one think it needed to stay on?"

"No, she was a great vet. She didn't want to talk to the media." I answered.

With Faith being featured on *Ripley's Believe it or Not, CNN, MSNBC*, and in national and international magazines, Dr. Delbridge chose not to discuss the condition of her patient. Faith was more than just a patient actually, the world was interested in her progress. I switched vets when I found Dr. Hartford.

He was good, he was close, he was willing to answer questions. I added that I thought the new vet was cuter than Dr. Delbridge too, but you have to understand, he's a guy, and I went to school with Diane Delbridge when we were just little kids. She was the first and only choice for me when it came to helping me and my little dog. She's the best vet on the planet if you ask me.

"Cute matters I guess." He laughed, and I suppose our old battle of the stubborns had to be put aside. Dammit. This guy was actually a nice man and he seemed interested in my little puppy. I can't ever hold grudges . . . . God's mean to me that way. Just as I find a really good grudge and get going on it, He breaks my stride, softens me up and there I am forgiving people. My son does rub off on me after all. Laura would continue the grudge, but she would categorize it, place a value on it, and make appropriate accommodations for any future responses to the individual. Caity forgives everyone, but she never forgets. Once burned Caity will forever dismiss. Forgiveness must take a bit of faith as well, as I have found out that it really does feel good to have the peace that comes from letting go of the feelings I held against someone. But just a little grudge now and then, that wouldn't be too bad, would it?

Chapter Fifteen

At the close of spring 2003 I had heard enough about war when I turned on my television set. I was about up to my eyeballs in financial problems, having not been hired by anyone with any the slightest idea of what it cost to live these days and to raise a family. I was sinking a little too deeply in my own self pity about being overweight, and there wasn't much to look forward to either. Something had to give. Somehow, someway, I had to find a way to smile again and that's when the idea hit me: I called the CBS local news station KWTV-Channel 9 because my best friend Jeannie's husband had worked there at one point and I remember him telling me that news anchor Kelly Ogle (another cute man) simply loved feel-good stories about family oriented things. Family, church, morality, good things to put into the news because quite frankly, the world had proved to be a pretty nasty place. Anytime Kelly could come up with a little story about something really cool, he was going to show it, and make the biggest effort to spread the joy. Kelly was out the day I called and whoever it was that answered the phone at KWTV didn't feel it necessary to pass along my little tale about a two-legged dog in Oklahoma City that walks upright and leaves everyone smiling in her wake. Linda Cavanaugh, however, at the NBC news station of KFOR-TV channel 4 was in. She, like Kelly, is a prominent, wonderful anchor with many years of experience, grace and charm. She wanted to do the story on Faith, and she wanted to do it that night! Sorry Kelly, I tried.

Linda sent out a cameraman to my house to pick up a few shots, maybe of the dog running around the yard with the kids, maybe taking a stroll down the street. This couldn't be a very big piece, she knew just where it was going to be placed in that evening's news and the story needed to be written on the QT as it was already getting close to 5:00 p.m. When Dennis Anderson came to the house what he saw was anything but usual. We were there, smiling of course, waiting to greet him, to shake his hand, and to introduce him to our furry buddy. He got on his cell phone and called the station with news about Faith being remarkably unusual. He had thought in his mind, he confessed, that Faith walked on her front legs, dragging her rump in the air somehow. He admitted that seeing her walking upright was more than just a little surprising. He stayed quite a while filming and asked me if he could come back if he needed more footage. Sure, why not, this is the sort of thing I think Faith was made to do. She was created to be the smiling, laughing dog without a care in the world. Go ahead Mr. Cameraman . . . shoot away! Come back tomorrow, the next day, and any other day if it makes the people giggle or gives them hope that they can do more than they first thought they might be able to do.

We didn't really interview with KFOR that day. Laura told the camera a few things about Faith; the fact that she is terribly spoiled, that she eats too much, we take her for walks, and then there was a little blurb about thanking God that she was in our lives. It was barely noticeable on tape when the story aired but it stood out on its own somehow. People have commented several times about Laura giving God the credit for making Faith and/or giving her to us.

"Now Faith is an ordinary dog, she chases the cats with the best of them." Linda concluded in the story on the night of June 23, 2003. Within hours KFOR called me to see if they could run the story over the Associated Press. Why not? Again, I thought that if someone out there in the big, bad world could use a smile, it may as well come from the story about our puppy. She was laughing, laying by my side when the phone rang and I gave my permission for the story to be shot across the world instantly. Within a few more hours the people of Germany, Sweden, England, Holland, and France had called me. I was literally on the phone from 4:03 a.m. to 9:14 a.m. Central Standard Time, talking to news people all over the world. Laura gave an impromptu interview to a London based radio station, and agreed to be called later that afternoon to be live on a particular show that details stories with strange and bizarre twists. Stories the world finds both odd and fantastic at the same time. Pictures of my daughter Laura and my dog appeared on the covers of tabloids within days. I was called by the editor of the *National Enquirer* as he wanted to run a feature story about her. My mind raced as I suddenly imagined Martians from outer space wearing Faith-costumes, landing in the desert and demanding to be taken to Pamela Anderson. Nothing was going to be out of place I was promised. The *National Enquirer*, according to their leader, was capable of telling full truths as well as sensationalized news. I agreed to the interview and pictures being printed as long as the stories written were true, and any picture of Faith was flattering. The agreement was made and into our house came Mr. Stephen Holman, not only a resident of Tulsa, Oklahoma and a photojournalist for the Tulsa World, but he is also a contract photojournalist for the *National Enquirer*, *The Star*, *The Globe*, *National Geographic for Kids*, and several other major magazines. This could explain the sudden onslaught of global coverage immediately following the breaking story in the *National Enquirer*.

"LISA MARIE HAS A MELTDOWN!" read the front cover of the July 29 issue of The *National Enquirer*, and I didn't care. I had been called the day before it was released and told that Faith was on page 30. There she was! Walking and going places. Her left arm flinging around, useless, and splayed backward. Standing on her own two feet, crossing the pavement, going through the living room, playing tug of war with the other dogs, and basically just having a good time. My little dog, my daughter Laura, even Caity was in the magazine with Ean. You know what I did, I stood in line at Wal-Mart and purchased 40 copies for myself. The lady didn't have to ask me twice to explain it. She laughed out loud and picked up her PA telephone. "Ladies and Gentlemen in Wal-Mart, today on sale at every counter in the magazine racks we have the *National Enquirer* featuring one of Oklahoma City's most admired residents. Faith the two-legged dog is on page 30, come and get your copy. Her mother is buying out the store!! Hurry!" It was so cute the way my daughter blushed every time I showed another customer. She finally decided to run to the pet department and look at the fish swimming in their tanks until I was finished showing off. That took a while.

Making my way to another Wal-Mart just down the road, to every 7-11 store in the area, and to a few bookstores that I knew carried the *National Enquirer*, I continued to embarrass Laura over and over again. Caity didn't mind at all, she wasn't the least bit concerned about the coverage because there wasn't a picture of her baby belly fat plastered on the subsequent pictures. Could they have chosen a less flattering picture of Laura? Perhaps, but at least they chose others where she is smiling and looking more attractive. It's just that every time we see that particular first photo showing up on the internet, in other tabloids, on news stations across the nation, and in magazines we didn't have communication with, Laura is quick to point out that she really isn't that fat. That the belly pooching out is just a fluke, which it was of course. Faith looks good, and that was a plus for us all. Proud parents we were, our little doggy was making it big and all because she had the guts to stand up to the world with a little faith of her own.

Laura and I decided that because of all of her efforts, Linda Cavanaugh and the rest of the great people working for KFOR-TV needed to meet Faith in person, or in dog. We drove her to the station and she was immediately recognized. We were allowed into the lobby of the station during a time that news was being written but not necessarily broadcast. Tammy Payne and Lance West were just about to go on camera for the 5:00 p.m. show, but they had time to do a little hugging before they went on the air. I remember a page doing a little clean up duty around Tammy as she tried to remove a few dog hairs that she managed to collect in the petting process. Linda Cavanaugh couldn't have been more beautiful. She graciously allowed us to go backstage, to walk around the news room meeting literally every employee at KFOR-TV. One in particular, Ali Meyer an up-and-coming news anchor who, like Linda, is tall, thin, well mannered and loves dogs. She plopped down immediately to Faith's level and began giving her kisses. I thought to myself, this must be a fairly cool place to work if people come and go wearing great looking clothes from the waist up, and are able to report on the good and the bad of the world. Trophies were everywhere, indicating that the news, weather, and sports had all been given a great deal of recognition not only in the state, but from across the nation and the world as well for great coverage. Faith's story was just going to have to be accredited to KFOR-TV, it was Linda Cavanaugh who had the foresight to put it on the air and it paid off in more ways than one.

While Laura and I were at KFOR-TV, a phone call came into the newsroom. Had I not been there to see it happen I might not have believed it. One of the guys answering the news desk phone told Gunnar, one of the best producers in the building, that *I* had a phone call from *Ripley's Believe it or Not*. They were calling me at the new station. I never did find out if they had called my house first and perhaps Caity had told them where I was that afternoon. I took the call, and within a week I was hosting a blond, young, female producer named Jeannie for the internationally well known show *Ripley's Believe it or Not*. She and her crew wanted to film a day in the life of the now famous two-legged dog. What we filmed was anything but the typical day in the life of our dog. What a boring show that would be: getting up from the bed to go pee, play with the other dogs, coming back to bed, eating a little here and there, chasing the cats, going back to bed, and maybe making a visit to the neighborhood grocery store or Petsmart if we were feeling particularly outgoing. What we filmed was a day in the life of a movie star perhaps, but not my dog. They had us setting up staged scenes of breakfast, bringing friends over to talk, going to the park to chase geese, taking a trip to the ball park where Faith was admired by hundreds of spectators. Next we went downtown to Oklahoma City's more prestigious tourist attraction Bricktown. While walking the canal, taking a boat ride, doing the in-and-out game of every eating establishment, watching people fly out of the restaurants to see her, we enjoyed the faces and the expressions of people who for the first time saw her walking on her back legs . . . . like a human. The entire process took over 10 hours to film, and needless to say, after the filming, dog and owners were exhausted.

During one of the segments a group of mentally challenged people were visiting the city from out of state, they were so happy to get a chance to pet Faith, but the editing floor holds more important moments than we will ever imagine, I suppose. It would have been great to have more shots of Faith visiting with people who are so overwhelmed by her that they laugh and cry at the same time. For these people, and their caregivers, Faith represents hope and the ability to give from inside of yourself when you think you can't go any further. There was a few seconds in the telecast where Faith is meeting with a young blind boy. Because the boy and his family did not speak English, it was difficult to translate their excitement for the chance meeting; however, facial expressions and laughter again were the tools of faith, showing the nation, and the world, that with just a little hope and a little faith in ourselves as well as what may be waiting for us just outside a downtown restaurant, we can make life a little happier when we believe that we can make it a better place. These are the moments I believe I have forgotten all the loss in my life. In the middle of a crowd of people who are hugging and petting my little dog, I forget that I was saddened by the death of my friend earlier in the year. Perhaps it is his spirit that comes out when Faith is being so happy.

I recall a time on stage in August of 1979, that he looked as if he were wagging his tongue in complete elation! Maybe it was my imagination, but there did seem to be a correlation between the events of my life and the introduction of our dog Faith. More than once I have had to ask myself if God hadn't sent down an Angel in order to bring about my joy which I had somehow misplaced. Why not use a little legless dog to show the world that anything is possible? I couldn't imagine there being a less likely hero. "Sometimes", as Linda Cavanaugh reported "these stories can leave you scratching your head in wonder!" Was she ever right.

After Ripley's aired my phone wouldn't stop ringing. It wasn't always someone from another state or country wanting to talk to Faith, or to do a show about her. We had calls from German TV shows and Switzerland, the Germans came out to do a story and filmed us in our day-to-day lifestyle, much like the *Ripley's* people had done. We were under an exclusivity contract with *Ripley's* until their show ran, and the German producers guaranteed me that they too would wait to air their show. The *Oklahoma Educational Television Association* (OETA) of Tulsa came out to do a show. Their taping was only about four hours, and to be honest, I liked it a little better than I did the *Ripley's* coverage if only owing to strange camera angles and tricks of the trade using fading and whatnot. OETA's show was clean, pure, and to the point. Royal Ailes, a rather innovative producer, if I may say so, was a bit more understanding of my goals for Faith, and was quick to use video, home movies, still shots and interviews for his production. The OETA coverage aired the same month as did *Ripley's*, but for a more local audience. Using the growing resume my dog was accumulating I decided to contact a few car dealers in the area to see if they would be interested in loaning me a good new vehicle to drive Faith around in so we could get to the hospitals, children's homes, and other places I believe in my heart she is actually suppose to be visiting. I would love to be full time employed as my dog's chauffeur, taking her to places where the sad and lonely can actually be made happy, but this avenue I was taking didn't seem to be getting me anywhere. It didn't matter to any of the local dealers if Faith was able to walk upright, or walk up stairs for that matter, her owner, me, wasn't solvent enough to afford the payments on a new car. Didn't I mention I wanted them to loan it to me? I thought it would be good publicity for them and good transportation for me. This idea, to date, has not caught on. I am unable financially to do what I believe Faith was made for because I simply do not have the financial means to do it. I can't take off work and travel to the hospitals outside of our city, I can't take off work and go to the area homes either if I am expected to work and pay bills. This is one more area in my life that I believe will be handled in time, with a little faith on my part.

After the *National Enquirer* and before *Ripley's* came out I got a call from Margaret Dunbar of Big Dogs Sports. Big Dogs is a fantastic clothes line of sportswear with hoodies, tee-shirts, fleece, gear, and so much more. They have a website at *www.bigdogs.com* and anyone who isn't familiar with Big Dogs can go and see for themselves the fun line up of clothes items available. The logo on the Big Dog lines is a black and white St. Bernard, sometimes it is a girl dog, and sometimes it is a boy dog, but it is always big, strong, and I couldn't help but notice, a four-legged dog. When Margaret called me with an offer to make Faith an honorary Big Dog I had to let her in on the not-too-secret secret that Faith actually only weighs 26 pounds. She isn't the least bit BIG in terms of size. This news wasn't news to Margaret, a fan of Faith's. She had seen her on the pages of *National Enquirer* and had read about her extensively on the internet where her growing list of sites and credits was becoming incredible. I couldn't believe people were interested in chat rooms dedicated to my dog and her condition. Margaret wanted to send us a few things, gifts, toys, collars, etc. She wanted to know if there was anything she could do to help Faith as she saw Faith's "Paws-ative" attitude toward life. I told her I would let her know. *Ripley's* and Dunbar had talked about product placement during the *Ripley's* show, but alas that didn't happen. Ricki Lake didn't mind allowing me to hold a Big Dog squeaky-toy the day we interviewed with her on her show about the very best of Ripley's for the year 2003. It was amazing, as we flew to New York City with Faith in the seat next to me, not under the plane with the cargo I had to stop for a second somewhere over the Great Lakes and think to myself that I would never in a million years think that I would be going to New York to be on a show to talk about my dog, even if that dog was the most amazing animal on the planet. American Airlines deserves a lot of credit for allowing Faith to fly up in the cabin with me, and not in the cargo with other animals. Recognizing Faith as a celebrity they have an entire paragraph dedicated to this in their flight manuals. You can imagine the looks on the faces of the other passengers as we pass through security wherever we go, through the boarding area, and onto the planes. Whenever we fly, we fly American. I can't say enough about the traveling comforts this airline has brought to myself, my family, and of course, to my dog.

Chapter Sixteen

On that first flight to New York we were waiting in the airport in Oklahoma City when Laura noticed a group of soldiers coming in from a flight that had just arrived. She wanted to introduce Faith to them because they may have been in Iraq, they were certainly America's finest, and she just wanted to say hello and thank them for their dutiful service. One of the guys, a private that was probably in his late teens looked at Faith and pulled out his cell phone. "Commander!" he shouted, "That dog we saw in the magazine in Kuwait is standing right in front of me!" I was just as shocked at hearing this as I'm sure he was at seeing Faith. He bent down to pet her, and all of the soldiers began calling people, taking pictures with the cell phones and cameras to show everyone they knew back at their base camp in Kuwait that they were greeted at the airport by the two legged dog. A brave and handsome soldier with an arm wrapped in a military sling asked if I could pick Faith up so he could pet her. Seemed he had shrapnel in his leg as well and he couldn't bend very well. I thought my eyes wouldn't stop pouring out tears. Here he was, asking me if I could trouble myself to lift 26 pounds of a little dog and he had been on the front line obviously, he had fought for me, he had given up part of his body, and I was much more than thankful to him for it. I told him I would salute every soldier I would ever come in contact with because it meant so much more to me now. So much more.

I picked my dog up, and I held her out to him. I heard it first, then I saw it. Hundreds of people in the airport were standing and giving these guys an ovation for their bravery, their work, their courage to be where they were, and for doing what they were ordered to do. The first private we met looked up and he saluted the crowd. I only thought I had tears in my eyes when I lifted up Faith to the wounded man, now I knew I did, but I didn't care.

One of the times we flew back from New York, and I think it was the first time; we flew through Chicago O'Hare Airport to get to New York, but through the St. Louis Airport coming back. What a joyous smile Faith put on her face when she encountered the moving sidewalks in St. Louis. If you ever get a chance to play on the moving sidewalks please do. Oklahoma City needs to install a few of these things if for no other reason but to give me something to do with Faith on afternoons when we get a little bored. If I lived near the St. Louis airport I would take Faith as often as possible. That little dog can fly when she gets aboard these things. She won't stop running. It is the funniest thing in the world to watch, but to realize the expressions and the looks of utter amazement on the faces of the people both on the moving sidewalk we're on, and the ones opposite to us, to see Faith running as if in place, going a million miles a minute, bent over to balance herself, and racing me to the other end. She nearly pulls off her collar each time we get on one. The only thing more fun than the moving side walks may be the concrete paths of Central Park or the streets of Times Square at night.

Getting to NYC to do these shows wasn't easy. It sounds good doesn't it? You get a call from a nationally syndicated show, they want you to be on their show, and you go, you get paid, and all of the sudden you're talking to famous people, doing what the famous people do, going where they go. Well, in the years I spent working in Hollywood in the 1980's there were a few things I learned about the "famous" so to speak. Not much of what I knew about them was of much interest to me; however, my daughter Laura was excited, thinking perhaps she would be meeting Rupert Grint, the good looking red-headed boy who plays Ronald Weasley of the Harry Potter fame. Why he would magically appear in NYC at the same time she was there is beyond me, but I never rain on my girl's dream.

Journal Entry

October 27, 2003

9:30 p.m. 24 hours from now I'll be in my hotel with Laura. Ricki's people said they didn't have enough money in their budget to bring Caity along with us. I don't see why not. They had enough to give me $400 for missing work. It would mean one more ticket, we could use the same money to eat on, and the hotel room would be shared. They just didn't want to let her come I suppose. I have had such a bad time of it with these people. They want too much. First it was Laura's birth certificate, a note from her father, which of course I explained to them we don't do notes from him, we don't even talk to him. They wanted him to say it was OK for her to be on TV. I faxed them the orders from July 27, 2001, explaining that I had sole and full custody. That was enough, but then they wanted proof of her name being Stringfellow. It isn't Stringfellow, it's Stickley, but Toby Keith's real name isn't Toby Keith now is it? She goes by Laura Stringfellow. We listed her as

Stickley on the plane for their manifest, but she will be called Laura Stringfellow from anyone addressing her, and that, is by her request not mine. I had to have her birth certificate, a social security card, which wasn't a problem, but please! Next thing you know the airlines will require a rechargable Starbuck's card to get on board. Faith has to bring her vet's notes saying she is free of disease and disorders, that can't happen. She has a major disorder, hello, she doesn't have front legs. It's OK, I think they just want proof that she has had her shots and a statement that proves she doesn't have worms or something. No muzzle was being required on the plane, and that was good news. We were able to walk right on the plane, and that really is something to see.

Before the news story about Faith's abilities to walk upright I had a few other things going on in my life which required more than just a little faith to get me through. Because I'm a professor of English, and not employed full time at any one university, I was asked to take a summertime job selling insurance for a company called Conseco. It is true that Conseco had been in the news recently regarding their own financial difficulties of which I had absolutely no idea about; I was being hired to go door-to-door in small towns and communities on the west side of Oklahoma, literally trying to find people willing to buy cancer policies. I had no intention of keeping the position for any longer than I needed to, but the fact is, I really enjoyed my work. There were elements of it of course, that weren't conducive to feeling secure, for instance I was living in tiny hotel rooms in towns I had never heard of. There was the element of surprise when and if some good ol' boy with a key from last month's visit may be waltzing in on me, which happened when I was taking a shower. Thank God he was polite enough to apologize and leave the room. My job required a great deal of leg work on my part and a daily schedule of working at just after dawn to just after dark, which in the middle of June is usually after 9:30 p.m. The hours were long, the work tiring, and because I was driving alone most of the time, I was completely on my own when it came to needing my car towed into town from out in the booneys, to having my tire pop out from under me out in the middle of nowhere. That's not true exactly, I was in the middle of the countryside just outside of Fargo, Oklahoma, which is just North and East of Gage, and its just North of Arnett, so it wasn't like I was nowhere. I was in the dustiest, loneliest, most isolated area of the greater western section of our great state, but at least I had the prairie dogs, lizards, snakes, deer, and LeRoy "Chuck" Bailey to help me. Like Chuck, Fargo is a loner. Not much going on in Fargo any day of the year, and any year of the decade. Chuck was a member of the "Liars Club", which is a group of older gentlemen who met at the gas station (*The* gas station) and cafe on the main road. It was up to Chuck to keep tabs on everyone for me, because I knew he would know where they were. I involved him immediately, from the first day on the job when he bought a policy from me. I don't know if he felt sorry for me because I had never held a baby lamb before, maybe it had more to do with the fact that his beautiful wife of so many years had passed away, and our company was instrumental in getting him the benefits as soon as they were needed. Chuck was a die-hard Conseco fan and I needed one when I broke down not thirty feet away from a make shift meth lab.

"What are you doin' over there?" He called to me.

"Car broke down . . . . got a flat."

"Bound to happen. Let me help." He said.

"Is that a meth house? I smell something . . . ugly." I asked.

"Meth? Why, I don't know, maybe, probably, sure why not? It'll probably blow up like the rest of them do. If these kids that make the stuff ever took a Science class and passed it they may end up saving themselves a whole mess of trouble." That's Chuck. That's Fargo, well, that's Oklahoma period, but there is still more of an element of this behavior and feeling of genuine friendship in smaller towns around the state. After he helped me get my car going I took full advantage of him and used him for references until the day that I left the town some four weeks later. Monday through Thursday I worked Fargo, I had the entire city actually, all 580 people, and that included the 366 that lived out of the city itself. I had the opportunity, though not the pleasure, of selling insurance to the family of the biggest, fattest, strongest, and most adorable yellow Labrador I had ever seen in my life. Colonel was indeed huge, in fact, I believe someone in Fargo told me they had seen Faith on KFOR-TV and they mentioned that Ali Meyer needed to come out to Fargo to meet up with ol' Colonel. 248 pounds of yellow dog. He made my little Faith look like . . . well, a little dog.

I sold insurance for Conseco until such a time that a problem developed between what I was selling and what was being proceeded and issued. In the insurance business these numbers are never the same, but for unknown reasons my sales were not being issued, and this could only lead to one conclusion, I wasn't being paid. Looking back at it I can say without a doubt that my leaving Conseco when I did was probably one of those answered prayers that I actually felt more than verbally prayed. Bailey was great, as were all of the other members of the Liars Club; some of them have mundane lives, some not. One of my favorite members was a man I'll call Jack. Jack was a smaller man in stature, but in so many ways he reminded me of my friend who had passed away. He was bearded, about the same height and weight too, but there was something about Jack that made the light bulbs explode when he walked into a room. I saw it happen and thought immediately that he had to be producing some sort of electrical charge that he's not even aware of. "I can't keep lights in my house!" he exclaimed when I gave him a look that obviously required an answer. "I can just be standing there, maybe in the hallway or something, and if I stand there too long the lights blow." Strange, yes, but no doubt one of the more interesting facts about Fargo, Oklahoma. Jack had been many things before he retired. He had worked on the assembly lines, in the trenches digging ditches, he had driven trucks and been a rancher; today he relaxes in his home, a trailer at the edge of town and enjoys going through his scrap books (in the dimmed light of the kitchen) pouring over the many exotic places his work and play have taken him. In his living room is a large picture of him standing on top of Kilimanjaro I think.

There couldn't be a more energetic man in the world, and yet this one had been stopped physically by an accident. Still, with injuries, forced early retirement, and living in a tiny little community, Jack's smile was larger than life, much like his experiences. We had an opportunity to discuss cancer policies of course, one of which he may or may not have signed up for; but we had an opportunity to discuss Christ, faith, life after death, and issues that meant a little more to both of us. I told Jack about Maurice, how he had passed earlier in the year, and I told him that at times I could feel him in my house, even near me. Jack had that smile again, he told me that happens to him as well with a dear friend, a woman he had met on one of his excursions. They had been pen pals for a while, and after several years of contact she had stopped writing. Not being able to reach her by phone or letter he assumed the worst. Within a month or so of his feeling that she had passed away she came to visit him in a dream. He told me that she had died, and that it had been a peaceful death; that he wasn't to cry for her, or worry about her family. All things were taken care of in her life and now of course, in her after life. He had the feeling that she was telling him that they would see each other again, and to bring her point more to the surface of his heart, she told him a few names of relatives of his that had greeted her in Heaven.

Being a Believer, Jack took what she said to heart and let it go no further. This was the first time he had revealed his story. I was honored to be the one he told it to. I know he wouldn't mind me mentioning it; just thinking about what can be our driving force is remarkable. The issue of faith is so dear to you, and to me. It's private, it's public, it's hard to pin down. For me it is the feeling that I can't make it unless I give up the reins. I can't make the air that I breathe, but its still my responsibility to draw in the breath. I know that having the faith to let go of whatever the situation is and to let it work itself out is often seen as the lazy way out, but to tell you the truth, it's actually much harder to let go than one might think. For years I thought I was in control of my life, and all the things I had to do to be successful were totally up to me. Well, going through the divorce in 1997, and the subsequent battles in court over custody, child support, contempt of court charges, and so much more; I learned that I am not in control. I thought I was, but I am surely not. It became so very clear to me the day the judge ordered me not to call the police; a single act of stupidity on her part, which led to hours, days, weeks, and months of tragedy for myself and my children. If I couldn't be allowed the very basic of rights, what was I to expect? I let it go. When the same judge told me I was not going to be going to law school, even though I had been given a full ride at one of the best law schools in the southwest region of America, Oklahoma City University School of Law, I found myself buried in despair. She was literally telling me to my face that I was not allowed to go to law school and seek custody at the same time. In her opinion, not the law's opinion, going to law school would take too much time away from the children. I had a choice to make. Because the ABA, the American Bar Association, did not allow first and second year law students to work, she determined that I would be asking my ex-husband for full support. This wasn't the case, but nevertheless, she ruled and ordered me in chambers not to seek a degree in law. Not at this time, she further instructed. If I wanted to pursue one the day after Caity turned 18, then so be it. She basically admitted that she could not make this ruling in court, however, if I chose to go against her (almighty) powers, she was going to see to it that I was no longer a contender for parental guardianship. How dare she! I stood in the corner of her office behind the courtroom. I stared at her in utter silence.

I had completed my Bachelors degree at Oklahoma City University, and had sufficient grades to mandate a full ride to a law school that she knew was the best. She knew that my years of experience as a legal assistant had led me to the decision of wanting to be a lawyer, and that I would actually someday pursue the bench; this was my destination, not her's, and her ruling was both unconstitutional and wrong. I let it go. I didn't have a choice. I let it go. For grins and giggles I applied for law school at Harvard Law about a year after the judge's ruling. I obtained a telephone interview and was told that based on my grades and writing sample I would actually be given a face-to-face interview. I thanked the proctor and declined. But it is nice to know I have the door of opportunity still available to me someday. One of the nicest things about my decision to continue with an educational path is that I now have a Masters in Literature, and am just about to complete my PhD. in Administration and Leadership. If I didn't have the credentials at the time of the offer for a face-to-face, I would surely have them now. All is not lost, there is still another tick to go on the clock, and as long as there is, there is reason to pursue the dream. I believe in chasing dreams and in doing so, I believe you may run into a judge or two, perhaps a custody battle, a bad relationship, a co-worker that won't let you breathe five seconds without reporting it to the boss, or maybe you'll run across your boss doing cocaine . . . that can set you back! I believe that letting go is so very important, and that the only way you can do it is to trust that the One you leave that trust with is capable of doing what is best for you. I love the words of the Psalmist when he wrote: "I know who I am believed, and am persuaded that He is able to keep that which I've committed, unto to Him against that day". Go ahead and call me a holy-roller, it won't be true, but if it sounds like I may put too much faith in a God I haven't seen yet, it's because there really isn't another way. Fighting the fights alone makes no sense. Fighting the battles with others who feel the same that you do about faith makes far more sense. At the very least you have a network, a frame, and a gaggle of friends (are they actually called gaggles, because I know that a group of owls is called a Parliament) and you have a much better chance of regaining the confidence you need to continue the basic things you have to continue doing on a routine basis, not to mention the tough moments that come along.

PART THREE

Letting Go

Chapter Seventeen

The concept for writing this book came easily to me. The little dog that was given to us, or rather taken by my son without asking and then obtaining permission from Janet and her mother, would take more than the normal amount of love, time, effort, money, and support. We knew that. No one had to bring that bit of information to the surface. I saw her face . . . I lost my heart. It would not have mattered if she had no legs, this dog was going to be mine, and like everything else in my life, she was going to make it. She didn't really have a choice. There she was, laying in the palm of my hand, gnawing on my finger, looking up to me with the expression of both determination and a hopeful stare asking for help. She was going to make it. It would take countless hours of physical assistance yes, we were going to have to bend way over to place our hands under her, to guide and lead her across the patio concrete, the carpet, the tiled floor and the backyard grass, but she was going to make it. We were going to have to watch her to be sure she didn't fall off the couch or stumble off the stairs, get into the water bowl without being able to get her head out, or to crawl into the shower when we weren't looking. That was actually quite scary, and an experience neither she nor I will forget.

I stepped on what I thought was a loofah, but instantly the loofah squealed . . . loofahs don't squeal, and this was one of those times I lost all control and screamed out loud. No one was home and I thought I had killed the dog! Thankfully, she recovered, I recovered, and if for any reason she may have had soapy water in her lungs before I stepped on her, it had definitely been let out by the compressing of my big, fat, foot on her tiny, wet, yellow body. This dog can be under your feet, between your legs, tripping you, and generally being the biggest nuisance in the freakin' world, but something about her face and her expression let's you know that she's only doing it because she loves you.

At the time when our family was emerging from several years of battles of emotion, finance, stress, and court ordered visitation, this puppy brought to us an awareness that we are not the only reason the world turns on its axis. God allowed us to literally become the saving grace for Faith, one of His tiniest Angels.

Like ourselves, when we were struggling to survive, and to balance our lives having to relearn how to cope with the simplest things life had to offer, Faith was born without the use of her arms, her voice, the love of her mother, security, warmth, she was even neglected the right to six weeks of nourishment before being carted off to be the welcomed present for someone who had always wanted a dog just like her. There are no other dogs just like her! She may be the only two legged dog in the world that walks upright all of the time, and even this was not afforded to her at the time she was born. Faith was unable to do anything without help, and we were the ones who were being given that challenge and that responsibility. I constantly hear people say "God bless you for what you've done. Most people would have put her down." I feel a bit embarrassed when they say it, because it was my first instruction to Janet. There was no way the dog could make it if her own mother wasn't allowing her to live at that age. "God bless you for keeping her, you're a Saint." Well, I don't know about that, but I can tell you that I do believe she is one, and I bless her on a daily basis. I think she realizes we love her, but I don't think she has a clue of how proud we are of her.

Before someone can begin to think another person (or owner) is proud of them, there has to be something that the person would be proud of. Faith doesn't have any idea that there is something wrong with her. She knows she doesn't have legs, she figured that one out when we went to Dolese Park during the filming of *Ripley's Believe it or Not*. It had been the first time for Faith to visit the park's lake area and we let her go to chase the geese. We knew she didn't have legs, and we all naturally assumed she realized it as well. Not. The dog ran up to the geese on her back legs, which you can imagine only frightened the poor dears ever so much more than normal four-legged predators coming at them; she ran straight into the lake and didn't stop when the water went over her head! Come back, you senile animal! You don't have front legs, you can't doggy-paddle! Luckily for Faith, and I suppose everyone, Laura swims. She was out in the water in a flash, pulling her wet puppy back to safety. The initial reaction for all of us was to gasp with open mouths, but once we saw Faith's tongue hanging out, wagging and her tail thumping the air over and over, we realized that she wanted to give it another go. What a dog. There wasn't the least bit of fear in her, and she wasn't that upset to be without legs, she simply ran up to her waist in the water the second time, slow going, yes, and every duck or goose in the park spread the news rather quickly, but she had fun and she continues to have fun as often as we go. We have pictures.

Understandably, this book is an inspirational book for those, who like me, have faced difficulties and couldn't find ways to ease the pain long enough to find a little peace. It is also for those who have experienced depression and need to know that there are answers to the silent, often never expressed prayers kept so deeply inside of their hearts. I have pains in my soul from time to time too, doubts that what I'm doing is wrong, or that what I'm thinking about doing is going to be a mistake. Depression has never really been an option for me, though I think it snuck in without permission on an occasion or two. I was always too busy to recognize the symptoms. Depression to me was a state of mind and if I could just push it back with work, keeping my mind busy, my strategies going, making plans, finding new things to think about, I could effectively break the depressed feelings into pieces. This worked for a while I suppose, it wasn't until the day I was stopped and forced to give everything up (not by choice) that I realized that I had not effectively broken the feelings into pieces. I had managed to organize these feelings, and to put them into neat little piles, somewhat like Laura would do, which would someday need to be dealt with . . . but not today. That was my strategy. It was one of those denial tactics I suppose. I'll fight it off, I'll win, I'll win; I have no other options. What an idiot! I finally found peace through the assistance of helping the yellow dog in my lap. Though through our love and time she learned to grow, walk, and take the world by the tail; I learned to let go and to let the natural order of things take place.

God has not left His throne and the last time I looked, all of His twinkling stars were still aligned in their places. So then would I be realigned. I had to believe it, because it was a promise, because it was true. I've learned that I can now fully understand how the frustrations of the daily struggle, the future goals, and the needs of our families can be such an oppression. These feelings can lead someone to not only feel depressed, but to begin feeling overwhelmed, overrun and incapable of climbing out of the hole they've created for themselves, or the hole they were thrown into, which ever may be the case; but there really is a way out. With just a little faith and a lot of hard work. When we were hurting it took much more than the faith alone. Promises are good, but they do require work, work that can only be found in the hearts of the person who truly does want to make a change. Sometimes finding our own way out seems impossible and I'm all for asking for help.

My dad, because he is a normal guy, when we were growing up, would never stop and ask directions. It didn't matter how lost we were, and sometimes I think I do that with my personal life and my goals. I get stuck, I dig myself in, and even though the phone book is sitting right there, and I can ask for help for something medical, financial, emotional, physical . . . . I don't. I think it would be a total waste of time, it might cost something, it may set me back, it could be made worse if I involve someone . . . all bad excuses, but excuses I have used many times. The calm before the storm is a warning, and the calm which follows the storm, to me, is a promise that I was brought through said storm. I tend to pray a little more, and pick up the phone more often nowadays. I don't mind asking for help because I don't want the one I see in the mirror to be the one I used to be, I want to see the person I want to see. I wish I could be the person my dog thinks I am, or maybe the person these people I meet on the street think I am. They bless me, say how great I am, and they thank me for what I've done. Once a lady in New York City even called me a hero. That hurt. I'm not a hero, I smiled of course, and I thanked her, but I did what I had to do, and it was something that needed to be done. Not one time was I thinking to myself that the time, effort, and energy we put into Faith would bring about a book about her experiences, or that those experiences were going to be so wonderful. The book falls into its natural place after these experiences, and perhaps because of my educational background; Faith is Faith because of her own choice to live and God's grace to make it a reality. All the work in the world, all the bending over, the feeding through an eyedropper, and even the breathing into her nostrils after I stepped on her in the shower, would not have made a bit of difference in her life if she herself hadn't seen fit to stay alive. She wanted to live, and she wanted to run, she wanted to chase the geese, eat the bratsworth out of the hand of the generous man we met on Broadway who wanted nothing more than to pet the head of the famous two-legged dog. Faith wasn't aware of her fame, she was aware only of the garlic and peppered spices coming off that sandwich. She is one heck of an inspiration, and still, she is 100% dog. Something we can all take a lesson from. I think that I have learned to be more of what I was made to be, at the same time I've learned to fight my way through the harder times by letting go and letting faith take over. Ode to a dog.

The people at the *Maury Show* called us when Faith was just a year old. They wanted to do a show about miracles and felt that Faith's abilities were warranted to be brought back out to New York City and to do this particular show. To be perfectly honest, I wasn't that big of a fan of the *Maury Show* because of the usual genre of the show. Issues of civil conflict, domestic violence, secrets lovers, etc., these were the mainstay of the show, and I wasn't sure that I wanted Faith to be associated with it. I did however, agree to go if they would bring Caity with us. I wasn't going to leave her at home with her brother again, wishing she had been given the opportunity to see the Big Apple, and getting to be involved with Faith. Faith has always been Laura's dog really. Just after his dynamic rescue of Faith, Reuben had moved out of the house into an apartment and he wasn't going to be taking his beloved cat Nova, let alone a dog. Reuben is more of a cat person, which in and of itself strikes me as being unnatural, but I'll save that discussion for another book. Laura had been assigned Faith really, as Matrix was my dog, and Caity had chosen to take up with Ean. Because of her relationship with Faith Laura had been called Faith's owner on the initial KFOR-TV newscast, and we just sort of let that happen. It was true however, that the family was complete in taking turns to raise Faith. Each of us made extreme sacrifices of sleep, time, effort, and even losing our food from time to time when Faith, with her 40" nose reach has been nondiscriminatory in taking food right off of our plates, or from our hands as we aren't looking. If you aren't literally watching the dog at all times when you have food anywhere near her, she will end up with it. Again, we have pictures.

When the *Maury Show* agreed to bring Caity out with Laura, Faith and I, we were on our way again to the big adventurous city of New York City. Little did Caity realize that the great people of New York City have so much fun with Faith when she is spotted walking through Central Park or down Broadway's Time Square. Manhattan is the only borough we have actually been privileged to visit on these trips, but people from all over the area have recognized Faith because of the magnificent news coverage in the City. Faith has appeared on the front page of the paper in NYC, she's been mentioned on *Regis and Kelly, David Letterman, MSNBC,* and *CNN.* She had been featured on AOL front page, and in the Harry Potter websites. She was seen on the New York City based *Ricki Lake Show* before it was canceled, and she appeared on the nightly news during the week that the Westminster Dog Show was in town; as the cameras couldn't help themselves. The prim and proper dogs of showcase quality simply had to wait a few seconds to be admired when the yellow mutt from Oklahoma nosed in on their limelight, literally walking her way into the eyes of the New York City citizens. Calls of "Faith . . . Faith!" caught up with our ears as we strolled from 42nd to 51st on Broadway in early February 2004. A lady in dark dress, prepared to cross the street to see the Broadway production of "The Producers" had left her companion to see the two-legged wonder. She petted Faith and told me she had seen her that day on the morning news. She had told her husband that she was such a fan. I had to grin. We were standing in the middle of the sidewalk, bustling with people, people teeming out of shops like Quicksilvers, the MTV Store, Roxy, even an adult video store, people pouring out into the streets to see Faith because of the daily coverage.

At one point a woman in a wheelchair, who had recently lost both of her legs to amputation due to her severe case of diabetes was made aware of Faith's appearance. We couldn't see her or even know what she was planning to do, but in time she had wheeled herself off of the sidewalk and into the street, wheeling her way North in a southbound lane, just in order to get to us. I couldn't believe it. She was crying, tears rolling off her cheeks, and her hands shaking from being frightened of the traffic, the people cursing at her, telling her to get out of their way, honking, and waving gestures at her; but she came up to us at the intersection of 47th where there is a bit of a ramp available to her. "Faith!" She cried out and I saw her wheeling herself against the traffic which had just gotten the green light. Almost instantly I handed a police officer standing on the corner the leash I had Faith led by, I ran to the lady in the wheelchair and pushed her to the corner, up the ramp, and closer to her prize. She hadn't believed in anything she told me. She hadn't been a Christian, she hadn't been a religious person at all until after the last operation and something told her that she was not going to be around much longer. She was going to die, and there had to be a plan made for her. It wasn't until she received a burial plot advertisement in the mail that it all made sense. She took up the offer and purchased a single plot for herself. There was no one to be buried beside. There was no one who would be wanting to be buried beside her she reasoned. She had no family to speak of. Her only daughter was in another country, in France she believed. She hadn't spoken to her in years. It was an easy choice she stated because she had the money now and needed to make the plans so that her friends weren't forced to do that for her.

That morning she had decided that she might even go to the pawn store and purchase a gun. She'd have to wait a week but that didn't stop her from deciding that it was the best thing to do. She had lost all . . . faith. Before she left the house and called a taxi for help to get her to the pawn shop she had seen the strangest thing on television. It was a rerun of the *Ripley's Believe it or Not* show where Faith was featured, walking tall, going in and out of the water, struggling to catch the geese, and being loved on by a little Hispanic boy who was blind. Faith had made a difference in her life instantly, and she was sure that she would be OK. Her day was spent trying to find someone who could help her find Faith through the network she had seen *Ripley's* on, was it Fox? Was it CBS? She couldn't remember. The day was spent in joy, rather than depression and it wasn't due to anything she could explain. She told me that she laughed all day long and that she had picked up the phone to make a few calls to friends that she hadn't even talked to since the operation. They didn't want to be bothered, she had told herself. They had lives, they had families with both legs, they had people to see, places to go. She'd make the calls anyway, and just by fluke . . . or maybe by faith, she was going to see one of her friends who worked on Broadway at the Viacom building where MTV is broadcast. She was wheeling her way down Broadway when the muttle on the streets was that there was a yellow two-legged dog inside of Quicksilvers. IT COULDN'T BE! But it was. Faith was in New York City that very day, and she was walking up Broadway. Carolyn Gold pushed herself to the utmost limits, because she felt she could, and because she felt that she had to. This is what Faith was created for. *This* was the reason Faith was given life.

I couldn't help myself, I picked Faith up and plopped her yellow butt onto the lap of this absolutely beautiful woman whose tear-streaked face never stopped kissing her for the longest of times. I didn't have my camera with me, but as is always the case in Times Square, other people had their's. Camcorders broke out, instant 35MM cameras, and digital phones caught the moments as they expressed themselves so wonderfully. I hope Carolyn was able to get a few copies for herself. I gave her our website *www.faiththedog.net* and made sure she would be added to the long and growing list of Friends of Faith if she was to e-mail us and let us know how she was doing. From the time we left Oklahoma City to the time we came home from filming the *Maury Show*, even before the show aired, over 14,000 new hits had made their way to our site. We're going to have to get a larger space I'm afraid. We had to re-do it one other time, right after Faith appeared on *Ripley's*. I suppose it has something to do with the fact that she is so novel, but it has to do more I believe, with the fact that she is such an awesome example of dogged-determination. (I couldn't help myself on that pun.) Carolyn's desire to see Faith was so strong, and that desire doesn't stop with only people who have disabilities.

Every week I receive e-mails and letters from people who own dogs, cats, and other animals with disabilities, or in some cases their beautiful pets are about to have an operation to remove one of their legs following a diagnosis of cancer or perhaps the result of an accident. One such letter came from a woman named Renee Hart in California who has a rhodesian ridgeback named Huckleberry. She wrote because Huck was about to have his right front leg amputated after a run in with a car on a road near their walnut farm. A neighbor had heard the accident and came running. Renee mentioned that people she knew and talked with had given her a great deal of advise. Some had said she should put Huck out of his misery, she should put him to sleep because of the injury. Thank God she didn't listen to them. She had heard about Faith a year or so before the accident and she had remembered how Faith's life full and exciting. She knew that dogs, like people, are resilient and if we just give our lives a chance to work out the hard situations we come across we really can overcome much more than we thought we could. Dogs are no different. We have to think about their feelings when we make decisions which will ultimately effect their lives.

After receiving Renee's letter, and a donation from her to help get my book published, I called her on the phone to see how Huck was feeling. She said he had been so agile and so up and about that he had managed to lick off his bandages, walk around, stand up and get to around the house within a day or so of his operation. What a spirit! Who can hold something like that back? Faith has inspired so many people and when I think about it, I really do sit back and smile. I laugh out loud sometimes and just think how really exciting it is to be in her life . . . and then I remember; she's part of my life. God is so cool!

Chapter Eighteen

I have an English sur name, a name my sister made me promise not to tarnish in any way during the writing of this book. The name Stringfellow is not as I used to pretend it was, of Scottish heritage, it is decisively English, and with the knowledge of genealogy tidbits gathered from my sister, I can at least be sure that the first Stringfellows that we know about were literally the people who strung the instruments for the people of the great isle back in the day. We were the people you would see if your guitar strings broke. I remember telling my fifth grade teacher Mrs. Leard that the Stringfellows were the first people paid to hang people, that stringing them up had lent us the title of the "Fellow who strings". I knew I was lying when I said it, but it got me out of a horribly boring essay. In Mrs. Leard's class you could do oral reports or written ones. This was great news to a little brat of a girl with a vivid imagination.

Stringfellow is also a well known name in London, and I have to apologize to my sister at this point, and make it known that I am not the one who has given the name a rather controversial reputation. That was created by the very well off owner of at least two clubs by the name Stringfellows. There is one in London, that I know about, and still another one in New York City. I wanted to visit it while I was in the city. I wanted to flash my state license, proving my name was the same, perhaps it would have brought a smile to the face of the door keeper. Alas, I had a dog and a minor child with me at all times, and celebrity status or not, neither Faith nor one of my daughters would be admitted. Stringfellows may be controversial, but I had to bet they were at least law abiding. Still, the English connection between myself and my life, is never too far away. What does Kevin Bacon claim? Six degrees of separation?

I was standing in my college classroom teaching, minding my own business, because that is what I do. I had been teaching at Les College of Culinary Arts and Health Sciences for just over a seven weeks or so, when one of my students, a 21 year old high school graduate who had decided to wait a while before returning to the academic world, brought me a little gift. He extended his hand to show me that he had purchased a magazine. "That's nice" I said, but

I wasn't quite sure what he wanted to show me. "LOOK!" he exclaimed quite clearly, "Your dog is on the front cover!" And there she was. Faith was in the corner of the magazine, standing upright, walking, and just above her head was a little voice bubble. It read: So What? As if to say "So what, I'm walking, don't all dogs walk?" I have to admit I am quite accustomed to seeing my dog on the front covers of magazines, in the middle of magazines, and even on television from time to time. I picked up a Dallas publication once when I was in Texas and saw Faith kissing my daughter Laura; one of the syndicated photos purchased by Zuma Press, a Stephen Holman special. Zuma Press has sold the photos for whatever reason, and they have been reprinted any number of times. This time, well, it was different. I didn't do it. I did not give anyone my permission to put my dog's image in a nudey magazine.

My dog was on the front cover of the London based magazine *Bizarre* whose counterpart may be something along the lines of *Maxim* in America, however, *Bizarre* has a certain dark side to it as well. There are photos of very scantly dressed women in those pouting-to-the-point-of-provocation looks of course. The magazine also has third-world photos of beatings, raids by guerrilla soldiers, and even a picture of what appears to be a terrorist act captured on film! Frame by frame disclosure of the attack in all its inglorious horror. Somewhere in the middle of the girls, the guns, and the guts, walks a little yellow dog on her two back legs. She's walking through my living room again, as always, and again I thought that I should thank my best friend Jeannie Clarke for having the wherewithal to clean the room before Stephen Holman shot those immortal photos. The church pew ads a bit of talky-talk to it as well, as we're living in Oklahoma, the capital of the Bible Belt, but no, we aren't so religious as to think we have to have a church pew in our house for any particular reason. The pew belongs to my ex-husband's sister Dee, a woman I can say without being wrong, is a wonderful person, and for all of the things she has had to put up with she has come out as beautifully as the winter rose breaking through the late February snow. She is bright, colorful, has an excellent wit and to be honest, she found the connection between *Bizarre* and Faith to be perfectly normal. I thought it was, well . . . bizarre!

"Yes, I see Faith on the cover of the magazine. Did you buy it for me?" I asked.

"Yes. But I need the money back. If you don't mind. I'm a poor student."

"Not a problem." I paid the $6.00 and took the magazine with its young, nearly naked lady on the front. Immediately the students who were in the room waiting for class to resume wanted to view the magazine. They even said it was because Faith was on the front cover but I had to laugh at them anyway. They couldn't get that look in their eyes over a little dog. I said I would let them look at it during break, but first there required just a bit of doctoring. This sounds like I am such a nerd, but I am one. I couldn't tell you the difference really between a nerd, geek, or dork, but to be sure, I am all three of these unless the involvement with computers preludes me from being a geek in its fullest. I took a black *Sharpee* pen and drew a tank top on the front cover lady. I turned the pages and began "dressing" more women, and actually coming up with some fairly decent clothing line ideas in the process. It became a game between Caity and I. She was at the college with me that day in order to type essays for students who couldn't do it. She was paid in the past by students, but I had asked them not to do that again. When I tried to return their money only one of them was forthcoming and told me what he had paid. The others claimed that Caity, and sometimes Laura, were deserving of a tip for their help. Being home schooled my daughters have had many wonderful experiences which they would not be afforded in public high school. This demonstration of compassion and assistance is one such experience. Caity and I drew ruffled clothing, straight lined clothes, Viking uniforms, and even a little grass skirted bikini for the girl with a tiny g-string on the back cover of the book. No one complained about the girls being dressed and we made up little dialogs of the girls thanking us for covering them, as they were getting cold standing on their pages without anything to cover them. It was quite fun. I then found that stapling the pages together was needed, as some of my students were taking to rubbing off the *Sharpee* coverings. Fine people, I'll take that! I stapled every page with the exception of the pages which held photos and a little news blurb about Faith and Laura. You know the photo, the one of her youthful poochy belly sticking out, and her lips in the middle of saying something with an "Oooh" sound. She hates that picture, and there it was . . . . blazen on the pages of a racy little magazine out of London.

Break was over, and it was time to get back to the basics of teaching. This particular class was behind in their points for essay, and I had decided that a little bit of extra credit was in line. Show and Tell would save the day. I was teaching Art Appreciation, a class I was not actually supposed to be teaching as I was not accredited to teach anything dealing with Art, but I was asked by the Director of Education after I was hired, to be a TEAM player. He assured me that he would *take the hit* if anything happened. Whatever that meant. I assumed he would *take the hit* as I had given the college every transcript I had earned and a copy of my professional resume and educational vitae. How could I be expected to take a hit in any event?

There I was teaching, and listening to one of my students demonstrating the art which was required for her great grandmother to make the beautiful, antique quilt that required two other people to hold up. I was minding my own business, because that is what I do, when Johnny Prat, the Director of Education at Les College of Culinary Arts and Health Sciences, appeared in the window of the door. He was making a motion for me to meet him in the hallway but it did not appear to be that urgent. I left my record book, magazine, papers, pens, and everything else, including my stereo and CDs there in the room. Johnny immediately ducked his head down a bit and began walking me down the long hallway. Without an explanation of any sort really, he made mention that Hollie Haggard, our College Director would be coming along soon. Hollie and I had been in a private meeting about thirty minutes prior to this one. She had wanted to look at the magazine that my student had brought to me. She laughed at me because I had drawn clothes on the women and she commented that it wasn't "That bad", but still, she wasn't the least bit upset about the coverage that Faith received.

The only thing I could think of was that my daughter Laura had been in an accident, or perhaps Reuben had. It was just after 4:00 p.m. and I had Caity with me. I set myself, my nerves, and my heart for the worst. Johnny escorted me into the large conference room and gave me a pursed lipped face. He said he didn't want to say anything until Hollie had made it to the room. This was going to be something bad. I could tell. The prayers went out immediately for Laura, for Reuben, maybe my father, or mother. I couldn't make anything out of his face. What came next was completely a shock.

Johnny opened the door for Hollie, who was wiping her eyes with a white tissue. Black mascara covering most of the surface in just the time she had walked presumably from her office to the conference room. What could this possibly mean? Johnny lifted his right index finger and he said to me "Jude, this is not working out". He put up his second finger and added "You have to leave." He put up his third finger, making the symbol for the number 3, and stated "Don't ask me to explain, I can't say anything more", and he put up his fourth finger and said "Good bye". Of course I asked him to explain. To my surprise, and Hollie's chagrin, Johnny stated abruptly, using his finger demonstration a second time, that I was not working out, I had to leave, he could not tell me why, and that I had to leave right then. Not one bit of it made any sense to me. Not one explanation, and when I sought one from Hollie all I got was more tears. She stuttered something about me not being used to the types of students Les was bringing in, that the college students I had taught in years past with Oklahoma City Community College, Oklahoma Baptist University, Redlands and Langston University, had been "different". She stated that some of them weren't able to do the work I had assigned. After she realized that her attempt at lying was futile, she gave it up and said "You have to go. We can't say another word." This order wasn't coming from either Johnny or Hollie. I could tell, and the meeting Hollie and I had just minutes before the class began was all washed away. No longer was I being told I was a great asset to the college, words she had barely gotten out of her mouth before she was crying in my presence, having to recant it all. She couldn't say "Good Bye" easily, and Johnny was given the duty. She couldn't even look me in the eyes. I suppose you can't when you know you're dead wrong. What was it? I wasn't told.

The minute I was released I tried to find boxes to put my office things into. Caity was in the office at this point, my office partner Peter had been dismissed. He had been told by Johny and/or Hollie that I was going to be released, and that he needed to go home. He has subsequently told me that he was ordered to leave, and that he was told not to talk to me in the future. What is up with that? Walking though the halls it became quite apparent that the rest of the administration had no idea what was going on. I could hear them rustling around gossiping, saying "No way, you've got to be kidding!" and I remember hearing the distinctive voice of Chef Kurt Bombit telling the forty some odd students I had to leave behind that he was taking them to the kitchen, and that he was sure things would be worked out. I could hear students saying "That's not true!" but I didn't know what they were talking about. Although, by elimination of topics, I could tell it had something to do with my release. Had everyone been told before me? Chef knew, the administration was told somehow, and both Hollie and Johnny were just steps in front of me when I heard them talking. Obviously, this order came from higher up the chain, but no one was willing to say a word to me.

Caity and I drove to KFOR-TV immediately to see if Brad Edwards, a journalist with a news column called "In Your Corner". He may want to run a story about it. He may want to be in my corner. After all, Oklahoma may be an At-Will state, allowing people to be fired at the will of the employer, but there still had to be some sort of protocol, a written notice, reprimand, something! Brad wasn't in, but the receptionist, a woman of some news knowledge from the years she has been working the front door, told me that she believed this was a news worthy story, and she thought that because Faith was involved (indirectly because I was not going to be able to feed my little dog without a job) she felt that I should ask Ali Myer to do the story. Faith and Ali go back a ways now.

The following day proved immeasurable in terms of evidence against the college and in my favor. Students began calling me saying various different things. One said that I was fired for being immoral. I had allowed Laura and Faith to be in the "dirty" magazine. As if I had anything to do with that story or coverage. Another student called to say that I was being released because Hollie thought I was gay. Which was preposterous when you considered that there were at least four known homosexuals in the class. This particular student herself was gay and she said that Hollie had told another student that I was pushing my homosexual ways onto the students through the works of art we were asked to study. I dismissed this charge as Hollie and everyone else who knows me knows I am very heterosexual. I don't have animosity toward the homosexual people I know and don't know but that couldn't be the reason. It was my calling to teach. I was the TEAM player, remember? I was teaching something alright, but it was after all something I wasn't suppose to be teaching wasn't it? Who were those people I had seen in the kitchens that afternoon? Were they from the state educational boards? Were they with the accreditation people? They seemed to be hanging out in the administration offices after I was fired. It gave me cause to wonder.

When a third student confirmed that the consensus for me being fired was immorality because I had somehow "allowed" Faith and my minor daughter to be photographed and covered in *Bizarre*, I chose to contact the magazine itself. I called Matt Potter, no relation to Harry. He was the editor at the time. I explained to Matt the situation I was in because of the pictures of Faith being in his magazine. He instructed me to call an attorney. This was a few weeks after the event, and after I had obtained the information pertaining to the people in the office. They were indeed with the accreditation committees, or someone dealing with the rules and regulations of who was teaching what at Les College. I had taken the hit, as it were, that was in his own words, meant for Johnny. I was fired, in my opinion, because the administrators at the college didn't have the proper credentials to ask me to teach Art. For that matter I had taught a course in Math just a few weeks prior, and I had no more credentials to teach it than I did to teach Art Appreciation. My degrees warrant that I teach English, Humanities, Ethics, Philosophy and even an introduction course on Psychology, but I was certainly being used and played by the Director. This I was sure of. I called KFOR-TV and Ali did her magic. The story was aired and it came across as if the college, according to the students anyway, and what they were being told, fired me because Faith was in a nudey magazine. I asked her to put in the story the bit about a possibility that the college had not filed the proper papers with the state as well.

My morality was in question, for that I wanted to file a lawsuit against Les College of Culinary Arts and Health Sciences. For defamation of character, as well as for monetary loss of wages. I was told by my attorney that because I had not been employed for more than 90 days I would not have a good case. At-Will literally means that a company, in this case a school, can fire someone at will without having to meet any criteria. Where it is entirely unjust and unfair to the employer, it keeps legal costs down when employees sue for retroactive pay and such. Les got away with it, but in the end, again, because of faith that something would turn up, I got the best of it. Funny how that works out? Can we call it fate? I don't think so.

I can't sit around and let petty people and the decisions they make ultimately affect my decisions, my life or my destiny. With each day that passes since losing my job I find another reason why I probably shouldn't have aligned myself with the small college, but the students are the ones I long for. I've tried a million times to get them out of my head, but I can't. To call them by name without their permission would be wrong. Perhaps when they read this book they will know who it is that I'm talking about, but in each and every case I found a new awakening and a sharing of faith. Not to mention a sharing of Faith my dog, because I brought her to the school on more than one occasion.

One student that stands out is a little Asian woman. I'll call her Kim. She had the heart of a saddened warrior when we met. She had been through a difficult marriage, and she felt that because of her vows to stay married she was trapped. She tried to find joy in her life, and she had done so through the life and relationship she had with her little daughter. But now, it seemed that God had taken even that from her. Kim was far too shy to bring this to my attention, but one of the reasons I ask for autobiographical essays at the beginning of my courses is to get to know the students themselves. Kim was brave as she wrote the stories about her life and what it was like to hate a God that she was brought up to love. For years I have studied graphology. I'm fairly good at it too. I can look at a good sample of handwriting and if for no other reason but to entertain myself, giving me a little more insight to the author of the paragraph or two, I am able to tell some of the more deepest secrets about a person depending on what it is that they write about themselves. In Kim's case she had all but eliminated the first hump of her "M"s when she wrote words like "mine", "month" and "Mom". They were apparent more or less when the word held an "m" in the middle, words such as "time", "remember" and so forth. I could tell from the very flattened balloons of nearly every one of her "y" words, or words rather that ended in a "y", that she and been without physical touching, there wasn't the least bit of intimacy in her life; even though I knew she was a married woman. There were other indications in her writing which led me to believe that she was angry at both her mother and her father, but that her father had been the most hurtful. He had abandoned her. This I could tell through the way she curved the top part of her capital "I" and how she barely created a bottom hook for the end of the "I". No opportunities for familial love. Kim was hurting. I pulled her to the side one day and asked her if I could help pray with her. She wasn't inhibited with me. She fell into my arms crying. She was putting on the oriental face of bravery, one I had seen so often in my foreign students at Oklahoma City Community College when they had been forced to leave their native homes and to become educated in America. Lonely, making their way in a strange and incredibly harsh world, no friends, no family contact if they did not receive good marks. Why this goes on I can't tell you, because this sort of alienation of students is not isolated and it is not manipulated by only the Asian cultures. So many of my students report to me that if they don't pass "this time" their parents will disown them, they will never spend another penny on education, and words that must bring about responsibilities. Kim was hurting deeply. Tears and a gripping fist told me that she was more than tired of carrying on with her false bravado.

"Professor Jude, I am crying. I am hurt. This hurt." she sobbed.

"Tell me Kim, what is happening?".

"My daughter, Professor, my little baby she has diabetes. I don't ask God much. I don't. I mad at Him. He make my baby sick. He make my baby to die soon." her English barrier apparent, but beautifully articulated through her love for her daughter.

"Kim, we don't always know why God allows things that seem bad to happen to beautiful and innocent people, children, or the elderly. There has to be a reason. Let me pray with you."

"He not listen. I pray. I pray every day. She is sick and I can't make it better."

"Let me pray anyway, maybe where two hearts are gathered."

I told Kim what I found in her writings. Not what I had read in the words about her favorite color, food, why she was taking classes at the Culinary college, or why she wasn't in her country anymore. I told her what I read in the innuendos of the letters themselves. Her breakdown was complete. She wanted to stay in my office and cry, and I held her. I think I held her for about an hour. We prayed together. We prayed not only for her daughter but for her own faith, her joy, she wanted the joy to return.

I have a new friend for life. I can walk away from Les, and Les can walk away from me, but forever and that last day I have a true and genuine friend named Kim. Before I was fired she was seen holding my arms as I walked down the hallways leading to the kitchens where she would finally let me go, but not before she would kiss my cheek and whisper in my ear that she loved me. She also told me to check out the bottoms of her "y" words. She had been making amends with her husband as well. There was a certain *JOY* returned that had not shadowed the bedroom for nearly a year. Kim was more than happy about her new promises from God. She told me over and over again that every day she has found the miracle. The miracle, she would say. The miracle. I can only imagine what a burden she must have let go of. I hope it had something to do with her eternal desire to be a Believer again. I'll miss Kim for sure, the administrators told the students that they were not allowed to call me. If they were caught they would be expelled from the school. Kim took the time to tell me that much before she said she could not keep a secret long and that if we were to talk she would want to tell everyone.

I'm going to be honest and say that I'm going to miss the pot heads that smoke their weed every day just before coming to my class. Without them the class would be different. In some ways the class would be more orderly, yes, but it would not have the flair of youthful rebellion that these two brought. You never knew what you were going to get when you asked a question of one or the other of these two. In their defense, neither had graduated from high school, having been too high or sleepy to attend on a regular basis. Both had been beaten by fathers, step fathers, siblings, and in one's case, a neighbor, who subsequently had raped him at the age of 14. I read this again in his writings, but not because it showed up in a curly cue, he flat out told me. I couldn't understand his candor, but this was what Hollie had meant when she told me that these students, some of them, were not the same as the others. They told me things. They put it out there for the world to see, almost daring me to disapprove. I never did. I think they found that the most interesting part of our teacher-student relationship. I couldn't be bought off for a good grade, and I couldn't be embarrassed easily. Though there was that one time when one of my cross-dressers asked me to join him at the club after class. I think I would have loved to have watched him strut his stuff for the runway, but I declined. You never know what that sort of thing can do for the reputation of the college if a teacher openly supports such a controversial event. Little did I know that just having someone take your dog's picture could be such a problem. I held the hand of another student when she got her tummy pierced. She cornered me after class and asked me if I would be her pseudo mother. I told her I would not sign anything. I squeezed her hand harder than she squeezed mine, and it was her belly getting punctured. I watched another get married in a boat. I watched another one ride a horse in a rodeo, and took another student home after he had too much to drink once, at the school! Another time, he and I spotted each other at a restaurant over the weekend. He felt comfortable enough to ask, and even if it was the wrong thing to do, I felt it was the right thing to do. I helped him walk up the stairs, and asked his roommate to take good care of him. Twice I had taken him home, and twice I remember thinking he had too much to offer to give it up in booze. Nothing was said on Monday. Nothing happened. Teachers are often much more than a class room figurehead. I knew that. I missed the college students at Les more than I missed some of the others because the others seemed to have more opportunities. More life chances. I may become a writer and write for the rest of my life, but I will never give up teaching. It seems to be what I am, not what I do. I don't always know exactly what it is that the students are expected to learn. With Les I was teaching a course in Math where I was sure that most of the students had a better working knowledge of what it meant to divide a decimal; however, teaching isn't about being right all the time, or about setting an example every time either. Sometimes its about being where you need to be, where you are needed, and being available. Teachers have it better. I know I feel that way about teaching and when I'm in the middle of a conference with a kid who for the first time isn't able to depend on anyone other than himself or herself for the work; I remember the best teachers I have ever had. They come to mind immediately. Faithfully. Joyfully. I want to be like them. Let me be that teacher, I ask. The one they remember when *they* want to remember a teacher. Bring my face to their mind. Bring my smile back to them.

Journal Entry:

February 3, 2004:

I've decided to stay home for the next six weeks and write the book *With a Little Faith*. If I get hired I get hired. But I'm going to try to write this anyway. It needs to get written. I need this. I need to dive head deep into writing and to get a publisher. I need to write. I need to write a poetry book too, but this book comes first. If I can get this done I can make a good effort at becoming an author. If I can find a publisher I can get an advance. I'll work on the book from 7 to noon. I'll get up at 6:00 a.m. and pray, read a few lines from St. Augustine and drink my morning coffee. I have to do this.

Well, I did get up, pray and drink my morning coffee, but it was more or less around 9:30 or so. What happened to the early morning hours were predictable. I can't even imagine why I thought I could lie to myself. I don't wake up early. What was that all about? I think my idea of work is getting up early, putting my best effort forward, and getting it done. The trouble with that way of thinking is that it works for others but not for me. The alarm goes off at 6:00 a.m. just like its suppose to, but my head is reminded that I didn't get to bed before 1:30 the night before because I was reading the latest William Bernhardt thriller. I can't put it down! Bernhardt is a great deal better than Grisham if you ask me. He's funny, he's witty, and . . . he's from Oklahoma City. He and I actually worked at the same law firm, but not at the same time. I was fired from that one too, but only because I refused to back down to the Queen of the joint when she demanded that I use a certain font and I explained to her that the attorney I worked for preferred otherwise. Queens always win.

What I can do is start earlier I told myself, maybe stop writing around 7:00 p.m. so that I can pick Bill's books up a little earlier, but then I would have to start my writing some time before 11:00 a.m. since I usually go about eight hours at a stretch, and that would require that I got up earlier than . . . . this isn't going to work. Besides, I tell myself nearly every day; if the dog is laying on my legs and she's made that sigh, that noise that indicates that she simply cannot be disturbed, who am I to wake her up and force her to do more? She's a celebrity! I'm just, well, the owner.

Chapter Nineteen

Faith seems to be showing up on all sorts of magazines these days. I saw her in a few last month and thought to myself, "Hey, they didn't ask my permission. I could be fired!" and then I laughed. I'm not working! Her image has become somewhat of a public domain. She could be marketed I suppose, perhaps I will get a license to make Faith dolls, magnets, notebooks, or posters. I think one of Laura's friends said there are Faith posters in Germany, but I have not seen any evidence of this. Faith isn't about making money or being the next *Benji*. She has a completely different calling, one she hasn't given much thought to I'm afraid. She lays about the house and expects me to make those types of decisions for her. She will be the one to show up, smile, putting her ears back up on the top of her head and walk from one end of the block to the other to show off her abilities to do it. Some dogs grab a raggedy ball and tempt you with it, trying to pull you into their game. Faith is more likely to take off out the front door and stand outside the car until you open the door letting her in. She loves to ride, and she loves to hang her head out the window slobbering on the passengers in cars behind us. She is such a dog at times! We'll be standing in line at the airport waiting to get our baggage scanned and trying to look all proper like. This isn't a time to be silly and bite the cords of the scanners, but there she was in Newark! I had to apologize. "That's OK, we know Faith!" I was happy to see a friendly face because her next dog-like activity had more to do with the fact that flying four hours and waiting in the airport an additional two hours before that, led me to understand why dogs are usually carted and placed in the plane's enormous belly.

If pooping in the airport wasn't illegal before, I'm sure I'll soon see signs that say "Do Not Poop in the Airport" posted at the terminal gates. Where is a plastic baggie when you need it? We had just left the airplane in Dallas for a connecting flight to Oklahoma City when Laura felt a definite pull on her arm. Faith just couldn't wait any longer. I tried not to laugh, but honestly, pooping on Texas! This was so . . . . Oklahoman! My dog was a true Crimson and Cream (yellow) Sooner! I had to write to Coach Stoops about it, and of course, I cleaned up the mess. You haven't lived until you're asked to sign autographs seconds after you've mopped up a mess like that! "For her next performance, Faith will be doing stand up at the Improv!" I made my way onto the plane to an eruption of applause. We Okies do like our little ironies you know. The idea of Faith choosing Texas to releave herself did not escape any of us. Even a few die hard Longhorn fans found it hilarious. "When a girl's gotta go, a girl's gotta go" was one of the more lively comments.

Big Dog Sports contacted us again through their Marketing Director Margaret Dunbar. She was yet another person who just happened to run across another story about Faith in a national magazine. She told me that she had never seen a dog with more courage, and that she wanted Faith to be, what she called, a "leader of the pack" for Big Dog Sports. There wasn't much time to plan a trip to California for Faith to be in the parade, and so the hope was that Faith would show her support for Big Dog by wearing t-shirts and bandannas with Big Dog logos. Big Dog also ran a little story about Faith in their Christmas catalog, stating that one of Faith's endeavors is to go where disabled children are so that she can be an inspiration. They mentioned Faith's "paw-sitive" attitude and for that we're very thankful. Big Dogs Sports' people aren't the only ones who can't get enough of Faith. I mentioned *Bizarre* Magazine earlier; since her first steps on television in June of 2003, Faith has appeared in more than 60 magazines, on more than 24 television shows, and has been talked about by millions. I tell my students that you'd think I would be a millionaire by now, flying around the world with Faith doing shows and talking to people who need a little encouragement. It hasn't happened yet. In fact, it's quite the opposite.

Chapter Twenty

September 2004 was a great time for publicity for Faith. Someone had placed a faux story on a Harry Potter website about Faith being in the next movie. The movie they were talking about was the Goblet of Fire. I was just as surprised as anyone when I woke up and prepared myself to go to work, (by this time I had been employed by the Oklahoma City Public School District as a 9th grade English teacher) to find a host of television news vans parked outside my little house. When they began asking me about Goblet of Fire I was completely caught off guard. I had an attorney for Faith, but I had not been told whether or not we would be invited to be in a movie. I was certainly excited about any possibility of Faith being in a Harry Potter film. Wow, that would be really cool.

I could just about imagine Laura, my red-head, being so prim and proper on the set, while trying her hardest to get a look-see at Rupert Grint. They would instantly fall in love of course, and he would be completely swept away with her because she not only looked quite a bit like Lindsay Lohan, she was intelligent, liked anime, could hold her own in a conversation, and she was, after all, the owner of the world's only two legged dog Faith. This was a dream of course, but one worth dreaming. I had to explain to the news media that I was not at liberty to discuss the matter as I had not discussed it with my attorney. This bit of information led the media hounds to run off to their word processors and camera people and to state that I knew I would be in the film, and then all sorts of stories began hitting the internet, the papers, the magazines, and of course international news stations. Fox ran a great story about it, I asked Phyllis Williams of our local media to run the story herself. Because I didn't know if the story was valid or not I took it upon myself not to find out until a bit of coverage had been reported. It can't hurt to have the possibility thrown out there for someone with authority to take the news and run with it. It just might pan out. After the story hit CNN and other national and international headlines, we were told that the people of Birds and Animals Unlimited, the trainers for all of the Harry Potter films, were talking about the possibility of the use of Faith in one of their films, but it was the New York office doing the pushing we were told, not the British branch of the company, as they were determined to keep all of the Potter films British right down to the last actor, even if it was a dog. This of course, didn't work out for them as the panthers in the movie Faith may have been in are not from Britain at all, and they were not trained there either. So, that leaves a door open doesn't it? Perhaps Faith can be in the next film, but I won't hold my breath. If she is, she is. Faith has more to do than act in movies, she has people to see and faces to kiss. The summer of 2005 found my son Reuben playing as an extra in a independent film called Wisteria, the story of an evil older man from New York named Albert Fish. Fish used to kidnap children and actually eat them. The film was being filmed in a city near where we lived, and on a whim we took Faith down to see the casting crew. Faith wasn't picked, as it was a very serious film, however, Reu plays the part of a city cop. During the filming of the movie I had the opportunity to bring Faith onto the set for a little brevity among the crew. One of the best decisions I could have made for a lazy summer. Faith was immediately loved by everyone on the set especially a really interesting actor by the name of Vyto Ruginis. Ruginis has been a million things, and if anyone were to look him up on the internet, they would find that he is a seasoned character actor. The role he plays in Wisteria is that of a police detective in the late 1920's and early 1930's as Fish was being sought by authorities.

Vyto, sometimes in costume, sometimes out of costume, would sit on the grass beside Faith and I and we'd talk about film making, about people and the way they handle certain situations. "Faith for instance", offered Vyto. "She doesn't know she's different does she? She walks, she barks, she eats, she chases squirrels, just like a regular dog. But Faith has a message that anyone can understand. You have to try in life, you have to do things for yourself." I truly appreciated what Vyto had to say about my dog, and he was truly touched by the way Faith made her day to day life seem seamless. She wasn't acting like a diva, or something special, she was . . . and she is, a dog.

It was through the filming of Wisteria that Faith and I met an attorney from Washington D.C. When he came out of a local nursing home where his mother was a resident. As he wheeled his mother out of the home in her wheelchair it became apparent to me that both he and she were staring at my dog. Being rather used to people staring at Faith, I stood up from the grassy patch I was resting on and began walking over to them. They weren't alone, a former mayor of the City of Guthrie was with them, as well as her sister. It seemed a small group had gathered by the time we made it over to the attorney and his mother. Amazed and full of questions I tried to answer as much as I could about Faith for them, and just as she always does wherever she goes, Faith was able to make a new bridge between my life and the life of someone who would be working with me in the future in terms of formulating Faith's career. Clif McCann, the attorney e-mailed me after seeing Faith's website and suggested we have the name of Faith the Dog made into a trademark to protect her from anyone in the future using her image for anything less than admirable. Who would have thought? I would never have imagined a couple of years ago that holding a little two legged dog in my hands, trying to make her stand up and walk, would lead to me needing a trademark in order to protect her rights. I didn't even realize dogs had rights! Hey, everyone . . . dogs have rights!

Before the fun and excitement of filming a critically acclaimed independent film, where my role was very interesting: I was the personal assistant to an extra, I had been employed by an Oklahoma City Public school where things were not always as they seemed. It didn't take long to figure out that it was going to take a great deal of faith, the ordinary kind, just to survive the twists and turns of this ride.

I was employed for only one year, the term would be terminal I was told. I was not expected to come back, it was not a matter of me being a bad teacher, but the district had a way of making teachers apply for their own jobs year after year, and this particular position was a new one, one that would probably not be made available the next year, or any other year subsequent. It was months before I realized that the school I was working at was under the government's eye. They were being scrutinized for having one of the lowest ranking test scores in the state, and because of the massive turnovers in administration over the past few years, a new principal had been hired. He was from another state, he was going to make things happen, he was going to turn things around. He ran into the brick wall that is secondary education in the inter-city schools of Oklahoma City. At least I had the comfort of knowing that whenever I was being screamed at by an administrator it wasn't always something I was responsible for. Sometimes, as it turned out, it was the fact that the scores were too low, the English Second Language students too many, and the expectations of bringing up benchmarks, advanced performance indexes, and other standardized scores was simply an impossibility. The school is still on its way out at the time of this press, however, the faith shown by the students to continue to try and to continue to want to be educated amazes me. Not everyone wants to be taught, I'm not so naïve to believe that the school I taught at was one of the schools imitated in the movies where principals, teachers, and students work together to pull out of the slump that time has created. This school had the makings of a success story, unfortunately for the district, the Superintendent and the principal himself are not living in reality. Times do change, but not over night.

On the afternoon of February 28, 2004, I was in my classroom, we were working on Romeo and Juliet, a standard for any 9th grade class. We had seen the movie, and we were discussing it when over the PA system our 11th grade vice principal made the announcement that the student body could be released to go to the gym for the Brotherhood Assembly. This was going to be a great celebration of all of the mixed cultures of our school. My favorite two events were going to be the rap hip-hop sounds of a student who is only 4'6" tall, and he's Hispanic. He is so funny and so much fun to know. He can rap! He can dance! He was going to be really outstanding. The second group that was really on my mind were the stomp group. A group of African American girls from all grades who had been working hard on a skit which included a plot as well as their stomp dances. I couldn't wait.

The announcement to dismiss came a bit early according to my estimation, but that was nothing new. If one thing was sure about this school, it was that nothing went as planned. Nothing was as it seemed, nothing was done the way it was suppose to be done, but we the teachers had better follow any and every directive given. This announcement was a fool's folly. Every student exited without order to the halls, scampering, running, trying to get the best seats, or simply trying to get out of the building and off of the grounds without being caught. Like I said, it was a normal school with normal kids attending it.

About five minutes, a full five minutes after the first announcement was made, our 11th grade vice principal made a second announcement when he realized what his first call to dismiss resembled. "Teachers", he implored, "At this time, please only release the students who are to be a part of the Brotherhood Assembly". Right! Oh yes, let's just go into the crowded massive halls of the school and somehow, because we're miracle workers, call to order the groups and throngs of heads and feet that are bobbing through the corridors at this time. Perhaps we will even be able to be heard over the laughing, screaming, yelling, radios, cell-phones calling, and locker doors slamming. That didn't happen. I managed to wrangle four.

Another full five minutes goes by and the same lazy-lipped principal calls out one more time. "Teachers, at this time, please escort your students to the assigned areas of the auditorium where you normally sit." WHAT? What on Earth is this man talking about? We didn't have assigned seats. We didn't normally go to the assemblies at this time, even if we did have normal assigned seats, it would not be for this group of students. We were in third block I believe, and we normally had assemblies during fourth.

Suffice it to say that the panic that was once among the halls was now billowing its way into the orifices of the grand auditorium. As my class was upstairs I believed my non-assigned assigned seats would be upstairs. I was wrong. Of course I was wrong. I couldn't possibly expect this school to have any realism. Not after all the years it ran so well in complete chaos. I walked the four students I managed to corral into the auditorium on the top level of the school where I met with another English teacher, one who will not be named. She mentioned to me that she believed I was to be downstairs, and that she would check it out if I were to watch her area and not let anyone sit in it. I did exactly what I was told. That's just it. I always did exactly what I was told, but I was never really quiet about it. I usually made a comment about it being ridiculous to one or another of the other older teachers, who usually had another comment to the same effect to me. This was our way of venting without being completely terrible about it.

As I stood there guarding her area I was accosted, literally stepped on by my own vice principal who felt that it was her duty to yell in my face, causing her own spit to hit me squarely in the eye. As I tried to wipe it off, I also tried to understand her ranting over the music, the drums, the announcements from the stage, and the hundreds, now nearly a thousand kids seated on the second level. She was muttering something about me being downstairs, and that I had no right to be in the other teacher's area. When I tried to explain my position to her, I was awarded more spit. This exchange was witnessed of course, not only by other teachers, but a wonderful ROTC Sgt. Major, who refused to allow it to go on. Calling to my vice principal by name, he told her to back off, to stand down, and she did not. He told her once more that he would not allow her to mistreat me. She finally backed off of my foot and I breathed a frightful breath. I was so upset about what had just taken place that I immediately went down to the office to place a call to my union representative Rick, who I had been very accustomed to calling.

When I reached the office I was told by one of the three secretaries that I had a call, it would be patched through to the visitor's phone by the front door. I took the call. It happened to a news reporter from the Oklahoman, our city's largest paper. He wanted to do a story on Faith. I told him I had another story for him, one that would be amazing to his readers about the district and the way that teachers were being man-handled at the school. He was very interested, so interested in fact, that he put me on hold while he got another tape to record my every word. It wasn't long before my vice principal and the 11th grade vice principal had found me. I think they were actually looking for me. I could hear the music from the auditorium and knew that the assembly had started. Their real position at this time should have been monitoring the students, but here they were on a witch hunt, looking for their stray teacher who they had reason to believe was calling the union to file a formal complaint. Let me just say that the reporter, as well as myself, got two ears full when the 9th grade vice principal was in my face again, this time without the accoustics of the music filled auditorium to block out what she was screaming. Every eye of everyone in the office was bulging and staring at us. I simply turned the phone toward her mouth and let the reporter do his job. He wanted me to spell her name, and right there in front of God and everyone, I did. When I completely ignored her she became enraged. She was stepping over every professional boundary there was, but with the main principal out of the school, she felt that as supervising principal she had the right to belittle, berate, humiliate, and cause as much disturbance as was humanly possible. With her 6'2" frame, I wasn't sure she was actually human, but believed her to be some sort of Amazon from another world.

When the dust settled I returned to my classroom, where I picked up my purse, my lunchbox, and I left the building. I signed out, I said good bye to the ladies in the office, and I smiled at the main principal's secretary Shirley. She's the nicest person in the entire school, and I wanted her to see that I was not ruffled. She smiled back, shook her head, and said "Ms. Stringfellow, you do get yourself into trouble!" I answered back "Just doing my job!" As I had been in scuffs with the administration since the first day of school when it was very clear that following the laws and the proper procedures of ethics in a public institution of education was not on their minds. Someone had to stand up for the kids. This took faith, a little moxie too, I knew I would not be coming back, but I had no idea I would be asked to leave early.

On March 3, 2005, I was escorted from my room the second the last bell rang. Here stood the Amazon and the main principal with a mandated letter from the former asking me to leave and not return. Not until a formal hearing on the matter could be held. This formal hearing was scheduled for the last week of the year. My students, over 100 of them, would be given substitutes, less than educated persons without the reasonable responsibility to see to it that the advanced performance indexes, the benchmarks, and the standardized scores of the students were brought up. They were babysitters and they were bad at that from what I was told.

At the hearing I was vindicated. I was told that she was wrong, that she had no right to do what she was doing, naturally I assumed this meant that I would be given a chance to return and see to it that the next year would be a better year. I was wrong. I was asked not to return as I was causing too much of a problem when I let the union know, and the state of Oklahoma know that the school district and the school administrators were not following standard operating standards of what is expected at an inter-city high school. I was guaranteed that my file would be sealed. I was told that I would be paid, I was told that I would receive the insurance benefits, and that I would be given the standard reference that anyone received if anyone called for a performance or personal reference. Faith is a funny thing. I was expected to show faith in the same district that treated me so badly. I was expected to show faith in the very people that lied to me, spat on me, and even wrongfully walked me out of the building in front of hundreds of students who wondered if I were being arrested for something. Faith is a funny thing. I had to show it, it was this moment that I chose to be quiet, and to let the actions of the administration be seen by the students who knew me too well to know that I would never do anything illegal. They knew. They had faith too, but it wasn't in their school, it was in me. I had to be strong and I had to let them go.

Chapter Twenty One

The summer of 2005 found me in quite the bind again, as I faced the hard cold facts that telling the truth to people who don't relish being truthful can cost a person much more than they ever expected. My Dad used to say that I speak my mind even when my mind should shut up. He's right, I don't hold back what I'm thinking and although it is most likely the truth that I'm speaking, I have had to learn to speak less and save more. I interviewed with quite a few school districts over the summer months of 2005, and in every case I was called back for a second, and sometimes a third interview. It was obvious to me that the administrator liked what I had to offer in terms of being a high school teacher, but for reasons unknown, I was never hired. I received a letter or a phone call, in one instance I received an e-mail, all stating that they were choosing another candidate to fill the position of being their needed English teacher for the upcoming year. I knew something was going on, something sinister such as my previous employer telling tales about me, or perhaps telling more than is legally allowed when an employer calls for a reference. It's easy to do really, and no one would be the wiser. Trying to prove that you've been talked about by a previous employer is about the hardest thing in the world to do. You can't record the conversations being held between two parties you don't even know are talking to one another. It would be easy for one party to say to the other "Hey, buddy, I know I'm not suppose to ask, but . . . what kind of an employee was Jude anyway?"

My mouth has gotten me into more trouble by speaking the truth about a situation than it ever has by speaking a lie. For instance, at the Oklahoma City Public School that I worked at in 2004, I was very open and very honest about the fact that my administrator had stepped on my foot and that she had spat on my face while she was barking at me. I had mentioned it to the principals where I was interviewing that I had need to involve my union. The kind-hearted secretary told me about a week after I had been asked to leave, that the same administrator that had spat on me had physically grabbed one of my students by the back of the neck and forced him into the wall. This woman, the administrator, takes matters of control into her own hands and uses her size and her position as an intimidation mechanism. The boy may have been afraid of her, but I was not. I immediately called the parents of the kid to let them know. They stated to me that because they were illegally in this country they were not going to bring the administrator to any form of justice. Through broken English they thanked me for caring, but asked me not to contact them further as the school had already "warned" them against talking with me. While checking my history or my background at this particular school, it wouldn't be very hard for a new employer to find out this sort of information. I was literally the only teacher that I remember who was stupid enough or strong enough to stand up to the woman that called herself a leader of the school, to let her know that she would be held accountable someday for what she mistook as power or authority. My mouth gets me into trouble, yes, and my pen records it for life. I have more than 300 journals which I have kept on a near daily basis since I was quite small. Using about 20-25 composition notebooks a year now, I'm sure I'll reach over 1,500 before I'm finished. When I die, I have asked my friend Victoria Reddling, my counselor and spiritual leader, to go through them and to publish the parts that could be published without embarrassing my family too much. She is also to ask my friend Will Orr if he wants his name to be published in a book that I have written, and if he does, she is to ask him if he wants his name to be changed to Bill or something. For that matter, several friends should be consulted before I mention them in books without their permission. Wouldn't it be best to ask David Parker, a man who is like an uncle to Reuben, if he would want to be in the book? After all ink on the printed page can be very loud. Ink can be deafening when it needs to be, and my experiences at Oklahoma City Schools is not only recorded, it is recorded in detail, I should give the same consideration to my friends, lest they pretend they don't know me when I meet them on the streets.

Faith is a multi-faceted thing. You have to have it in order to see yourself through to the end of whatever it is that you're planning to do. I needed a job, I had to have one, it wasn't as if my kids could feed themselves, nor could my mortgage be paid simply by hoping . . . hope is great, I hoped a great deal, but faith is the only thing that truly gets me through these times. I guess I can best explain it by adding another word to the mix; work. You can't just have faith, you have to work at whatever it is that you want. Let's say I wanted a job. I did want a job. I had to have one. I could sit on my butt and wait for the phone to ring, which would be more indicative of hope, or I could get up, buy the paper, go through the classifieds, circle the ads that I would be qualified for, make the calls, go on the appointments, tell my side of my story, thank the manager . . . and . . . pray. I also have to work. I have to build a resume, take that resume to the places I want to work. Set up interviews, show up for interviews. I can't just hope or want to be hired. Faith without work, according to the Bible, is dead. I don't want dead. I want life. Life is good. Have you ever sat at home and stared at the phone because it was supposed to be ringing for you? The person on the other end, say a friend, doesn't realize you're about to pounce the receiver when they call. When they call, and you pounce, they seem so surprised to hear you utter in disappointment "Oh, it's you. I was hoping it was someone else." Oh goody, now you're upset and you've just upset your friend as well. No, I think faith, the real faith is just waiting normally for the phone or the letter in the mail asking you to come to work, or telling you that whatever it was that you wanted has happened. You have to put forth the right effort, do the right things, and dot the i's as you cross your t's, but you don't have to worry. Faith, well, faith is when you do what you have to do, you call on whomever it is that can make it happen, and you just let it happen. Hard? You bet it is. It's the hardest thing in the world because you can't control fate, but you can . . . and you should, control faith.

I've been drawn out, held out, freaked out, and made to question my own faith a million times, but the truth is, my time is simply not God's time. Looking back, OK, having 20-20 site, I can see where being God is something I just wouldn't want to do. He's really got a tough job, and asking me to show a little faith in Him is not that big of a deal. He's never let me down . . . and if that sounds corny, or churchy, you'll have to forgive me. I'm a little corny and I'm a little churchy from time to time. (Don't read every page of my journal if you're thinking you'd like to put me on some sort of a pedestal though, you'll soon find out that I'm a lot like you.) Have you ever had to wait for something and you really didn't think you had the time to do it? If you're like me you grab the notebook, scratch out all the things you have to do, things you have to pay right now, things you can't get away with not paying, or not doing. If you're like me you can't find the time, the money, the resources, or the information you need to get the job done, but you can't stop either. Stopping would mean giving up, and if there's one thing I do better than speaking my mind, it's holding on. I could be a bulldog I suppose.

Thinking in terms of what is next for Faith I'll be honest with you and say that she should be seen by as many people as she can be. Whether that is through commercials, movies, music videos, or just being on the covers of magazines and newspapers, Faith is meant to be there to help people who otherwise have difficult times in their ordinary lives. When we go to places to talk about our mission, places like the Angel Tree in Bethany, Oklahoma, a place where kids whose parents are incarcerated, we talk about hope. We talk about what God can do for anyone, you, me, Faith, and others who are willing to put forth the effort in their lives to stand up and do the walking.

Walking by faith, not necessarily on two legs. Carolyn Gold wheeled herself to us. I'm talking about putting on the protection of faith, and doing whatever it is necessary to fight the battles using wisdom, and hope, prayer, and others as your weapons. The actions of doing so is the product of faith. Faith really is the substance of things hoped for. Substance meaning, the thing which that hope or dream is made of. Getting up and making things happen is only part of it. Being willing to work for the goal, being willing to be there for someone else whose goals are being met, and in doing so, perhaps even further your own set of goals in a direction you never dreamed of. Faith is the evidence of things not seen. Can you see it? Take a walk with me someday down the streets of a really crowded city, on the moving sidewalks in the airport, up the escalators at the malls, or maybe down the hallways of a nursery school, hospital wing or community center. When you do, watch the people as they see the laughing little yellow dog. They lose something when they do. They lose their fear of the day, they lose their burdens, they drop the very thought that was bothering them just a few minutes before. For them, this moment is all there is. And in that moment, they see faith in the body of a miracle. They see Faith.

After Thoughts

This book was written and ready to go at the end of Spring 2005. It was at that time that I was told by the Oklahoma City Schools that I would be receiving a lump sum pay out for the contract we had signed in August of the following year. Strangely, just two days before the call came from the district telling me that I would be paid, I was released from the only position of employment I had regarding teaching at the college level as well. Budget cuts again? I wondered. However, I had already signed a contract with the college as well, and demanded that my pay not be affected by their decision to release several instructors. I was the only instructor paid for the summer months who had been released. Something in my head had told me days before to go to the school and to sign my contracts. It wasn't a phone call, or a mailed notice, it was a voice in my head and my heart warning me that it was the thing to do. I'm glad I listened.

The film *Wisteria* comes out in October 2006. You should be warned that it is a bit on the gritty side, however, Vyto and my son make the film worth going to see no matter how you feel about gritty tales.

Faith has her own website. It was set up by Matt Layne, a fantastic man, a fan of Faith's, and great webmaster. He is with Timeline.com and is wise and talented beyond belief. I decided to add a blurp on the website about needing help to get the book published. It worked. In the front of this book I mention the names of the people who graciously, generously, and wonderfully, without self thought, gave to the project, but I can't leave that alone. I want to be sure and thank them one more time. Thank you Debbie Minshall and family, Ginger and Dennis Handy, Ericka from Seattle, and Xlibris for the finished project of this book. Greg Haigh at Xlibris has been with me throughout the whole mess as I have anguished to get the book finished. He has been amazing. Ginger Handy gets a SECOND thank you because she, the crazy woman, bid on an auction I held on Ebay and she won the "Thank You" in the book. She already had a thank you! But, for Ginger, you can never say it enough. Thanks AGAIN. Thank you to the readers who have found this book an inspiration, thank you to my kids who have let me have the time to write without being interrupted . . . . too much. Thank you Faithy, I call her Yellow Dog most of the time now. She is truly an act of God.

A Study of
N. F. S. GRUNDTVIG

DANISH REBEL

by
Johannes Knudsen

Muhlenberg Press, Philadelphia

Copyright
1955 by Muhlenberg Press

Library of Congress Catalogue
Card Number 55-7763

Printed in U.S.A.   UB758

Contents

To My Wife

Introduction

Locked in the language of a small country yet sought in other lands with eagerness and anticipation, N. F. S. Grundtvig (1783-1872) has become almost legendary outside his native Denmark, where he is a great national and religious figure. Proclaimed abroad as a prophet and condemned as a heretic, he has incited a curiosity which has not yet been satisfied. The fault of this lies not in the man who wore his heart on his sleeve and sent to the printer almost every page he wrote—a five-foot shelf will not hold half of his first editions—but in inadequate presentation and interpretation.

What first evoked world curiosity in Grundtvig was the remarkable system of popular education, the Danish Folk Schools, which bore the imprint of his name. For several decades now, even in studies published in the English language, he has been hailed as a great educator whose ideas have spread across the globe. Grundtvig the educator has long been esteemed a great though somewhat enigmatic personality. But the presentation of his educational ideas has not penetrated the depths of his thoughts. Such studies have excited a residual frustration which only a more comprehensive analysis can remove. On the other hand, indignant conservatives have proclaimed Grundtvig a rank heretic and a dangerous rebel. The man was a crackpot, and his followers were both heretical and sectarian. True, he wrote some fine hymns in his own language, but otherwise he was a secularized if not an outright pagan figure. Apart from these two extremes Grundtvig was known to a smaller circle as a bold historian, a linguist, and research scholar of note, particularly in the field of mythology and medieval history.

The picture has changed. A better acquaintance with the church life of Denmark and the growing dilemma of Protestantism, whetted by the barbs of Søren Kierkegaard, have combined to increase the curiosity about Grundtvig and motivate a body of research. It is indeed strange that Kierkegaard, his great opponent in Denmark, should help pave the way for an understanding of Grundtvig outside Denmark a century after Kierkegaard's death. Unlike Kierkegaard, the individualist, Grundtvig's conception of the church and his ideas about man were corporate. For him neither physical nor spiritual life can be lived alone. The body of a people is the spiritual entity into which a man is born. It enfolds him and carries him, gives him life and strength, guides and guards his life. The life of the people is determinative for the life of the individual.

Any presentation of Grundtvig must inevitably stress the dynamic character of his personality and his life activity. His problems were never abstractions; they always pointed toward actual circumstances. And his answers were always directed toward the solutions of life situations. Some of these situations seem dim and distant to us today, but they were real enough a century ago, and many of them are real today even when they appear in a different guise. For Grundtvig life was serious, so serious that his main problem became that of life and death. Church life, national life, education—all these were considered, not in terms of trivialities or exclusively practical aspects, but in terms of their ultimate implication. The forces that were at play were either vital, life-giving forces or they were destructive, death-bringing powers. "My antithesis," he once said, "is that of life and death." Nothing less could suffice. This conflict is essentially a religious conflict, and as few others Grundtvig saw it as such. It was more than that; it was a Christian conflict. Grundtvig was never a non-religious humanist. He was a Christian who became a prophet, a scholar, a poet, a patriot, and an educator.

It sounds trite to say that Grundtvig believed in the power of the spirit. Yet, fundamentally, this is the key to understanding the dynamic quality of his personality and ideas. He believed firmly that the Spirit of God and the spirit of man, separately and jointly, were active against the powers of destruction and death in the world. And he believed that man, not by his own strength but by the power of God's Spirit, was given victory in the struggle between the contending forces.

His problems grew out of two strong personal commitments, one to his country and one to his Christian faith. He was intensely interested in the survival and future happiness of Denmark, and he believed firmly that national, i.e. cultural, greatness could grow out of a realization of the cultural values of his people. But the question of national survival led him to the question of the pertinency and validity of the Christian revelation. In his struggle with issues he found a new way to express the character of revelation and of the church, through a dynamic concept of the historic fellowship of faith of the church and the power of the living word. This renewed the church life of Denmark and carried the work of the Reformation that step forward which the static forces of orthodoxy had blocked.

Grundtvig was fundamentally concerned with the basic nature of man. This was essentially a religious preoccupation but it had important consequences for national and cultural life. Again his barriers were static concepts developed from a stereotyped church view, but he found new impulses in his contact with British church and public life. He gave renewed significance to man's creation in the image of God and his freedom in human affairs. He found inspiration and motivation for individual and social activity, and out of these insights rose the views on education which inspired the Folk Schools of Denmark, the most spectacular fruit of his labors.

To an unusual degree Grundtvig was absorbed in the ideas of his age. To interpret his ideas today his original contributions must be shorn of their nineteenth-century dress. It was a century of marvelous progress and wonderful accomplishments, but wars and crises have changed our outlook from that of our grandparents. We have become pessimistic where they were optimistic. Their unshakable belief in progress has been replaced by a cautious emphasis upon consolidation. They saw the beacon of freedom; we see how self-interests have abused our freedoms and we are learning that freedom must be supplemented and supported by mutuality and responsibility.

After the depression and the static years that followed the Napoleonic wars had run out Grundtvig lived in an age of expansion and progress. He grew with a generation that discarded old standards to construct new ones. His was a time of national growth and a great expansion of society as well as of human thought, but he antedated the great systematicians of the second half of the century. He accepted the ideas of growth and development held by Lessing, Herder, and, for a while, Schelling, then lived just long enough to hear Darwin's bold theories of evolution. He shared the social expectations and the national hope of the early reformers of his century, but preceded Marx's materialism, and the roar of Bismarck's conquests did not begin until he had reached his eighties. He lived through the death agonies of the old mercantilistic system and broadened his outlook with the Industrial Revolution. This must be considered as we try to evaluate and place his ideas. Yet we must reach even further back, into the ideas and ways of the eighteenth century, for Grundtvig was of university age when the new century rolled around.

One difficulty in interpreting Grundtvig is a difficulty of personality. He had many peculiarities of behavior. His loquacious participation in public affairs irked his contemporaries and prevented them from appreciating his real contribution. But after a hundred years a man is judged by his monumentality and not by petty idiosyncracies. Grundtvig's language is even more of a barrier. He wrote in cumbersome and long-winded prose, filled with exuberant expressions and a terminology all his own. It is difficult to read and harder to translate. His poetry was superb at its best, but it is so steeped in the imagery of his people that translations lose either the beauty or the meaning of its highly concentrated expressions. It seems wise in most instances to make a prose translation of the contents at the sacrifice of the form.

Grundtvig was a warrior. Practically all his prose writings, even to some extent his world histories, are polemical. He was always battling for something and therefore always battling against something. As a result he pressed his ideas so strongly that they became one-sided in their emphasis. This we must understand, particularly in regard to the things he does not say. There are other sides to the issues for which he fought, and Grundtvig's emphasis often varied with the controversy in which he was engaged. The inference is not necessarily that he was inconsistent, merely that he was polemical and dialectic.

Also he had a strong tendency toward doctrinalization of his own ideas, an inclination stimulated by his friends and followers. Having expressed an opinion somewhat extremely in a polemical writing, he would seize it, defend it, and establish it defiantly as a dogma. In his later years the most tragic example was his dogmatization of a particular theory about the historical origin of the Apostles' Creed.

In our search to find what his message means to us, we must remember that Grundtvig was open to change. He was pitted against many individuals in his arguments, yet it was always an issue for which he was fighting. If he realized that he had made a mistake, he changed his view, though often belatedly. In his early youth, like all Danish patriots at the time, he was incensed against England, the great archenemy of 1801 and 1807. Then after his journeys to England (1829-31) he became an Anglophile. Through most of his career he believed in an enlightened monarchy. Yet after participating in the constitutional congress of 1849 he became a convert to the democratic cause. In 1866, as an octogenarian, he even sought and won election to the upper house in order to fight for the democratic constitution against reactionary amendments. His conception of church government underwent several important changes to conform with his theology, and in numerous other instances he made similar adjustments.

His changing views must be considered as a part of growth. One emphasis grew out of another, with certain basic attitudes never absent, though not always obvious. After his conversion experience of 1810-11, at the age of twenty-seven, Grundtvig was always a committed Christian. This unwavering loyalty to the Christian faith must be taken for granted in everything he did or said. In 1816-19 he developed certain basic philosophical ideas about evidence, and these never left him. Nevertheless he continued to grow and to develop new insights and understandings. As he himself has said, faith never changes but its interpretation must always adjust itself.

Grundtvig developed slowly, in striking contrast to Søren Kierkegaard, whose meteoric career and enormous production came to an end with his death at forty-two. Grundtvig was only beginning his active public life at that age; he enjoyed thirty-seven years more of development in his ideas. Many of his most important commitments came as delayed-action results of earlier influences. Typical of this is the impact of Romanticism brought to Denmark by Henrik Steffens in 1802. At the time Grundtvig refused to be swept away by the common enthusiasm, but several years later he became a fiery Romanticist and gave Steffens credit for being one of the most important influences of his life.

Grundtvig cannot be interpreted apart from his personality, for all the affairs in which he participated became personal issues. This fact brought him many a battle scar and it often beclouds the situation. He was never a spectator but always a participant, and the ideas he promoted were always formed through personal passion and concern.

Because Grundtvig's ideas were presented in a small country, their impact produced revolutionary changes in education, church, and government, affording a laboratory in which they could be tried out.

1

In the Grip of Life

Nikolaj Frederik Severin Grundtvig was born September 8, 1783, at Udby, a village located fifty miles south of Copenhagen on the island of Sjaelland. His father was a clergyman of the old Lutheran school who was quite unaffected by current philosophies. A solemn and serious man, he devoted himself to his task of preaching, instruction, and care of souls. Grundtvig's mother was also a person of strong character, a sincere and devout woman who brought up her children in good manners and the fear of God and who inspired them to follow in the footsteps of their father and her own forefathers as men of the cloth.

Deeply rooted in the soil and history of Denmark, they were heirs to a thousand years of national, cultural, and religious life. For ten centuries the gospel had been preached and for more than nine the people had belonged to an indigenous church. During the Reformation this church had followed in the footsteps of Martin Luther and had been given new life and new character. Although it had become set in doctrinal orthodoxy, this pattern was warmed by Pietism until the intellectualism of the eighteenth century made it sterile. This modern influence had not touched the life of the Grundtvig home, but it was soon to envelop the life of the youngest son.

As a child Grundtvig lived the life of a village boy, but he had the added advantage of the educational resources of the parish parsonage. He was a voracious reader, especially of history, and followed current events through the weekly newspaper from Copenhagen. When he was nine years old he was sent to Pastor Laurids Feld at Thyregod in the central part of Jutland, the mainland of Denmark, to be prepared for entrance into Latin school.

His days of Latin school, or university preparation, were spent at Aarhus, the main city of Jutland. In retrospect Grundtvig had little good to say for the school. He criticized its deadening influence, and it is largely in polemics against the Latin school that he later expounded a free and popular system of education. The school was undoubtedly better than Grundtvig's evaluation. The fact that during his Aarhus days he became a young sophisticate who lost interest in current events as well as in religion seems to be no fault of the institution. The fact was, as Grundtvig failed to realize, that he was simply passing through the period of adolescence where preoccupation with personal matters often subordinates more generalized interests.

During the fall of 1800 Grundtvig, at seventeen,

passed the entrance requirements of the University of Copenhagen and was registered as a student. He was well prepared for the work, having studied the humanities plus Latin, Greek, and Hebrew, but after his graduation he had to compensate for a lack of French and English. His outward circumstances were less favorable; finances were meager, his clothes were poor, and his rather uncouth manners made him somewhat less than a social success. The lectures at the university made no immediate impact upon him, and he spent his time with routine studies, card playing, and argumentation. The greatest object of his concern was undoubtedly himself, as his diary plainly shows, and he tried his hand with very limited success at various literary efforts in poetry and dramatics.

True to the family tradition he studied theology although he had no interest in the ministry. His religious interest was so slight that the reading of a satirical poem caused him to confide to his diary that "gone was orthodoxy." The lectures did not impress him, "for our professors were poor at keeping abreast of the times, so that our theologians knew little about Kant and our philosophy was kept strictly to Leibnitz and Wolff." [1] He was taught the epistemology, or method of reasoning, of Wolff by Professor Børge Riisbrigh. A redeeming feature of the general dullness of his studies was his friendship with a fellow student, P. N. Skougaard, who reawakened his interest in history.

[1] See Appendix, pp. 221-31.

Two major events, which apparently made slight impression on him at the time, were later to have great significance in his development. They form a typical example of the delayed action so characteristic of Grundtvig. The first event was the battle of Copenhagen, April 2, 1801, when a British fleet attacked the city.[2] He joined a student corps which was organized at the last minute and which saw no action during the battle, but he was more concerned with an imminent examination and the following vacation. Years later he showed that the battle and the defeat had made a deep impression upon him, but at the time the shell of his sophistication had not been shattered.

With a similar immediate reaction but with an even greater delayed impact he attended the lectures given at the university by his somewhat older cousin, Henrik Steffens. Steffens had returned from a period of study in Germany deeply inspired by the new ideas of Romanticism and by the philosophy of Schelling. He lectured at the university to a large and enthusiastic audience during the winter 1802-3, and in a very dramatic way the lectures inaugurated the era of Romanticism in Denmark. Adam Oehlenschläger was directly inspired by Steffens to become a poet, and through him, Romanticism influenced Danish literature. But the general enthusiasm was not shared by Grundtvig. He commented briefly on the lectures in his diary and several times he remarked that he could not understand them.

[2] See Appendix, pp. 237-39.

The story is told that Steffens and Grundtvig met at the dinner table of a mutual uncle. "Do you attend my lectures?" Steffens asked. When Grundtvig replied in the affirmative, Steffens continued: "But do you understand them?" "Yes, some," Grundtvig answered drily.

Years later he was not so reserved. Through Steffens' lectures, he stated, "I received, without being aware of it, a living impression of and a respect for the spirit as the wonderful living power of the word, whose effect is the irresistible conviction that there is an invisible reality beyond the reality of our senses. Years were to pass before this made any noticeable difference in my view of life and knowledge, but it was this impression of a living word about the invisible reality and about the sovereignty of the spirit which formed my first step from the spiritual world of the eighteenth century to that of the nineteenth."

Grundtvig was graduated from the university *cum laude* in the fall of 1803. He was then twenty years old and far too young to serve in the church, had he so desired. The next year was spent in a rather desultory fashion. He toyed with the idea of writing a historical dissertation but gave it up. His time was spent with reading, most of it history, and he taught himself the Icelandic language so he could read the old sagas. Lack of finances compelled him to spend much of his time at home, although he made numerous visits to an older brother who had a parish on the near-by island of Falster. He had previously tried his hand at preaching, both at home and in his brother's church. On one of the sermons he commented in his diary. "It treated the thought of death, in part as a guard against vice and in part as a motive for virtue." But he was more interested in social life, and he recorded successive infatuations for the daughters of a near-by pastor with alternate expressions of lyric enthusiasm and common sense reflections on the problems of matrimony. Finally, he was compelled by circumstances to seek employment. He accepted a position as a private tutor at an estate on the island of Langeland, far removed from the intellectual life of Copenhagen to which he was greatly attracted.

The three years he spent at Egeløkke Manor saw the first great crisis of Grundtvig's life. When he arrived he was a sophisticated but somewhat uncouth young intellectual with an overdose of self-interest and very little concern for the issues of the day. Then he was hit by a bombshell. He fell in love with his pupil's mother, the twenty-eight-year-old Constance Leth. It was an all-absorbing passion which tormented him for at least two years and which defied all efforts to combat it. There is no evidence or reason to believe that he made undue advances to the lady. Apparently he gave vent to his feelings through poetry and in his diary, part of which is intact. But there can be no doubt that he was deeply shaken by the experience and that he discovered realms of emotions within his own soul which dethroned the calm power of reason of which he had been so proud. When the passion was finally spent he was a chastened and more deeply serious young man. On his twenty-third birthday in 1806 he wrote in his diary: "O Thou who art eternal! Thou art the only one to whom I can confide my quiet despair. With a pure heart and a childlike faith I look to Thy heaven and pray, pray sincerely, that Thou continuously wilt bless my work and, if possible, grant peace to my heart!"

Simultaneous with this infatuation he was taken up with world literature and the philosophy of Romanticism.[3] Undoubtedly his emotional crisis had some influence on the new interest. Above all, however, he experienced the delayed impact of Steffens' lectures, and he was, of course, advancing to the normal interests of a young man twenty-three years old. Shakespeare and Goethe were his first discoveries and from them he proceeded to Schiller, Fichte,[4] and especially to Schelling.[5] The latter captivated him completely for a while and he confided to his diary: "I departed from life with Schelling in his *Bruno*." In order to get books he started a reading circle on the island and kept it going for a while despite the inhabitants' general apathy and natural resentment toward him as a revolutionary young firebrand.

When Grundtvig commented that he "departed from life" with Schelling, it is to be understood, in accord with the ideas of Romanticism, that he was carried

[3] See Appendix, pp. 231-34.
[4] See Appendix, pp. 234-35.
[5] See Appendix, pp. 236-37.

beyond the realm of ordinary, practical living into the "real" world of the spirit. Schelling had proclaimed a wonderful new harmony and in this the storm-tossed soul of young Grundtvig momentarily found relief and release. The key to the harmony was an intuitive longing and such a longing he found in the frustration of his love. He therefore made a sincere, though perhaps momentarily inspired, effort to commit himself in a mystical manner to Schelling's way. He tried to sublimate his love by identifying it with the longing of which Schelling spoke so that he could rise to the vaunted union with the Absolute. His diary records: "She . . . is not the object of my longing but only its expression . . . My longing was awakened by my emotions and therefore both objectives are combined without becoming one . . . I cannot give up my longing, for then I would succumb to myself and become nothing; but continue to attach it to an earthly object I cannot do without destruction of my own being, and transfer is impossible. Or is it possible? Can I not transfer it, if not to someone else, then to myself? But then I must separate it from the object which is now its expression for me . . . Only when I become conscious of that toward which I long can I separate it from her to whom it has so long been joined, and my own spirit can become its expression. If I can reach this goal, I am saved. Then I am raised above the law which compels man to seek the solutions of his problems outside himself. In the union of my soul and the highest goal I have reached an enjoyment which leaves our finite life behind and ascends toward the supreme and ultimate goal."

The experiment failed and the attempted realization of Schelling's philosophy was in vain. The next item in the diary reads: "Again I have been silent for two months, and disconsolately I take the pen for the results are not happy. Only dimly do I recall the thrill of my last item. Only momentarily could I appear as the object of my own longing, I whose soul is torn by persistent disharmony. Never has my passion been more violent and consuming than since the moment when I thought I was raised above it. And how could it be otherwise? Did I not increase it by identifying it with my longing toward the highest goal?" Our interest in this crisis is not his passion, which his strong nature eventually overcame, but the personal test of the religious philosophy of Romanticism. Some years later he refuted this philosophy and presented strong arguments against it. Although the refutation was made with theoretical arguments there seems to be no doubt that it grew out of this practical attempt at personal realization. As usual, however, he was slow to accept the consequences of a vital experience.

In this emotional turmoil Grundtvig's youthful and rather arrogant abandonment of religion was completely forgotten. With moralistic fervor he now preached in several of the churches on Langeland, and when a general argument arose in regard to a new liturgy he even took part by publishing a pamphlet called *Religion and*

Liturgy. His fervor was far ahead of his thinking, however, and although he criticized Schelling as inadequate, he still defined religion in terms of the Romantic philosophy. He called it the "relation of the finite to the eternal" and defined the religion of Jesus as the "reconciliation of the finite with the eternal." The traditional concepts of the church slipped into the discussion, but he interpreted them in terms of Schelling. Grundtvig was moving toward a more positive Christian point of view, but he did not realize it and for the moment other interests captured him.

One of these interests was his patriotism. The war with England had settled down to the intermittent skirmishes of a naval blockade,[6] but this blockade brought the war to Langeland, a station in the guarded movement of troops. For the second time the war was brought close to Grundtvig and this time it struck home. When England laid siege to Copenhagen in 1807 and seized the Danish fleet, he reacted intensely, perhaps primarily against his own previous apathy, and became a bold critic of the Danish people for their indifference to peril. He published an apocalyptic poem called "The Masquerade Ball in Denmark" in which he castigated the people for making merry on the brink of catastrophe. The poem is so overdone that it is almost hysterical, but it did reflect a sincere concern. Furthermore, in taking its spokesman from history and legend it gave expression to the interest in which Grundtvig momen-

[6] See Appendix, pp. 236-37.

tarily found release from the press of emotional turmoil.

From his early childhood he had been fascinated by history. His adolescent indifference toward it had been dispelled through the influence of Skougaard, and after his graduation he had resumed the study. He had even considered a historical dissertation. Thus in Grundtvig the growing interest in ancient Nordic history and mythology found an eager champion. Already in 1806, while he was still at Langeland, he had published an article, "A Little About the Songs of Edda." In 1808 he moved to Copenhagen where he found a position as history teacher in a private school. He then embarked upon the historical and philological studies which were to absorb so much of his time and through which he gained a renown entirely apart from his work within the church. For the time being he threw himself into mythology.

The classical tradition which had permeated all of Europe since the Renaissance had exclusively emphasized the Greco-Roman mythology. But interest in the old Nordic gods had been growing, particularly in Denmark, through the influence of the mythological dramas of Johannes Ewald. Romanticism had given further impetus to this interest which placed the Nordic mythology fully on a par with the classical. The poet Oehlenschläger had used its themes in poetry and drama and the time was ripe for a more scholarly treatment of the subject. This is what Grundtvig undertook, and he was ready to publish his *Nordic Mythology* in December, 1808. He treated the ancient tales as a cosmological drama which reflected the faith or philosophy of the Nordic people, but his best contribution was a scholarly discussion of the historical sources for our present knowledge of the myths. While not all his conclusions were upheld by later research, the little book was epoch making and won him much renown. He followed it up by two poetic accounts of the old legends, *Scenes from the Decline of the Heroic Epoch of the North*, published in 1809, and *Scenes from the Wars of the Norns and the Asas*, in 1811, whose accomplished purpose was to awaken interest in the life of the past as an inspiration for present-day activity.

Grundtvig resumed his work with the myths in a second and larger study in 1832, but he was never more engrossed in the subject than at the time of the publication of *Nordic Mythology*. He became so immersed in his research and waxed so enthusiastic about the ancient gods that he went to great extremes of expression. All his newly kindled fervor was, for the moment, pointed in one direction. With a friend, C. Molbech, who shared this interest, he visited an ancient sacrificial mound. In a poem published in the papers he then described the sacrificial grove in exaggerated terms, ending with the proclamation that he was so filled with sacred devotion that he had thrown himself before the altar to worship the ancient gods. A few years later he described the lyric outburst as "fool's talk," and declared that he had, of course, never bowed the knee to any

idol. This is undoubtedly true, but the poem nevertheless reflected a state of mind which had gripped him and
which has rightfully been characterized as "Asa intoxi-
cation." [7]

During the period of these Nordic studies Grundtvig
was a fellow of Valkendorf College, an endowed
residence for students and recent graduates, and he became fast friends with a number of younger scholars.
Through these he was introduced into the intellectual
society of the city where he was received favorably and
was regarded as a poet and scholar of promise, although
his extrovertive behavior seemed somewhat peculiar. A
future career seemed to open up for him and through
his teaching he managed a satisfactory living. But other
forces were at work to alter the picture, and again they
include the delayed impact of influences and ideas.
Furthermore, his all-but-neglected family ties claimed
his attention. His parents were old and ready for a
retirement which finances did not permit. They pleaded
with Grundtvig, who was now past the minimum age
for ordination, to come to Udby as an assistant to his
father so that the burden of the parish work might be
eased. The son was reluctant to give up a promising
career and he hedged. His mother finally wrote him a
letter of bitter reproach. Under pressure of this situation
Grundtvig started plans for his ordination, and March
17, 1810, he preached a trial sermon—which was to have
wide repercussions.

[7] "Asa" is the joint name for a group of Nordic gods.

His interest in religion, expressed in *Religion and Liturgy* in 1806, had been subordinated to his interest in history and mythology, but it had not expired. The new situation revived it, and the demands of the sermon brought it forth. The sermon does not merely reflect an immediate interest, however, for Grundtvig wrote in his diary in 1815 that "it is not, as many probably would believe, a rush job, for I had worked intermittently on it for two years without being satisfied with its form." The fact is that the reformer and critic, who had given vent to his feelings in "The Masquerade Ball," now chose the form of religious indignation. Grundtvig's blistering trial sermon was titled, "Why Has the Word of God Disappeared from His House?" In it he excoriated the preaching of the ministers of Copenhagen.

The sermon was preached without an audience, and although the professor who was assigned to criticize it was a little perplexed, he passed it, knowing that it was just a private performance. But Grundtvig, who had been bitten by a desire to publish, sent it to the printer. Its publication raised a storm of indignation and criticism from the clergy in the city. There was even talk of a lawsuit for defamation of character, but the matter was officially settled by a reprimand through the university, given many months later. The Copenhagen ministers did not forget, however, and there can be no doubt that their resentment kept Grundtvig from a Copenhagen pulpit for many years.

While the matter of the sermon and his ordination

were pending Grundtvig spent the summer and fall of 1810 in relative idleness. He was tense. For the past two years he had undoubtedly worked too hard and he was ill at ease over the conflict between his ambition and his filial duties. The problems raised by his sermon also plagued him. About twenty poems written during this period show an intense preoccupation with personal religious problems. For the demands of his teaching he read historical works but concentrated upon the history of the church. Inspired by this reading he started a series of poems about the Crusades, undoubtedly regarding himself as a crusader, and he grew highly indignant during the reading of Kotzebue's *History of Prussia* when the author spoke disparagingly about the "withered cross of Christ."

Then the tension came to a head and the crusading spirit gave way to personal crisis and despair. Years later he described the situation: "I was suddenly crushed by the question: Are you a Christian? Do you have the forgiveness of sin?" The agony increased until he worked himself into an extremely depressed state of mind, and in January his friends intervened to take him home to his parents. His father received him with calmness and thanked God that the crisis had come.[8] After some weeks of quiet the depression waned, and as he in the meantime had been appointed assistant to his

---

[8] He used the word "Anfaegtelse" for which there is no English equivalent. It is the same as the German "Anfechtung," a moral and spiritual crisis.

father, he was ordained into the ministry and settled down, for the time being, to the parish work at Udby.

Although it is difficult to understand and fully describe a religious conversion, there are several elements of Grundtvig's crisis which are made clear in his writings, especially in his letters. It is first of all quite evident that he reacted against his own previous Rationalism and Romanticism. The trial sermon would not have been so violent if he had not be striking at his own Rationalistic past. The first break with Romanticism had come at Egeløkke, but Grundtvig had not immediately seen the consequences of the rejection. His *Religion and Liturgy* was still filled with the terminology of Schelling, while for several years he permitted his Romantically inspired enthusiasm for history and mythology to be the outlet for his religious aspirations. Whether that manner of release ran its course and failed of itself, or whether he was brought up short by the demands of the trial sermon and the requests of his parents, we have no way of knowing. But his own statement at the time gives us some insight. In the preface to the poem, "New Year's Eve," dated December 31, 1810, he wrote: "With pain and shame I must confess that I . . . have participated in the pride in reason. I will not mention the period when I, echoing the time, contaminated the house of the Lord with useless and sacrilegious talk of duty and eternal merits and of the virtuous man, the honest teacher of the truth, Jesus, who did not hesitate to pretend he was more than he really was and who substantiated his claim with apparent miracles, for about this I have been ashamed for a long time. But for several years I have regarded Christianity as the revealed truth of God through his Son, and yet I have dared to place it . . . under the yoke of human reasoning . . . By the grace of God I have now bowed my pride in reason. It now seems unbelievable to me how anyone can believe that Christ was more than a man and fail to believe his teachings."

In a series of letters to S. J. Stenersen in Norway during 1813 and 1814, Grundtvig gave an account of his refutation of Schelling. In referring to his own *Religion and Liturgy* he said: "Pantheist I have never been, but during my transition to Christianity I regarded many things through the glass of natural philosophy, especially the atonement, this rock of contempt, the one thing for which we need Christianity and against whose simple acceptance we struggle the longest, because we do not want to crucify our pride." He condemned the "basic falsehood which carries his [Schelling's] system," and he claimed that "the system is built on denial of God and denial of the liability of sin," for the natural philosophers "deny the living God and the reality of sin." It is evident from this that Grundtvig's rejection of Schelling's religious philosophy was based on Schelling's inadequate treatment of the reality and power of evil.

It would be wrong, however, to view the struggle merely as a philosophical contest. It was far more personal than that, and we have the evidence in a letter written to W. Østrup in June, 1811. "You know that I have been called a Christian for several years and that I judged myself to be one, but my Christianity was frail, and pride and impurity dwelt in my heart while I sought vain honors. I called myself a Christian and spoke harshly to all non-Christians, but contrary to Christian love I wrote satirical verse, and instead of working in the vineyard by assisting my old father I exalted the old pagans and their idols in song and writing . . . In a wondrous way the Lord then laid hold on me last fall and I felt that I was removed from paganism and placed in the service of Christ. With Christian enthusiasm I sang of Denmark's history to the praise of God, and diligently I studied the Holy Scriptures. From that moment I gave up everything that seemed unchristian except the pride that had taken possession of me and which only changed its form, inasmuch as it fooled me into believing that I was a holy and God-pleasing person, whom he had chosen to restore Christianity . . . This pride on the one hand and a nervous condition on the other gave me strange visions. There is no doubt that I would have become the vainest of enthusiasts, if the good God had not taken pity on me and removed the veil which evil foes had placed before my eyes. Suddenly my blindness was gone; my pride and my lack of love were evident, and no remorse or regret over my sins was apparent. I was near despair, my mind failed me, but my heart remained cold." He continued with a description of his nervous condition and told how after several months he became more quiet and could start to work. "Wednesday before Pentecost I was ordained and came home immediately. From that moment I have felt the strengthening power of God and by his help I hope, in the name of Jesus, to become master of my warped thinking. Praise be God that I have gotten a more humble and loving heart during the long struggle, and I hope to be confirmed in the love of God and of Jesus Christ, so that in all things I may seek the glory of God and denounce the world and all that belongs to it."

Three months later he wrote to another friend, Johannes Boesen: "I cannot sufficiently thank God for the comfort and strength he has given me since I entered into the holy office." After writing that he had been comforted by reading about the trials of Luther, he added: "I have also learned from Luther that one should not be a Pietist with a long face but go joyfully through life as one who has the hope of his salvation . . . Furthermore, I have learned that nothing is more unchristian than Pietistic spiritual pride which despises and condemns others."

Grundtvig's conversion had intellectual and moral elements which can be documented. The break with Schelling was the main intellectual feature, and it was the culmination of a long development which had begun in 1806. The moral element was a struggle for righteousness which eventually led to the honest self-appraisal that he was haughty and filled with a pride that was to be humbled. There are definite similarities in this to Paul's and Luther's battle to achieve righteousness. All were strong personalities who were humbled by their own failures and through their inherent honesty. In addition Grundtvig experienced a mental crisis which has been much emphasized but which seems to be a strong person's agony of storm.[9] What cannot be documented, measured, nor described is the "Damascus Road" experience when "God laid hold on him." The judgment and the grace of God experienced by the individual lie hidden in the mystery of the spirit. Only the fruits are evident, and in Grundtvig's case the fruits are found in sixty years of intense living. After 1810-11 when he was twenty-seven, he was committed to a Christian life, but the intellectual problems of clarifying the issues of that life gave him many years of agony.

[9] Hjalmar Helweg's *N. F. S. Grundtvigs Sindssygdom* (1918), has analyzed the mental element of this and two later instances of depression, 1844 and 1863, and has called them manic-depressive psychosis. While Helweg's approach has been criticized, because he relied exclusively on literary evidence, there is little doubt that the diagnosis is correct.

2

At Grips with Life

His twenty-seventh year, 1810-11, marks an important milestone in Grundtvig's development. Although his experiences were accentuated and somewhat confused at their climax by a mental depression, he regarded them as genuine and there is no reason to consider them anything less than a fundamental Christian crisis of sin and grace. This conversion left a permanent impression upon him. His life had become Christ-centered. All subsequent developments can only be understood and interpreted on the basis of this fact. No criticism which he made of the traditions and ways of the church and no proposals or programs for change should be evaluated apart from the Christian faith which broke through during these days. All his activity derived its impulse and dynamic from this faith even in the realm of scholarship, in practical education, and in politics.

In his own account of the crucial moments of repentance and despair Grundtvig emphasized the tenacity of the pride which he felt was the last and most important barrier of his self. In its ultimate form this pride "fooled me into believing that I was a holy and God-pleasing person whom he had chosen to restore Christianity." He had considered himself to be a crusader for Christianity, but he was humbled by the realization that the first object of criticism and judgment should be his own vanity and self-glorification. From this realization we might expect that his subsequent attitude would be meek and humble and that he would refrain from harsh and condemning criticism of his countrymen.

The opposite was the case. During the years that followed his conversion Grundtvig was no less sharp and condemning in his attitudes and expressions than he had been before. No sooner had he emerged from the depression which accompanied his crisis than he launched renewed attacks upon the clergy accompanied by energetic exhortation to repentance and change. The most important example of this is found in his appearance before the ministerium of the diocese of Roskilde, of which Udby was a parish. In October, 1812, he delivered a lengthy poem, "Roskilde Rhymes," a poetic account of the history of the diocese. The story was incredibly long and wordy, driving most of the listeners during the three-hour late-evening reading to bored inattention or sleep, and apart from two sparkling passages it has little value. The forceful exhortation to the clergy to awaken and preach with fervor was therefore largely lost. But Grundtvig was not abashed. He returned to the convocation two years later with a paper

"On Polemics and Tolerance" which was more direct in its criticism. Tolerance was a favorite term and a common practice of the Rationalists. Grundtvig, while recognizing the importance of tolerance toward people, attacked tolerance in regard to the great issues of truth and falsehood. He challenged the ministers to shake off their indifference and to join the battle for the truth, and declared the doctrine, for the most part proclaimed in the Danish church, to be false and foolish. Solemnly he proclaimed "that if the Danish clergy does not rise to battle for the Word and the faith, there will no longer be a Danish church in Denmark."

The people in general also received their share of criticism. In 1813 he published a treatise, *To the Fatherland*, calling attention to the growing unbelief and immorality and speaking of the judgment of God. "It is therefore obvious that we are standing at the border of the most awful immorality and ungodliness, . . . and that we are close to the situation where we consciously deny God and virtue . . . If there is a God, every single individual is in the greatest of danger which he can only escape by hasty flight from the land of evil and a serious conversion to God and humiliation under his mighty hand."

This devastating criticism of others appears to be a contradiction of the humble and repentant spirit which had prevailed during the conversion crisis. But Grundtvig no longer considered his motivation for criticism to arise from his own rather arrogant indignation. He regarded himself as an agent of the truth elevated above the limitations of personal ambition by the mandate which he had received from God in the renewal of his spirit. He was now a crusading reformer whose prejudices were raised beyond rational rebuttal by a claim of divine sanction and inspiration. This attitude lasted several years, and the sanctimonious character of the crusade can only be justified by the essential correctness of his views and the proof in action that he was not pressing for personal prestige or power. But it was hard to convince his contemporaries that he was not arrogant, hypocritical, and even deranged.

The explanation raises not only the question of the validity of such an attitude but also the question of its underlying causes. Why was Grundtvig during these years a prophet of doom and almost a rabble-rouser? Why did he continue throughout his life to be a prophet and a promoter even after he had shed his frenzied and fanatic judgments? Grundtvig loved his people and his church with a great passion. This love grew out of a forceful personality's virile love of life itself, a love which had caught fire in the glow of Romanticism and which had been intensified by dramatic war events. The passion engendered a deep concern as the tides of war turned against Denmark. The scourge of the Napoleonic wars seemed to herald the end of the world and his country was swept into the maelstrom of defeat. Financial chaos followed in the wake of war with Denmark bankrupt. Gloom piled upon gloom, and salvation seemed possible only through a renewal of the spirit and the effort of the people.

Renewal was to be found in the Christian faith, and Grundtvig proclaimed this hope of salvation. His criticism was caustic in "The Masquerade Ball" and in the trial sermon, but it was a criticism which had the positive purpose of furthering the cause that could save the people. The exhortation was not in words alone. In 1814 Grundtvig participated in the nationalistic fervor of a group of students who banded themselves together under an oath to give their life for king and country.

Grundtvig's concern, his criticism, and the proclamation of a new hope through the conversion of the people, were so forceful during these years that it does not seem amiss to call it an apocalyptic period. Apocalyptic writings seek to reveal the redeeming purpose of God through the judgment of turbulent events and the emergence of a new era. They grow out of a deep concern and conviction, they proclaim a coming catastrophe, they call for a purification and a change of heart, and they claim to speak from an inspired knowledge of God's will and ways. All of these elements united in Grundtvig's attitude at this time.

His personal affairs did not help to allay his concerns. The assistantship at Udby lasted only a short time, for his father died in 1813, and all attempts to get an appointment in Copenhagen were in vain. The opposition of the clergy in the capital kept him out. Plans for a professorship in Norway were also frustrated when that country was ceded to Sweden in 1814. By historical and literary efforts Grundtvig managed to earn a small income, and for a while he derived some satisfaction from preaching in the pulpits of his few friends. But the growing opposition to his polemical views and to his criticisms caused him, in 1815, to make the resolution that he would not preach in Copenhagen until he had received a regular call. Instead he published his *Biblical Sermons* in 1816.

Only gradually did the situation improve and his tension lift. In 1817 he was rewarded for his historical efforts with an annual scholarship of six hundred dollars. This was such an encouragement that, at the age of thirty-four, he decided to marry and establish a home. His bride was Elizabeth (Lise) Blicher, the young lady to whom he had been attracted even before he went to Egeløkke in 1806. They had been engaged since 1811 and had been compelled to wait a "Jacob's week" of seven years. Even yet their income was minimal, but in 1821 Grundtvig finally received an appointment as pastor at Præstø near his childhood home.

We are getting ahead of the story, however. Grundtvig's hope had rested in the Christian faith which he had tried to awaken in his fellow-countrymen through a call for repentance and exhortation to live a new life. In the process, he rejected both mythology and Schelling's evolutionary and pantheistic philosophy. He turned to the only other delineation of faith he knew at the time, Lutheran orthodoxy. Thus Grundtvig went back to the ranks of "old-fashioned" Christians, of whom his father had been one and among whom his uncle, Bishop Balle, had loomed as the "lonely champion of the Bible."

In almost exalted terms Grundtvig spoke the praise of Martin Luther, and in a treatise, *Why Are We Called Lutherans?* published in 1812, he called him the "saint of God, . . . the faithful servant of the Word, the soldier and warrior of our Lord Jesus Christ." Luther's great merit was that he had again called attention to the Bible. "Luther was the great instrument in the hand of God who again opened the Bible, the source of the sure hope of eternal life." Thus Grundtvig's new Christ-centered life became Bible-centered, for the Bible was the way to Christ and it was the source of Christian living. With an interest again almost amounting to frenzy he therefore started to read the sacred book which had been neglected in favor of literary and historical matters. His calendar records that he completed five separate readings of the New Testament during 1813. His *Biblical Sermons* are filled with tributes to the Bible. "God's Word is food for the soul which makes it wise unto salvation, strong for battle and victory, and nourishes it for eternal life. This Word of God we have, undiluted and in great plenty, in the Holy Scriptures. It is like golden apples in silver bowls; it is the heavenly food which makes the believing soul who receives it a participant in the living Word of God who became flesh and dwelt among us." The Rationalists also made use of biblical arguments. But Grundtvig declared that they misused the Bible, that their interpretation failed to consider the obvious understanding of Scripture which any person with common sense would get from an immediate reading. "It is plain that Luther's basic proposition, for which he risked his life and by which he won out over his opponents, was that the Bible was to be understood literally."

But Grundtvig was not content to express himself in sermons alone. In fact, the first major expression of his crusade after 1810-11 was a history of the world, *Brief Concept of a World Chronicle in Continuity*, published in 1812. The book was a hasty pudding insofar as it was written in a short period filled with other activity, but it was based on long reading and intense study. It was in many ways a landmark. It was Grundtvig's first major expression of his new judgments. It was his first historical survey, but it was also the first history in the Danish language which expressed the historical philosophy of Romanticism as interpreted by Henrik Steffens. This philosophy maintained that life is growth and continuity and that there is a dominant factor or idea which determines and guides the growth.

Grundtvig subscribed to this point of view in the introduction when he, quoting another historian, said that history "was a chain of great events, all joined, all fused into one, all running together for one purpose." This purpose could be opposed by man in the freedom of his will, but even opposition to the prevailing purpose could only further its cause. For Grundtvig the basic idea was the will of God, and it was through his providence that the world was guided. Christ became the center of history and faith in Christ was the dynamic of all great events in history. "Every deed of a people must have been a fruit of its faith." [1]

Grundtvig had turned to history because he was historically minded, but he wrote this particular history in order to proclaim a truth. His purpose was probably best expressed by one of his critics. "Surely his purpose was to expand and secure faith in Providence, to show his contemporaries the way to salvation, and to turn their souls from the corruptible world to the higher and necessary goal; in short he desires to glorify God and convert his fellow-man." [2]

The book met with vigorous protest, much of it justified. It was full of factual errors and even the author had appended almost sixty pages of corrections. The subject matter was poorly balanced, with minor contemporary characters being given as much attention as

---

[1] A recent analysis of Grundtvig's philosophy of history, William Michelsen's *Tilblivelsen af Grundtvigs Historiesyn*, 1954, has shown the influence upon Grundtvig in his view of history by Luther and the Romantic philosophers. Michelsen claims that Grundtvig agreed with Luther that God was the Lord of history and that human events have their cause in the sovereignty of God. They differ, however, in the application of this view. Luther, reaching, as he did, against the scholastic theology of the Middle Ages, claimed that God was a hidden God (Deus absconditus) and that his actions were masked. But Grundtvig, in polemics against the philosophers of the Enlightenment and Romanticism, who had obscured God, proclaimed the open manifestation of God's will and power.

[2] *Dansk Litteraturtidende* No. 25 (1813), p. 393.

major figures in history. Harsh judgments accompanied most of the factual statements. Competent critics quickly called attention to the prejudiced treatment of historical facts, but Grundtvig "silenced" them by stating bluntly that the truth was found in Christ. His was not a mere repetition of facts but a prophetic utterance.

The *Chronicle* of 1812 is best forgotten save for the chain of events and arguments which it set in motion. Out of this apocalyptic document came a long debate which contributed to Grundtvig's development and to our understanding of the issues involved. The first clash was with an old friend, the historian C. Molbech, who took Grundtvig to task for his "treatment of history." He maintained that history should be a "presentation of facts," that it must not be polemical. In response Grundtvig published a small book, *The Reply of the Chronicle*, 1813, in which he discussed his point of view in regard to history. He denied that historical writing should be impartial. Rather, it should be interpretation, and for a Christian the basis for interpretation must be the Christian faith.

"Should not a believer who has faith in the living God in heaven and who believes in God's judgment over our hearts, in reckoning and in judgment, should he not be partial, support those who were the friends of God and combat those who were his enemies? . . . When a Christian writes history, he can never regard an event without tracing its relation to Christianity. For him Christianity must be the judge of all men and all ages, for Christianity and truth are not two but one. This is what we understand by the objective truth of history and its universal interpretation."

It is quite evident that Grundtvig overshot the mark and failed to see the significance of impartial treatment of facts. Furthermore, it was in this booklet that he reintroduced as a serious method of argumentation the Principle of Contradiction[3] which he had been taught in his university days and which stressed the conclusion that of two contradictory principles one must be true and the other therefore false. Grundtvig used, or misused, this axiom to prove his point in the historical argument, and from this moment it entered into all his discussion. The weakness of the axiom was the difficulty, the near-impossibility, of establishing clearcut alternatives. Therefore it was necessary to postulate the alternatives arbitrarily. The strength of the principle was the unshaken conviction that the basis of all life is found in a relationship to God who is the center of all things. An example is his argument against Schelling. He claimed that Schelling's philosophy "confuses good and evil, light and darkness, and that it denies the reality of evil. Thereby it conjures up uniformity where there should be variety and establishes that harmony of contradictions which is the goal of reason." This Principle of Identity was for Grundtvig a denial of the basic truth of contradictions and particularly of the basic contradiction of good and evil. Therefore Schelling was to be

[3] See Appendix, pp. 221-25.

31

condemned. In this situation the argument was sound, but this was not always the case.

In 1814 Grundtvig was thrown into further debate. He had published *An Ancient Prophecy* concerning world catastrophe which he had applied to the Napoleonic wars as these reached their culmination. The document was confused and obscure, and the famous physicist, H. C. Oersted, reduced it to absurdity. In doing so, however, he not only argued that Grundtvig had been irrational in his fanaticism, but denounced Grundtvig's attack upon Schelling's philosophy. Grundtvig's reply was a considered and well-argued but sharp and final attack upon Schelling. He expanded and fortified his arguments with reasoned and logical exposition. In the eyes of posterity Grundtvig's argument is much more pertinent than Oersted's.

As the discussion waned and as the end of the war took the edge off the great tension under which he lived, Grundtvig settled down to consider the many problems which his crusade had brought to mind. In one sense he retired from the arena but in a more profound sense he came to grips with the problems of living. For four years, 1816-19, he published a literary and philosophical magazine, *Danne-Virke*, to which he was the only contributor. Many of its articles were speculative, and his argumentation is so wordy and involved that it is difficult to read. Nevertheless, he did an enormous amount of philosophical spadework which is essential for an understanding of his later development. Grundtvig has been underestimated as a philosopher, although he should perhaps be classified as a philosophizing prophet, inasmuch as his insights often were visionary. He had an uncanny ability to sense the essence of a matter. His shortcomings were his wordy arguments and the impulsive character of his thinking. He constantly revised and improved his insight and proclaimed each step in the development with force and long discussion.

Grundtvig lived in an age when the problem of "knowledge" was of tremendous importance. It was important to "know" what life was really like, life behind and beyond that which is immediately in contact with our senses, and it was important to establish the means by which we reached this knowledge. From the seventeenth century philosophers had claimed that the reality of this life could be reached by the power of reason, by human logic. Kant had maintained that this claim was a fallacy and that there was no road from man to ultimate life and to God by the way of reason. He had claimed that the only human approach to God and to knowledge of God was through conscience or the moral obligation with which man had been endowed. Romanticism, on the other hand, while sharing Kant's rejection of the road of reason, had claimed that the ultimate or "real" life could be reached through visionary intuition.

Grundtvig rejected all of these approaches. That there was a God and a life beyond the immediate human life he was not in doubt, but this certainty grew out of his religious experience and not out of any philosophical speculation. It was through faith that he "knew" God and this was the truth of life for him.[4] He was so certain of this and considered the conviction so important that it overshadowed everything else. It was for this reason that he had pressed the proclamation of "truth" so far in his *Chronicles*, even to the extent of submerging the simple and impartial requirement of factual history. In the *Danne-Virke* articles he had calmed down, and now he gave long and careful consideration to the matter. But he continued to start all his thinking with the one great reality of God as revealed in faith.

He defined philosophy as man's search for wisdom, but not a wisdom resulting from mere reasoning. The purpose of thinking was to make clear and understandable that which had been revealed through faith. Man's reason must always be "in the truth," founded in that truth which had been revealed. When we thus live "in the truth" we can begin to talk about eternal realities, for then our finite human values, which we can describe, can be understood as a picture of the eternal life which has been revealed. In other words, when we live in faith, we can understand the Creator through the world which he has created. The object of his study, thinking, and research was therefore not the transcendental truths with which philosophy is concerned but the evidence of God in the world, the manifestation of God in his-

[4] Michelsen has shown that Grundtvig's reliance upon "faith as the criterion for truth" was influenced by Fichte's "*Die Bestimmung des Menschen.*" *Op. cit.*, p. 284.

tory. In contrast to most of the philosophers of his day Grundtvig was not interested in God's manifestation in nature. The basis for his whole approach was that we know God in faith.

Grundtvig's consideration of God's manifestation in history required an emphasis upon growth and development. In this respect he took up the interests of Herder in the eighteenth century and the Romanticist philosophers of Germany. But that which grows and develops must naturally give evidence of its own beginning. Therefore we can know God through his acts in history. By this route Grundtvig reached the conclusion that man is the image of God. Through Christ, who became man, we can therefore see man as he was in God's creation and in God's purpose, and the man who finds himself in Christ is still the man of God's creation.

Here Grundtvig was influenced by John Locke, whose philosophy he discussed in one of his articles. Its emphasis upon experience and common sense and its down-to-earth quality particularly fascinated him. Although Grundtvig profited greatly from this philosophy, he did not go so far as to become an empiricist.

Grundtvig did not develop a complete and systematic philosophy. He tried to give sober and penetrating consideration to a number of basic concepts and to relate them to the one great reality of his life, his relationship to the God whom he knew through faith. Besides this, his important ideas were mostly those which had to do with the significance of history, the created world as a manifestation of God, the importance of man as the image of God, and common sense. He also discussed the significance of human speech, of the word, as the manifestation of God's creation in man. For him the important thing was not the idea but the creation, which finds its center and manifestation in Christ.

Alongside his philosophical discussion and as his major field of interest Grundtvig continued his historical work. He intended to write a voluminous survey of history, but after the first volume of 552 pages in 1814 the project was abandoned. In 1817 he published a new *Survey of World Chronicle, Especially in the Lutheran Period.* This book was a balanced product in which the most important mistakes of the *Chronicle* of 1812 had been corrected, but it maintained the prophetic theme of the earlier work. It was written in a poetic and forceful language which expressed clearly the continuity of history that Grundtvig had learned from Herder and the Romanticists.

Grundtvig next turned to medieval histories of the ancient North and translated two of them. They were the Latin history, *Gesta Danorum*, or *History of the Danes*, by Saxo Grammaticus, and *The Chronicle of Norway's Kings*, by Snorre Sturlason, written in Old Norse, thirteenth-century histories of inestimable value. Grundtvig's translations have had great significance. Many Danes have read the Saxo translation with personal inspiration and it was republished as late as 1941. The language of the renderings was robust and poetic, far removed from ordinary pedantic literalness, and the old lusty atmosphere of the tales has been retained.

Grundtvig also became interested at this time in the ancient Anglo-Saxon epic poem about Beowulf, the scene of whose activity is Denmark. Thorkelin's publication of the poem in Denmark in 1815 was followed in 1817 by Grundtvig's textual studies in *Danne-Virke* and in 1820 by his Danish translation. For many years he continued this work and in 1861 he published a critical edition of the text. For some time this work was forgotten, but today Grundtvig is recognized as a pioneer in Beowulf research. Kemp Malone says that "The first and greatest of Beowulf scholars, as everyone knows, was N. F. S. Grundtvig." [5] R. W. Chambers states that his dating of events in the poem to the first decades of the sixth century, by proving that Hygelac of the poem was the same person as King Chochilaicus of Denmark who is mentioned by Gregory of Tours, is "the most important discovery ever made in the study of Beowulf." [6]

Grundtvig competed with great fervor in several of the literary feuds which formed one of the principal divertissements of the time. He also carried on correspondence with many friends. Best known among the poetry he wrote at the time is "The Easter Lily," written in 1817. Inspired by the gift of an Easter lily

[5] "Grundtvig as Beowulf Critic" by Kemp Malone in *The Review of English Studies*, XVII, No. 66, April, 1941.

[6] R. W. Chambers, *An Introduction to the Study of Beowulf* (1932), p. 4.

by his fiancée, it tells in dramatic form the story of the Roman watch during the late hours of Easter Eve and the resurrection events of Easter Day. The dialogue reflects the difference between the pagan philosophy and the Christian faith.

Despite his many activities Grundtvig was a lonesome man who buried himself in books after his one-man crusade had ebbed out. He often referred to these years, as spent in the "tombs," but it would be more proper to call them years of contemplation and growth. They determined much of his later development; they gave shape to many basic ideas. The problems with which he worked were vital and the effort he gave to them fruitful.

3

Centrality of the Church

Grundtvig's appointment as parish minister at Præstø was entirely unexpected,[1] but it was very much appreciated. "I was called again to the ministry, and as it happened contrary to my will I was not in doubt that it was according to the will of God. This gave me courage to combat death, within me and around me, with the hope of the resurrection."[2] He moved to Præstø in April, 1821, and threw himself vigorously into parish work. Many years later his brief stay was still remembered. His confirmation instruction was as unforgettable to the children as his sermons were to the people. In April, 1822, he and his wife welcomed their first-born son, Johan, and his only personal sorrow of those days was the death of his mother at Præstø in September, 1822. It was at Præstø that Grundtvig completed his two great translations of Saxo and Snorre.

But his spirit was not at rest; since he had been called

[1] He had not even applied for the position, although in the state church a pastor applied for the vacant position and was appointed by the king at the recommendation of the bishop.

[2] Introduction to *New Year's Morning*.

back into the ministry he longed to proclaim the gospel in the center of things, in Copenhagen. The opportunity came earlier than he had expected. When in 1822 a vacancy occurred at one of the major churches of that city, Grundtvig applied and was appointed. At last, seventeen years after his graduation, eleven years after his ordination, and at thirty-nine, he had a Copenhagen pulpit of his own. On the First Sunday in Advent, 1822, he preached his first sermon as assistant pastor at Our Saviour's Church, famous for its steeple which is formed as an outside staircase. The clergy of the city still grumbled, but the people, especially students, flocked to hear him.

Still he was not at rest, but now the reason was within him. He was no longer an unwanted rebel or a voice crying in the wilderness but a regularly called pastor who proclaimed the gospel to an attentive congregation. This required not only a robust faith and a forceful delivery but also a clear concept of the validity of his message. The truth was that Grundtvig had not clarified his convictions. Feeling that he needed this clarity he laid aside his historical research, and resumed the reflection he had begun in the *Danne-Virke* period of 1816-19. These previous deliberations had paved the way for his present problems which directly concerned the validity of Christianity itself. But he now printed none of his writings. He wrote constantly, however, in order to "reach clarity through writing," as he later expressed it, and a large pile of manuscripts testify to his search.

Until recently very little of this material has been available in print. Grundtvig had been reading the works of Irenæus, the second-century church father, during 1823. From later references it was obvious that this reading had greatly influenced him. Too often it has been assumed that Grundtvig's presentation of new viewpoints in 1825 was the result of a sudden visionary insight. Nothing could be farther from the truth. Henning Høirup in his book, *Grundtvigs Syn paa Tro og Erkendelse,* published 1949, has excerpted and analyzed the unpublished and "apologetic" manuscripts of the period around 1823. They show how Grundtvig's insights were wrought out of a constant battle with the great issues of Christianity in its relation to the world.

Grundtvig never doubted the validity of his own religious experience. There was no wavering in his Christ-centered faith. His problem was that of demonstrating the validity of the gospel in the world in which he lived. In his early apocalyptic years this had been no problem. He had accepted and proclaimed the traditional conviction that the Bible was the source and norm of all Christian life. His statement that the Bible was infallible was not identical with the "fundamentalist" claim of the literal inerrancy of every word. Even in 1813, when he proclaimed with great fervor that the Bible was to be understood literally, he wrote in the *Reply of the Chronicle:* "The Bible contains all truth necessary for salvation. The main truths are evident to all at all times, but a certain part is from time to time

41

destined to throw new light on the main truths when it is necessary and possible. These parts are therefore by nature obscure until they are needed."

An example of the unclear thinking to which Grundtvig was given at this time is his discussion, in the introduction to the *Chronicle* of 1814, of the problem of the Old Testament. He maintained that the books used or quoted by Jesus and the apostles were to be given preference. The Books of Moses were to be considered "proof" and the Word of God; the Psalms and the Prophets were to be believed "on their word"; the others which were used by Jesus and the apostles were to be believed "in the things"; and the remainder were to be considered human books. In a sermon of 1814 he stated: "The Psalms and the New Testament must always be the dearest words of God, and the discourses of Jesus in the Gospel of John must be for us a biblical core." [3]

That the message of the Bible was the truth for himself and for the world, Grundtvig never doubted. A constant and thorough student of the Bible, he wrote sermons and hymns filled with biblical imagery. His problem was never mainly one of biblical criticism; it was rather that of how the Bible could be the effective instrument of the gospel in the world.

During 1810-25 Grundtvig maintained that the Bible was the adequate vehicle of revelation. In the apologetic writings of about 1823 he struggled with the problems of mythological and rational interpretation and of the

[3] *Biblical Sermons* (1816), p. 172.

relation between biblical truth and experience. "If we have a book we believe contains a divine revelation, then it must be completely so, or at least it must be said that every thoughtful reader could find revelation in it." [4] He defiantly proclaimed the Bible. "Assuming, as we must always do, that it is true that the Christian church is built on the foundation of prophets and apostles . . . then we cannot possibly be wrong when we say that God's word is everything which prophets and apostles have spoken in the name of the Lord, everything about which they write: The Lord saith! and all words that are related to these." [5] But the last statement not only shows Grundtvig's struggle, but also an approaching change. The foundation upon which the Bible rests is composed of apostles and prophets. The validity of the Bible rests upon their testimony which is revealed in that Bible.

It was at this point that his reflections during the *Danne-Virke* period started to influence his thinking. At that time, with his starting point of faith in God, he had reached the conclusion that we gain knowledge through the evidence of God in the world, manifested primarily in history. In the same manner he now discussed the validity of Christianity as demonstrated through history. It is here that Irenæus influenced Grundtvig. Irenæus defended Christianity against falsifiers by emphasizing the Scriptures, the office of the

[4] Høirup, *op. cit.*, p. 195.
[5] *Ibid.*, p. 195 f.

bishop, and the living testimony of the faithful. As Grundtvig thought this idea over, he once wrote, "the historical proof is the only one we can give for the truth of Christianity."

There was no radical change in his views during 1823. The uncertainty in the unpublished apologetic writings is undoubtedly the reason why Grundtvig, eager as he was to publish the slightest utterance, failed to make them public. We must regard them as significant studies only, showing us the ideas with which Grundtvig worked. The "discovery," as his new view of 1825 has been called, was therefore not a sudden and visionary insight but came as the result of lengthy debate.

This intense activity of 1823 is also reflected in Grundtvig's sermons.[6] He was struggling with a static understanding of revelation and was trying to build a more satisfying dynamic concept. On the threshold of a new insight, he had not yet found a satisfactory expression or achieved the clarity which was necessary.

He felt a new buoyancy or, perhaps a resurgence of his old enthusiasm. His words from the following summer explain it. "I worked with all my power at an apology for Christianity which should clearly prove how defendable it was and how completely undefend-

[6] The sermons from 1823 are not published, but Kaj Thaning has analyzed and summarized them. The analysis shows that Grundtvig's sermons reflect the same elements as the apologetic writings: the search for an adequate expression of the gospel, the challenge of traditional Lutheranism, the influence of Irenæus, the emphasis on the created world, and the emergence of a new anthropology. Kaj Thaning, "Grundtvigs møde med Irenæus," *Grundtvig Studier*, 1953.

able was all objection or indifference to it. This work was not in vain for it disclosed my own lukewarmness and eliminated it, but the form could never satisfy me. No matter how prosaically I started, my style soon became so poetic that it was not fit for launching upon the Dead Sea. When I finally attained a lucid style I was shocked to see that its life was gone. At the same time, however, I noticed with joy that I had again become alive. I was filled with a living hope that I might see the same wonder of God in thousands of people in the North." [7]

What released this newly gained enthusiasm into a definite awareness of its character was the Epistle for the First Sunday in Advent, November 30, 1823. Grundtvig was struck by the words of Romans 13:12: "The night is far spent, the day is at hand." [8] Not having reached intellectual clarity as yet, still many of his mental barriers were removed to make way for the return of the fervent hope he had known after 1810. The joy of this so inspired him that he wrote a long poem, *New Year's Morning*, which was published in September, 1824. The poem is one of the most remarkable of Grundtvig's writings. Its content is autobiographical, inasmuch as he reviews the various stages through which he had passed, but it is also filled with visions of the new day to come and with jubilant expressions of the joy he had gained. It is incredibly long

[7] Introduction to *New Year's Morning* (1824).
[8] It is interesting to note that the continuation in 13:13 was the passage which occasioned St. Augustine's conversion.

—312 stanzas—and the form of the verse is unusual, influenced by the epic poetry of the ancient North. But
there is a glorious rhythm in the verse and the effect of
reading it is almost hypnotic. Despite its length there
is a remarkably sustained note of joy. It starts by proclaiming the "peace of God," an ancient form of personal saluation which in this instance assumes a deeper
meaning.

> God's peace! Oh wherever
> Ye dwell in the land,
> On fields by the river,
> In mountains so grand . . .

This peace, as it is found in the days of the fathers, as
it was gained by the Saviour, as it is enthroned by love
in hovels of earth, this peace, which he enjoys, he now
offers to his friends and kinfolk in the North.

It is well nigh impossible to give an adequate impression of the poem to a reader unfamiliar with the Danish
language. Translation attempts either violate the content or lose the rhythm. The content of a series of verses
must be paraphrased. Of the critical period around
1810 Grundtvig writes: "I felt that I was utterly defeated and condemned. The requirements of faith were
impossible to fulfill; my heart was cold and hard and
I was condemned to the grave. In my despair I realized
that light without warmth is like the torture of hell. I
tried to fight my way to God but through the Spirit I
knew that only one person had ever lifted himself from
death to life. In my abasement and despair the Spirit

lifted me up and carried me to church where I was granted the baptism of repentance and the life which is found in the chalice of love. Then the Spirit bade me go and preach the wondrous salvation from the power of death." The poem adds little to the thoughts that had already been expressed in the apologetic writings, but it shows a great buoyancy of spirit and a strong confidence of faith. The one exception to this was his emphasis on the sacraments, which was to become more insistent in the next months.

Another great poem, which dates from 1824 also reflects Grundtvig's new inspiration. The poem has been changed into a hymn by slight alterations and by elimination of some of the verses, but it deserves to be known in the original form. It starts by stating, "I know of a land" (in the hymn: "O land of our King") which is a land of perfection and glory.

> I know of a land
> (O land of our King)[9]
> Where harvest embraces the flowery spring,
> Where all things worth having forever remain,
> Where nothing we miss but our sorrow and pain,
> All mankind is longing to seek and explore
> Thy beautiful shore.

This promised land is a natural part of the imagery and belief of a child. It is a dream of prophets who have described it as an isle of eternity in our human existence. Most people, as the vision of this land proves to be fleeting and disappointing, lose faith in it. Poets and artists

[9] Translation by S. D. Rodholm.

try to recapture the land, as in Romanticism, but their most brilliant effort is but a shadow of reality which breaks the heart of even the greatest creative artist.

Where human efforts fail, however, the Spirit of Love succeeds. For the land *is* real and not merely a dream. When the hand of love reaches down from heaven to touch our eyes, the wonderful land rises in a blue and distant haze beyond the tempests of a mighty ocean. The land can be reached, but only through faith, hope, and love.

> The highway of faith
> A footbridge o'erhanging the torrent of death!
> Although it will sway in the storm it will hold
> And carry us safe o'er the deep to our goal.
> He built it who went to the Father from us
>   By way of the Cross.
>
> The high-soaring hope!
> While here through the dusk in the lowlands we grope,
> Broad-winged in the baptismal waters newborn
> It lifts up our hearts to the land where the morn
> Of life in full glory eternally shines
>   And never declines.
>
> All-conquering love!
> A fountain of strength from the Father above,
> It fills with the word of a Saviour who lives
> The cup which we bless at the table, that gives
> The soul what it needs to grow up and bear fruit
>   In goodness and truth.

The joy and happiness of that land and its reality sparkles throughout the poem. Its hope is not confined to a future life. The kingdom of God is here and now, and although it falls short of the glory of the fulfilment, it is nevertheless real. The translation does not bring this out as well as could be desired:

> My spirit receives
> Through Christ what the world neither knows nor believes,
> This, while we are here, we but dimly can know,
> Though feeling within us its heavenly glow.
> The Lord saith: on earth as in heaven above
> My kingdom is love.

The two poems show that Grundtvig had entered a creative period. The fifteen-year-old struggle which had been carried on through changing circumstances was finally coming to a climax. A new hope was kindled, a new insight was at hand. The problem was not one of the vitality and validity of his own faith, which had burst through so strongly in poetic expression, but of the effectiveness of the Christian faith and life in the world. What was the means by which living and sustaining faith was brought into the life of man and the stream of history? Answering that this means was the Bible could not satisfy him, for the Bible had become a source of opinion rather than a source of life. Even the enemies of his faith, rationalizing philosophers who had reduced Christianity to moralizing and philosophizing, used the Bible as a source and argument for their conviction. What he sought was a dynamic concept of Christianity to replace the current one, which had become static and lifeless.

In his philosophical studies of 1816-19, Grundtvig

had already seen the significance of a historical approach. In the created world, especially in human history, he found the reflected will of the Creator. He had acknowledged the importance of the empiricist emphasis on growth and development. But he had not yet connected these concepts with Christianity or theology because he had been satisfied that the Bible was an effective vehicle of faith. Now that this answer seemed inadequate, he turned to other ideas, of which the first expression was *New Year's Morning.* There he stressed the church and the sacraments as the refuge to which the Spirit had brought him when he had been raised from despair. But there was still one element lacking. How did the church become and continue to be a living expression of the faith? The answer was that the response of the church which vitalized and activated faith among men, and which made the gospel a living power, was the historic confession of faith of God as the Creator, of Christ as the Lord and Redeemer of men, and of the Holy Spirit as the Guide and Comfortor. What is this confession, but man's response to the Word of God?

The emergence of this new view can be dated quite accurately. In March 1825 Grundtvig started to publish a new *Theological Monthly* with his friend, the learned theologian A. G. Rudelbach, as coeditor. The copper plate of the title page shows its orientation. On the one side of the picture Martin Luther stands beneath the cross with the Bible demonstratively held forth, and on the other side a bolt of lightning strikes the withered tree of Rationalism. The purpose of the magazine was thus a crusade for Christianity as represented by traditional Lutheranism and aimed against Rationalism. Yet in July the same year Grundtvig preached a sermon expressing his new view in which the primacy of the church replaced the primacy of the Bible. As an expression of the evidence of the living church in history he proclaimed the confession of faith. Then in August and September of the same year he launched his violent attack upon Professor H. N. Clausen, proclaiming the new point of view in polemics.

Grundtvig did not discard the Bible. He still considered it the sacred source-book of the Christian faith. But he corrected what he believed to be a fundamental mistake of seventeenth-century Lutheran orthodoxy in making doctrine, and the Bible as the source of doctrine, the primary evidence of Christianity. He replaced the primacy of the Bible with the primacy of the church. In doing this he did not believe that he was attacking Lutheranism as such. On the contrary, he considered his new view to be a defense of Lutheranism as it was originally conceived against the perversions that had taken place during the seventeenth and eighteenth centuries. On the other hand, his emphasis upon the historic church did not carry him into the realm of papacy or Catholicism. It was not the institutionalized church or the office of the church which was in his mind but the living and confessing church. When Grundtvig spoke so strongly about the unaltered confession of the apostles, he did not yet conceive of this in terms of the exact words of a particular creed. This unfortunate dogmatization came later. What was important to him at first was that the faith expressed in the confession of the apostles, the content of the confession, should be the same today as it has been throughout the history of the church.

The "enemy" against which Grundtvig battled during these years of preaching in Copenhagen was the sterile Rationalism of the eighteenth century which had been entrenched in many pulpits of the city. Among these pastors the most prominent was H. G. Clausen, dean of the cathedral. When therefore his son, H. N. Clausen, was appointed professor of systematic theology at the university, Grundtvig, with many others, considered the appointment a new fortification of Rationalism within the university. In this he was wrong, for young Clausen had moved away from the narrow Rationalistic views and was in reality introducing a new theology. But it was even more at odds with Grundtvig's new insights than the Rationalistic theology with which he identified it. Professor Clausen had been deeply influenced by Schleiermacher during his postgraduate studies in Berlin, and while he turned against the out-of-date Rationalism, he was also critical of orthodox Lutheranism. In 1825 he published a learned book, *Catholicism and Protestantism, Constitution, Doctrine, and Rites,* an analysis of the two great bodies and a statement of his own concepts of Christianity and the church.

Grundtvig received an advance copy of Clausen's book and a few days after its publication he launched a severe and polemical attack on it in a pamphlet called *The Reply of the Church*. Its impulsive and violent character caused a furor and had serious repercussions. Perhaps he should have resorted to the usual procedure of sober analysis and criticism in the *Theological Monthly*. But if he had, he would have betrayed his strongest loyalties and the *Reply* would not have become the important milestone in church history which it now actually is. It was the dramatic form of the controversy which brought to the fore the underlying issues and called them to the attention of the age.

For Clausen the church was a body whose purpose was to promote common religiousness, which again meant that it was to promote the religious idea as the universal principle. The "idea" was for him Christ-centered, but his concept of Christianity was strongly doctrinal in his exposition of Christ as the revelation of the religious idea. In his characterization of Catholicism he claimed that this body promoted Christianity through historical authority, while Protestantism related itself directly to the revelation of the New Testament. But the Bible was incomplete and therefore it became the task of the theologian to discover and proclaim to the Christian what Christianity was.

Many things in Clausen's book could justifiably be criticized, but these last two items in particular aroused Grundtvig's wrath. The contention that Protestantism was not historical but that it related itself directly to Scripture completely ignored the life of the church. The idea that the task of interpreting the Bible, and thereby interpreting what Christianity was, should lie exclusively in the hands of the professors of theology, Grundtvig called an "exegetical papacy." Over and against this doctrinalism he placed the evidence by which we can know what Christianity is, the historic confession of the church. The church as the body of Christ continued the revelation which had been given through the historic and resurrected Christ. Characteristic of the church was its confession which from the beginning had accompanied the sacraments.

Rising again in a fervor which had been absent for years, Grundtvig introduced his battle call by saying that he was appearing as an ecclesiastical opponent of Clausen. He claimed to speak on behalf of the church and declared pompously that Clausen was a false teacher and that he should either recall his statements or withdraw from his office as theological professor. Then he took up Clausen's definition of the church and called it an air castle which did not correspond to what actually had been the understanding of the church through history, particularly in the mind of the reformers. The church is not, he claimed, a society to promote religiousness; it is a community of faith known by its confession of faith. Historically it had made the sacraments of baptism and Communion the essential requirements for membership. "Thus we meet Professor Clausen and all those who present their own dreams as Christian revelation and their own imaginings as Christianity, with the unshakable and known fact that there has been and is one Christianity on earth. It is distinguishable from all else by its incomparable confession of faith by which it has, in all languages and in all its varying forms, proclaimed and still proclaims faith in Jesus Christ, crucified and risen, as the certain and exclusive way to salvation for sinners, which through baptism and communion leads to the kingdom of God and the land of the living." [10] Grundtvig called for a dynamic concept of the church and proclaimed that it was found in the confession of faith which was man's response to revelation.

Grundtvig's pamphlet was a battle cry and the battle came. Troops rushed to the two banners and undoubtedly most of them supported Clausen because he had been personally attacked. Even many of Grundtvig's friends reacted against this polemic, failing to see that Grundtvig considered it his duty under his ministerial oath to attack wrong teaching. Though he admitted later that he had been too personal, for the moment he could not distinguish between the matter and the man. For this he was punished, for Clausen did not rise to great heroics in defense of his cause. He prosecuted Grundtvig for libel, with the painful result that Grundtvig, after months of delay, was found guilty and placed under a humiliating police censorship requiring that everything he published be approved by the authorities.

[10] *Reply of the Church*, p. 25.

This unheroic feature of the battle and the violent nature of the attack did not prevent the little booklet, however, from becoming the fanfare of a new movement, a new awakening, and a new theology. Years were to pass, however, before his thoughts became clarified and the movement gained momentum.

4

Frustration, Growth and New Insights

Grundtvig's newly won dynamic concept of revelation and his emphasis upon the body of Christ, or the church, as the vehicle of revelation may not seem radical to a twentieth-century reader, but it was revolutionary in his day. Not only did his friends and followers have difficulty in being consistent with its requirements, but even Grundtvig himself failed to see all the consequences. Unfortunately he fortified himself in several instances against attack by dogmatizing his own views. It was several years before he reached the conclusions which grew naturally out of his new insight, and he had to struggle hard to rid himself of many traditional concepts to which he was deeply loyal. For the moment therefore the picture was far from clear. More than a decade was to pass before his polemics subsided, the first adjustments had taken place, and clearer formulations were achieved.

It was a bitter disappointment that the immediate result of the battle call was not a spiritual engagement but a lawsuit for libel. Grundtvig had undoubtedly laid himself open for this by his unbridled attack. It was natural that Clausen wanted to clear his name when he had been called a false teacher who should be dismissed. That side of the matter, however, could have been settled by the personal apology which Grundtvig offered when the waters were somewhat calm again. As it was, the lawsuit ground its way despite Grundtvig's plea for a dismissal, and it ended in legal absolution for Clausen.

The immediate frustration of this situation prevailed through the winter. The tenderly beautiful Christmas hymn which he wrote in 1825, "Be welcome again, God's angels bright," offers a profound understanding of the joy of the Christmas message on the background of gloom and sorrow. What was particularly disappointing was that the most popular preacher of the time, J. P. Mynster, who later became bishop, while sharing the criticism of Clausen's book, nevertheless condemned Grundtvig in no uncertain terms. Even occupation with historical matters during the winter and spring months could not break the gloom, and it was only the expected festivity of a coming celebration that lightened the atmosphere.

Grundtvig himself had called attention to the fact that the year 1826 marked the one thousandth anniversary of the missionary preaching of the Christian gospel in Denmark by St. Ansgar, and he looked forward to the celebration of the event. When he heard that the officials of the church had granted free use of hymns for the occasion, he wrote three hymns and had them printed. One of these was perhaps the greatest hymn he ever wrote, "O day full of grace," a recreation of a medieval hymn about the sun which in its rising and setting was a symbol of Christian life. To his dismay he was informed through official channels that he could only use hymns which were found in the official hymnal. With the consent and support of his wife he resigned from the ministry in May, 1826, and for the second time he was without office in the Danish church.

The cause of his resignation has been much discussed, but there was undoubtedly an accumulation of dissatisfaction, chief of which was the libel suit which made continued service in the church impossible for him at the moment. Again he turned to literary efforts for a living. He still retained the annual stipend of six hundred dollars and after three years he was granted a further scholarship by the king for studies in England.

In the meantime there were several major problems which rose out of his altered point of view and demanded solution. Some of these were theological, some concerned the church, and some went beyond this to man in his relation to society. Grundtvig proceeded to tackle these in an effort to clarify them. The theological problem quite naturally fell into two parts with which his mind had been occupied for some time and which are mentioned in the unpublished works of a few years earlier. Both parts concerned the truth of Christianity. The first one was: What is true Christianity? or in other words: What is the historic content of the Christian faith? The other was: Is Christianity true? or: Can the Christian faith be the true faith for me? These were the titles of two series of articles which he wrote in the *Theological Monthly* during the next few years. They have been gathered and printed under the title *Concerning True Christianity and Concerning the Truth of Christianity*.

The major portion of the first series of articles consists of an analysis of the content of the Christian faith as it is known in the Lutheran tradition. He tested this tradition by Scripture and found that Scripture verifies all the tenets of the faith. There is no doubt that this argumentation is aimed at the Rationalists who denied much of the tradition, particularly in regard to the person of Christ, and the argumentation or "proof" was the biblical one which Grundtvig had used before 1825. For this reason it is assumed that these articles were written earlier and had been permitted to go to print even though their author had changed his point of view. Only in the latter part of the first series is the new criterion seriously presented. From the beginning Grundtvig had sought an expression for the truth of Christianity which was so simple that all could understand it. At first he claimed to find it in the Bible, but discovered that those who denied the truths he believed made equally effective use of the same Bible. This could only mean confusion, individualism, and conflict. Finally he found the answer in "the living testimony which went from mouth to mouth in the Christian church, independent of all changes and all academies in Christendom." This testimony was "the faith and the hope which Christians from ancient days had confessed and to which they had been baptized."

In the second and much more lengthy series of articles he started with the insight which had become clear to him by the end of the first series; that we find true Christianity in the church's testimony concerning its faith. He argued at length that this view was not contrary to Lutheranism but that, contrariwise, it was a fulfilment of the original Lutheran point of view. He claimed that this point of view would place Scripture in its right relation to revelation and would strongly encourage the reading of the Bible for knowledge and guidance. He also guarded against the misunderstanding that the emphasis upon tradition would lead to Catholicism, and he condemned the papacy in strong terms. Christianity was true because it comes to us by the authority of the Christian church, and is found in the sacraments. In the course of the series his argumentation became more cogent and more clear. He saw that he was not concerned with a "proof" of Christianity but a witness or testimony which, as a living word, brought the faith to the individual through the church and made it real. The doctrine of the church, the ritual, the office of the pastor, the fellowship, the prayers, and Scripture; all were defended and put in their proper place. But the claim for the primacy of the corporate testimony of the church through its confession became more emphatic. Rather than taking a "stand" on the Bible we should place it, he claimed, on the altar to be read. He emphasized the organic relationship between the revealed and living word of God and the word which we confess.

Through the whole series of articles Grundtvig was adjusting himself to his new emphasis, and his "apology" for Christianity which did not succeed in 1823 was now pouring forth. While this was not his final word in the matter, he grew more firm in his conviction. A discussion of the "inner" nature of the church and Christianity must necessarily, however, be accompanied by a discussion of the "outer" character of the church, especially as Grundtvig had accused Clausen of "false teaching" and had demanded that he retract or resign. Grundtvig had identified the state church of Denmark with the church of Christ, an identification which was common in his day, but with his new point of view this identification could not hold. Step by step Grundtvig therefore altered his views of the organized church, though several years were to pass before he admitted their full consequences.

The first stage of this discussion is found in a series of articles in the *Theological Monthly* in 1827 entitled "On Freedom of Religion." They were in part inspired by his own situation and in part by a development which had taken place in several parts of the country. As a reaction to the sterile preaching of the clergy a number of conventicles had sprung up, led by laymen who gathered the members of a parish for Bible study and devotional exercises. Such religious assemblies were prohibited by law and were duly prosecuted and the members even punished. A parallel existed in the Haugian movement in Norway. Grundtvig was not in favor of the "revivalistic" character of the assemblies, but he was incensed by the persecution. The eighteenth-century ideals of liberty, which had been suppressed by the reactionary lid clamped on all of Europe after the Treaty of Vienna, surged forth in the articles. Grundtvig started to campaign for religious freedom. No longer did he demand the resignation of Professor Clausen. On the contrary he felt that he could no longer be contained within the same church as those who denied the basic tenets of the Christian faith. He claimed the right to exercise his faith in freedom, even to leave the church.

The first two articles were rather moderate, but in the third Grundtvig worked himself up to a sharp criticism of the government, claiming the right of members of the Danish church to make a selection of another parish minister than the one to whom they were bound by law. As a result of the criticism the police refused permission for publication, the first exercise of the censorship with which Grundtvig had been penalized. The police action was a severe blow. In reaction he wrote another article called "The Literary Testament of the Writer N. F. S. Grundtvig," in which he threatened to discontinue his literary activity. The article is retrospective and self-critical, inasmuch as he called himself "half bard and half bookworm." It added nothing to the argument he was carrying on, but pointed nevertheless toward a new excursion in his thinking. The concept of history which had so radically influenced his thought in regard to the vitality of the Christian message was beginning to influence his thinking about the nature of man, the discipline theologians call anthropology. This next important stage in his development was to unfold under the impact of his three journeys to England, although his ideas concerning man and society were also inherent in the intellectual and spiritual development that had been going on since 1816. For some years due to circumstances, his investigation of the church and Scripture had had the upper hand. Next came the problem of the outward forms of the church. Finally, when the swells of ecclesiastical battle had died down, the consequences of his ideas on the relation of man to God and society could come to the forefront. In this instance it was the three journeys to England that acted as a catalyst.

Not all of his writings of these years were theological or polemic. After his resignation he started to publish a significant series of sermons called *Christian Sermons or Sunday Book*. Three volumes appeared, in 1827, 1828, and 1831. The first two contained sermons written during the time he was pastor at Our Saviour's Church and were actually delivered. The last volume was written after his resignation and therefore shows evidence of his newly gained insight into the validity of the gospel. It is somewhat more reflective than the others which are strongly evangelistic in character, but the whole series constitute a masterful Christian testimony. Cast in a forceful yet restrained language, far removed from the polemical tone of his pamphleteering, they bring a profound and powerful evangelical message from a preacher who was completely dedicated to the proclamation of the gospel. The *Sunday Book*, as it is called most often, is an important source for those who seek the rudiments of ideas which were yet to proceed from his fertile mind. These rudiments pave the way for an understanding of what was to break through in the early thirties, but they also, and primarily, are valuable as testimony to a virile Christian faith.

Grundtvig published one treatise after two trips to England that definitely belongs to the pre-England period. Because of Grundtvig's delayed-reaction pattern, the treatise reflected a former point of view, even after a new trend of thought had set in.

"Shall the Lutheran Reformation Really Be Continued" was published in a *Monthly Magazine for Christianity and History* in 1830. In the first section he claimed that the Reformation quite naturally should be continued, because it was a renewal of life and a renewal in the church should not only be kept alive but should grow. Furthermore, Luther had cleaned house, which was good. His successors, however, had been apt to consider his house-cleaning as the main thing, which was wrong if we consider the church a living fellowship with a living faith. We need the intellectual support of the faith, but Lutheran theologians had placed too great an emphasis on their intellectual answers, and had made those interpretations the most important condition for the truth. Therefore we must give primacy to the testimony of the faith instead of the interpretations of scholars.

In the second section he considered the relation of church and state. After a summary and analysis of the development up to the Reformation he stated that the mistake was that of making the state an instrument of the church. The state was to enforce the true doctrine and practice, which was intolerable because power in the state fell into the hands of those who denied the true and original character of Christianity. Therefore there should be an opportunity for those who dissented to rid themselves of this domination and form free churches. He did not advocate abolition of the state church, but he called boldly for a reform which would free "old-fashioned" Christians from subjection to the tyranny and rule of those who did not share their faith. He would prefer to remain in the official church, if possible, "for it was clearly of the nature of Christianity to work for civic improvement and enlightenment . . . It calls its spirit the Holy Spirit and it aims to create a communion of saints. The seal of this is a profound, active, and sacrificing humanity, and it therefore cannot be alive without creating a good friend, a good neighbor, and a good citizen in all ways."

The final section discussed the relationship of the church to theology, and here Grundtvig fired his sharpest missiles at the mistakes of the Reformation as he, perhaps inadequately, saw them. He was careful not to leave the impression that he discarded Luther's main contribution, expressing his regard for Luther in very strong terms. He even claimed that Luther would be grateful to him for carrying on in the same spirit to correct some of the things which Luther could not accomplish. His criticism was mainly that Luther had failed to realize the significance of the living, or oral, testimony of the church and that he had underestimated the significance of history. Conversely, he had overemphasized Scripture by making it the judge of all things and had restricted the order of salvation to the doctrines of the Augsburg Confession. To correct these shortcomings Grundtvig placed the primary emphasis upon the confession of faith at baptism as independent of Scripture and as a necessary requirement for membership in the Christian church. The confession, which for him was identical with the Apostles' Creed, and not the Bible, is the rule of faith. We must distinguish more clearly between what we confess in the church and what we can leave to the discretion of individuals. Therefore theology must be more free, but in return it must not dominate the faith.

Realizing that this exposition might lead to the conclusion that he discarded the Bible, Grundtvig again paid high tribute to that book. He called it the greatest book in the world "full of heavenly wisdom and the inexhaustible treasury from which the Holy Spirit . . . gives to all what they need and from which He teaches the ordained servants of the New Testament, as scribes instructed in the kingdom, to take old and new for the edification and upbuilding of the church. Where the Bible is not the daily handbook of the clergy . . . and especially where it is placed on the shelf and locked for the congregation, there faith is dead and the Spirit has been sacrificed. Then the house of prayer has become an open grave and will soon be converted into a den of thieves."

As a final word in the article Grundtvig called for "real" bishops to safeguard the doctrine. He was thus at this time strongly leaning toward the episcopal system. He was tempted to erase this passage in a later edition when his episcopalianism had completely disappeared, but out of regard for the original text he let it stand. There is no doubt, however, that Grundtvig very soon gave up this view, even as he very soon reached greater clarity in his view of the church as a practical consequence of his basic view of revelation. In these changes or clarifications the journeys to England play an important role.

Grundtvig's own account of his three journeys to England, 1829, 1830, and 1831, gives us an excellent example of the difference between his immediate impressions and the delayed impact which so often changed these. Through the letters which he wrote to his wife, to the queen, and to others we gain the impression of a critical and even irritable man who was irked by the many practical difficulties of traveling and settling down to study in a foreign country. At least regarding the first journey, the stolidity of the British character, the formality of their hospitality, and their lack of enthusiasm for his study project contribute to an impression of something less than success. Between the lines, however, we read awe and admiration, and it is quite evident that Grundtvig covered up a feeling of inferiority with his brusqueness. Later on, when he not only felt more familiar with the situation but was far enough removed from disappointments and humiliations, he changed to an appreciative, even laudatory attitude. As in so many other situations he had to shed a previous opinion which had been expressed in pungent terms. During his youth and through the Napoleonic wars England had been the enemy of Denmark, and it was with some difficulty that he threw off his animosity. What brought him to England was scholarly research and he seemed at first determined not to like the country. In the end he became not only an admirer of England but a strong Anglophile.

The two things that impressed Grundtvig more than anything else were the busy and practical activity of the British and their inherent democracy and love of freedom. Regarding the first feature he made a characteristically outspoken statement in *Brage-Snak* in 1844. He confessed then that he had been embarrassed when the British asked him: What do you do at home? "No matter how I turned and twisted, the Britisher continued according to his custom, and the more I criticized British activity the more eagerly he asked: Yes, but what do you do? This confounded 'What do you do?' I shall never forget though I live to be a hundred years old, and it irked me to the bottom of my soul, because I knew that the stubborn Britisher was right. The first requirement of a man is that he does something which shows what he is . . . No matter how arrogant I was when I first arrived in England and felt qualified to criticize British activity which emphasized craftsmanship more than science, the practical more than the spiritual, and which regarded profit more than common good, my crest soon drooped when the Britisher met all my criticism with the simple statement: If you must consider in advance all possibilities and accidents, methods, and misuses, you never get anything done, and when he regularly ended up with the question: But then what do you do?"

The second feature of freedom impressed him mostly in regard to public and political activity. He was in England during the years when the battle for the right to vote was waged and when the old restrictions on the franchise gradually were repealed. The contrast with the absolutism of the Continent and particularly of his own country could not fail to make a lasting impact upon a man whose freedom of speech had been restricted. It dawned on him that liberty was more than an academic issue and a remote political possibility. It was the very essence of society, the basic requirement for sound human living. There could be no true spiritual life without freedom. From the day he realized this he became an ardent champion of political and religious freedom and devoted much of his effort in the years ahead to this battle.

In many ways the journeys brought Grundtvig new insights and relief from long-established inhibitions. His son has provided the best expression of this. "The three journeys to England, 1829, 1830, and 1831, had an academic purpose. But they caused a complete change in his spiritual life; they brought his personality to full maturity. They awakened in him a new and lively participation in the real life of the day: the civic and political no less than the ecclesiastical and scientific. He gave up none of his former interests, the Christian, the Nordic, and the Danish, but his horizon was expanded and he gained new strength and new courage to wield influence in many fields." [1]

British higher education also made a deep impression upon Grundtvig and inspired his Folk School ideas of the next decade. The only form of higher education which he knew up to that time was the University of Copenhagen, built upon the German or continental system. Previously he had learned of the newly founded

[1] Svend Grundtvig in the preface to *Mands Minde* (1877), p. xii.

London University which remedied the exclusiveness of the older universities. Although he did not visit it he studied its program. On his second journey he visited Cambridge University as the guest of Professor Whewell at Trinity College. At that time, acclimated enough to share the life and ideas of the men he met, Grundtvig became interested in English literature and British higher education.

Before he went to England Grundtvig had been an admirer of the episcopal system and legislation for dissenters, advocating them in his writings. He especially looked forward to meeting Edward Irving, the founder of the Catholic Apostolic Church and what has popularly been called Irvingianism. The interest lasted no longer than a meeting with Irving. Grundtvig found his inspiration elsewhere. It was the broad church movement which influenced him most. Although it cannot be proved that he was directly influenced in his subsequent ecclesiastical ideas by the thoughts of the Coleridgean circle, apparently he was, since he spent some time at Cambridge where this influence was greatest. At any rate, after his return from England, many of Grundtvig's suggestions for church reform obviously have their prototypes in English legislation and in broad church ideas.

The project which had taken Grundtvig to England and which he diligently pursued during all of his three visits was only a partial success. At first he met a great deal of indifference not only toward himself but also toward his idea of publishing the ancient Anglo-Saxon manuscripts in critical editions. He was not interested in the Society of Antiquaries, which he visited but of which he was not made a member, despite the fact that several other Danish antiquarians were selected. He had difficulty appreciating scholarship for the sake of scholarship. In his mind research should be used to unearth the ancient cultural values of the Anglo-Saxons where Danish and British interests were closely linked, but he found no response. The Society of Antiquaries was not impressed with Grundtvig until they discovered that an English publisher was preparing to publish his work with the old manuscripts. Then it decided to do the job itself. When Grundtvig returned for the third visit and discovered that his plans could not be fulfilled, he was undoubtedly greatly disappointed. He shrugged it off, however, with the remark that the goal had been reached for which he had gone to England; that it did not matter whether he or someone else published the manuscripts, just so the work was done. He continued his work with Beowulf, but was not ready to publish the critical edition until 1861.

When Grundtvig visited England a fourth time in 1843, twelve years later, his work with the manuscripts was recognized, but at that time he was more interested in the religious life of the country. For a long time he was not given the credit his Anglo-Saxon pioneering work deserved, but he is recognized today more than ever.

5

True Nature of Man

Upon his return from the third journey to England Grundtvig was forty-eight years old. His forties had been a trying and turbulent decade. His thoughts had been clarified in an important area, but it had been difficult for him to assume the consequences of this new point of view and there were other important areas where he had not made a clearcut decision and where new insights yet lay ahead. In contrast to this decade the next eight to ten years were much more relaxed and fruitful. His personal circumstances became much more satisfactory. The most important features of the decade were his literary and historical activities.

The activities of the past few years had not only made opponents for Grundtvig; he had also found many friends and followers. These friends were eager to hear his message and encouraged him to preach to them in private. Grundtvig was reluctant to do this though he longed to proclaim the gospel. He was opposed to conventicles as such, and it was only because the authorities adopted a contrary attitude that he even attended a few meetings. Fortunately the church authorities realized the justice of his desires and gave him permission to preach at vesper services at Frederikskirken, a church close to his home, only a few streets from his former pulpit at Our Saviour's. Thus from 1832 to 1839 Grundtvig preached in the evening, the number of his listeners growing from year to year. Much of his polemical sharpness had worn off and his sermons were edifying and devotional. He was seriously handicapped, however, by not being able to officiate at the sacraments, for they played a major role in his view of Christianity. He was deeply disappointed when J. P. Mynster, who had been appointed bishop, refused to let him officiate at the confirmation of his own sons.

Finally, in 1839, Grundtvig was appointed pastor of the chapel at Vartov, a home for old people. The chapel was small and the position was considered insignificant, but the appointment was for full pastoral activity. The Vartov church became the center of a remarkable congregational life which spread its influence through the whole Danish church and became the embodiment in practice of Grundtvig's new emphasis upon congregational fellowship. Fifty-six years old when he received the appointment, he served the church for thirty-three years, and it was in Vartov that most of his hymns were introduced and first sung. In 1861 he was given the rank of honorary bishop in recognition of his contribution to Danish church life. The years at Vartov were not without personal troubles. Twice, in 1844 and in 1863, he suffered acute depressions, but on the whole the period cannot be compared with the turbulent years before his journeys to England.

Soon after his return from England several major works came from his pen. First in importance was his enlarged edition of *Nordic Mythology*, published in 1832. Its lengthy introduction expressed new and different thoughts in regard to the nature of man. The new ideas came directly from his views on revelation and the church, but they also reflected the insights he had gained in England.

Grundtvig did not get along with the British anti-quarians, because he could not adjust himself to their ideas of science for its own sake. Knowledge was for him a means to the end of serving humanity. Sterile in-tellectualism, in historical scholarship as well as in reli-gious interpretation, was a curse. This attitude un-doubtedly stemmed from his faith which naturally ex-pressed itself in an intense emphasis upon God as the Creator. If God has created the world, we are responsi-ble to Him for our thoughts and actions, showing this responsibility in our work. Combining with this fervent faith in God the conviction that the history of the world, and especially the history of man, was an unfold-ing process, Grundtvig always looked at history in sweeping perspective. Even his first apocalyptic at-tempts at historical writing had been outlines of world history. By the time of the journeys to England he had given up the narrow orthodox interpretations which had characterized these works, but retained the perspective of universal history as the story of mankind created by God.

His work with the ancient manuscripts revived Grundtvig's conviction that there was a sound strength and a living culture in the ancient North which had been lost but could be revived and revitalized. In this connection he now included England in the "North," inasmuch as England had been settled by Anglo-Saxons from the North. The revitalization should come by a fusion of the ancient Nordic spirit with the Christian faith. These thoughts led him in turn to reconsider European culture and the basic nature of man created by God. The culture replacing the vitality of the North, and for that matter also the sound culture of ancient Greece, was the sterile intellectualism which had dominated Europe from the time of the Renaissance. In this connection he revived the ideas which Herder had expressed in *Auch Eine Philosophie der Geschichte* concerning the "ages" of history. Grundtvig believed that the natural age of a culture was five hundred years, the number of years which had passed since Dante inaugurated intellectualism in Italy. Coincidentally, he speculated, the beginning of this period also marked the end of the great and ancient Nordic culture which had begun with the development of a virile Nordic mythology and had ended with the medieval historians, Saxo and Snorre. Now in turn, the intellectual period, ebbing out in the pettiness of a rationalistic interpretation of

Christianity, had come to an end. There was room for the flowering of a new culture with the revived vitality of the ancient North and the Christian understanding of life as the important ingredients.

Something artificial about this whole survey shows up in the fact that Grundtvig had difficulty in placing Luther, whom he admired and did not include among sterile intellectuals. Furthermore, the choice of a cycle of five hundred years was arbitrary. The idealizing of the ancient North and of Greece was one-sided, as was the condemnation of Rome and the conviction that a new era of culture should arise through a merger of Nordic and Christian values. Because Grundtvig was too much of a realist to retain the extremes of this dream very long, his subsequent work, including his *Handbook of World History*, is sober and realistic by comparison. But he satisfied his soul by writing the introduction to *Nordic Mythology*, in the course of which he developed and clarified several important ideas.

He knew that there was an unbridgeable gap between his point of view in regard to Christianity and that of the intellectualists, be they in the church or outside its fold. But he also realized that he could not fight their ideas in the same way he had challenged H. N. Clausen, by demanding ouster from the church. Nor should he even demonstrate his ideas by leaving the church himself. A battle of convictions, a contest of spirits, could not use any form of compulsion; it could only take place in freedom. This much he had learned from England.

From this time Grundtvig no longer advocated a severance of relations with the "naturalists," as he called those who did not share his Christian faith. He recommended co-operation with them in civic affairs while continuing the battle undauntedly on the spiritual level. Consequently, he introduced *Nordic Mythology* with a stirring appeal for freedom. The power of the spirit, he proclaimed, which is the power of a living word, can only be effective in freedom. He knew what it meant to be deprived of freedom to write as he pleased, and therefore was ready to claim freedom even for opposing forces. Freedom should be given, not to promote evil, but because lack of freedom would promote the cause of evil, and only in freedom is evil effectively combatted. From that time on, this emphasis on freedom was never absent from Grundtvig's arguments.

In the building of a new culture the dominant and revitalizing force should come from Christianity. The natural soundness and strength of the Nordic peoples, including England, was an essential contribution, but the guiding viewpoint should be Christianity's view of man. This emphasis required a precise evaluation of that view, in which connection Grundtvig now developed ideas that were to become just as significant as his ideas of history and revelation. Earlier, and quite naturally, he had held the view of man maintained by Lutheran orthodoxy, that man was capable of nothing good by himself and that his fall into sin meant a total depravity. This view had not been Luther's but was a medieval Augustinianism which had entered Lutheranism and had won out. Grundtvig abandoned this view and emphasized the wonder of human nature created by God. It has been said that he restored the first article of the Creed to its significant place.

The point of argument between Christians and "naturalists" was not a different opinion about the basic nature of man. They agreed that man was created a child of God. Grundtvig saw the evidence of this in the remarkable achievements of mankind in many cultures, particularly the Greek and the Nordic. Man was created in the image of God. Inherent in man was the natural and spiritual power which could draw him toward the goal of human development for which God had intended him. The point at which he disagreed with the "naturalists," was the fall into sin. Grundtvig agreed with the "naturalists" that man had had a terrific "misfortune" which has radically disturbed his relation to God and to his eternal goal. For him history gave plain evidence of this fact. He called it the "fall" and the "naturalists" called it a "mistake" or an "aberration," but terminology was not the important thing.[1] What separated them was mainly the question of a remedy. The "naturalists" believed that the remedy could be achieved somehow by natural man. Grundtvig held that the remedy, the restoration, could only be achieved by a regeneration in baptism and a union with Christ, the

[1] Grundtvig did not at this point discuss his differences with the orthodox view of the total depravity of man which resulted from the fall. See Chapter XII.

God-man. To express it in another way, the difference was whether man should accept Christ and adopt his way of life, or whether man should be "taken into Christ."

The Christian point of view which, in Grundtvig's opinion, should revitalize culture and bring a new day to mankind maintained that in creation man had been given a wonderful life which contained the power to meet the problems of human living. This view should be combined with the heritage of sound human and cultural values from the ancient North which reflected the vitality of creation. On the other hand, the alliance or synthesis which had existed between the church and the barren philosophy of the past five hundred years should be broken. This philosophy had been dominated by the compulsion of Rome and the tyranny of knowledge for its own sake. Sterile science should be replaced by a revitalized "science" which conceded the basic views of Christianity and which gave the natural strength of man a living expression. It has been said that Grundtvig permanently shattered all synthesis of culture and Christianity, but it is evident that he only shattered the culture-synthesis which was the Renaissance ideal. He plainly called for a new "synthesis" of cultural strength and the Christian point of view. In fact, his criticism of science was primarily that it had been "analytic" by nature and that it had not reached a "synthesis," because it did not have the ability to find such a "synthesis."

This then was the "universal-historic science" which should be developed. It should start with the assumption that God had endowed his created world with a sound and natural strength and striving, especially manifested in the Greek and Nordic cultures. (Grundtvig knew little or nothing about cultures outside the European orbit.) As an obstacle to man's development toward his goal of realizing God's purpose there had been placed in his way insurmountable difficulties of evil, both within him and in his environment. The force of evil had joined in an alliance with an intellectualism which denied the radical character of evil as well as the basic content of the Christian revelation. This alliance must be broken and a new culture, expressing the Judaeo-Christian view of the creation of man and utilizing the natural historic strength and wisdom of the Nordic peoples, should be built.

The dream of a "universal-historic science" was fanciful, but inherent in it, although not expressed explicitly, was the idea that culture was developed through the natural growth and qualitative expansion of individual folk groups or peoples. Inasmuch as Christianity was historic, it should also develop according to the natural characteristics of a people. Also inherent in this view, to become a very essential part of Grundtvig's philosophy, was the idea that a full development of Christian life, in the individual as well as in folk groups, required a recognition of the created nature of man. The person who is reborn in Christ is the same individual who was created by God. His created quality has not been utterly destroyed by the fall, and while recognizing that regeneration can come only through the divine action of God, the created quality of man must also be recognized in order to appreciate fully his regenerated nature.

The means through which culture and national life should be promoted and civic development take place was a civic academy for folk learning and practical efficiency. It should promote learning independent of the academic tradition of the university and it should train public servants in practical efficiency through purposeful development and mutual acquaintance. Literature would get the practical application it deserves and science would be encouraged. This is the statement in the introduction to *Nordic Mythology* through which Grundtvig first introduced the Folk School idea.

Grundtvig was an energetic advocate of growth or development in the evaluation of history. He spoke of the stages of various cultures in terms of the ages of man—youth, maturity, and old age. Childhood and youth form the age of fancy, which a man tries his strength and develops his ideas. Middle age is the age of feeling when a man devotes himself to his work in intense activity. Old age is the age of reflection when accomplishments are past and evaluation sets in but when life ebbs out. He applied this formula to the whole of mankind, but also used it in the evaluation of the cycle of a single culture and in the life of a nation within that culture. While he in many ways thus led modern historical philosophies of the rise and fall of cultures, he nevertheless overemphasized the analogy so that it became a Chinese puzzle of ages within ages which decreased its value.

All this philosophizing took place in the introduction to the actual study of mythology. In his earlier and smaller study of 1808, he had performed a valuable pioneering study by pointing out that the Nordic myths were not perversions of events but symbols of the orientation of the ancient people. This analysis he continued in the larger work. He regards the basic situation of mythology as a struggle between good and evil with the gods, or the Asas, representing the positive values in an intense struggle with the forces of destruction as represented by the demons. All the lively details of the myths are interpreted this way with a great deal of human wisdom deducted from the tales. The myths thus form a cosmogony of strength and profoundness from which we can learn much about the conditions of human life. The battle between gods and demons ended in catastrophe after which a new heaven and earth came into being, a verification for him of the possibility of a new synthesis between Christianity and the ancient wisdom of life.

Nordic Mythology was received with indifference. It was many years before it was even reviewed. When the Folk Schools came into being, however, it was eagerly and extensively used as a source of inspiration, and today is regarded as a key to the understanding of Grundtvig's later development and ideas of humanity. It was followed a few years later by another monumental historical work, a *Handbook of World History, According to the Best Sources,* of which the first volume was published in 1833, the second in 1836, and the third and last in 1843. The subtitle, "according to the best sources," is not an exaggeration. "During these years Grundtvig carried a great many ancient authors and heavy folios with medieval sources from the Royal Library to his home in Strandgade, and there he stayed as a watchdog chained to his writing desk." [2] This work was also much read in later years and was another source of knowledge and inspiration for the Folk Schools as they were established.

Like his *World Chronicles* of 1812 and 1817 Grundtvig still described history in terms of development and of prevailing ideas, still operating with the idea of the ages of culture as expounded in his *Mythology,* but he had given up his strongly biased judgments. He maintained a Christian evaluation but claimed that he had learned "to distinguish sharply between church and school, faith and science, time and eternity," and "realizes clearly that just as forcefully as the Christian church must repudiate any attempt to shape it according to their wishes, just as unjust would it be to force ecclesiastical forms upon the state or the school." The

[2] Ellen Jørgensen: *Historiens Studium i Danmark i det 19 Aarhundrede* (København: Bianco Luno, 1943), p. 40.

guiding point of view was no longer a judgment according to narrow religious and moral ideas but faith in the power and triumph of the spirit. Man does not rule the earth because he is stronger than the animals. He rules it because he has a superb gift, "something royal and divine we call the spirit which expresses itself in many ways, but mostly through the living word of our mouth." The strongest evidence of this created worth is found in human history, the realm in which we realize God's ways by knowing the conditions and accomplishments of men. For God is behind all history. It is, of course, true that history is the story of society and the various national groups. "But when law and order, the foundation of the state, is not sanctified by faith in an almighty judge or by an inherited reverence for the establishment of the fathers, then the state exists only on paper, law and order being strokes of the pen which can be abolished by another stroke." History is the story of the spirit of man, and the spirit of man reflects God.

Grundtvig scorned objective historical writing. His history was intended as interpretation, but it was an interpretation "according to the best sources." He did not hesitate to express an opinion. This opinion at times was an arbitrary one that does not hold up upon sober judgment. But at many other times he presented judgments which, with a stroke of genius, presaged the results of later historical research. *Handbook in World History* must not be judged according to the results of modern historical science. It must be considered a monumental accomplishment by the standards of the age, reflecting in a magnificent way the Christian convictions he so fearlessly proclaimed.

Yet another work must be mentioned in this connection, his last major historical effort. In 1838, the fiftieth anniversary of the great agricultural reforms,[3] Grundtvig was asked to give a series of lectures about contemporary history. He consented and invited the public to attend at one of the colleges connected with the university. The amazing result must be regarded as the inauguration of popular lectures in Denmark. Before, lectures had been for the intellectuals, given only at the university or in learned societies. It was unheard of that the common people should participate and particularly that a series of lectures should be arranged with popular appeal. Grundtvig was no great orator. He lacked the self-discipline which eliminates irrelevant and personal references, and he always included too much small talk. But he had a forceful personality and was thoroughly acquainted with the subject on which he spoke. To an audience growing with every lecture, he presented a lively and impressive picture of world events during the past fifty years. Grundtvig saved these manuscripts, which after his death were published in 1877 by his son, Svend Grundtvig, a historian like his father. The lectures, under the title *Man's Memory*, are interesting reading even today. They are filled with personal observations and are therefore ex-

[3] See Appendix, pp. 239-46.

cellent biographical source material. They must, however, be used with the care always extended to autobiographical remarks made after a period of time.

6

New Thoughts on Church and School

Grundtvig's views of the church had been influenced by his experiences in England. He had, upon closer acquaintance, lost his fascination for the episcopal system and had instead been attracted to the ideas of freedom and tolerance which characterized the broad church movement. This new influence and events within the Danish state church now caused him to reconsider the whole problem of church organization. A decade earlier he had declared that the church as the body of Christ was the living embodiment of the gospel and the effective vehicle of God's revelation. It had become activated in history through the confession of the believers, the features by which it was knowable to man being the sacraments to which the confession was inseparably joined. The important aspect of the church was therefore its life and not its form.

The Danish church in Grundtvig's day was a state episcopal church. Practical administration to the slightest detail, including the ritual and even the choice of hymns, was controlled by the bishops, governed in turn by the department of church affairs and eventually by the king, the head of the church with the power of appointment. The administrative authority of the church was maintained very strictly, and deviations from routine reprimanded, as when Grundtvig in 1826 attemped to use hymns not authorized in the hymnal. On the other hand, the doctrinal conformity of the church had been relaxed considerably during the past generation. For more than fifty years the skeptical and rationalizing influence of the prevailing philosophy had been in ascendance. At the time of Grundtvig's insurrection most of the Copenhagen clergy, the deans, bishops, and cabinet members, as well as the theological professors, were Rationalists. The last "defender of the Bible" had been Bishop Balle. The prevailing interpretation of the Christian revelation was, in the main, a denial of all supernatural character. Main emphasis was placed upon a moralistic and intellectual interpretation of Christian teaching and living. The clergy changed the ritual and the confession at will, with little or no protest until Grundtvig attacked Professor Clausen in 1825.

The revolt against Rationalism, which Grundtvig to some extent was compelled by the censorship to abandon, was taken up by his close friend and follower, Jacob Christian Lindberg. Lindberg was a scholar of distinction. He lost a natural and deserved opportunity for a professorship in Semitic languages because he rallied to Grundtvig's cause. But he was also a sharply polemical fighter who always championed the underdog. He took up the argument against Professor Clausen where Grundtvig had been forced to drop it, and plagued that worthy gentleman with pamphlets and accusations for years. It was Lindberg's logical contention that Clausen could not continue to be professor of systematic theology with the views he held, if the purpose clause of the Danish constitution in regard to the church was to be maintained. Lindberg was, of course, correct. He caused the church administration a great deal of embarrassment, because it had sanctioned doctrinal laxity all along the line. The question was, however, whether the battle should be steadily fought along the lines of strict enforcement or in the spiritual realm only. Grundtvig had already modified his original stand and had asked for permission to leave the service of the church rather than force Clausen out of office.

The main attack on the Rationalists did not come from Lindberg's astute and persistent pen. It was a revolt of the people which brought things to a head. A popular revival movement had called for a return to the older practices and teachings of the church, demanding more personal and fervent preaching and devotion. The devotional groups, or conventicles, that had arisen, were prohibited and persecuted. Furthermore, an area of conflict had arisen because the individual was bound to the parish. In practice this did not mean that he could not worship in the church of his choice, especially in Copenhagen where tradition had broken parish lines. But the individual had to participate in the sacraments only in the parish church to which he was bound.

Many of the "awakened" lay people had been influenced by Grundtvig's emphasis upon the significance of the sacraments and the fundamental and "unaltered" character of the confession as a necessary requirement for the covenant relationship which was established at baptism. It was therefore natural that they reacted against the parish ministers to whom they were compelled by law to bring their children for baptism and who arbitrarily altered the ritual as well as the Creed to suit their ideas. The most flagrant "sinner" in this respect was H. G. Clausen, the dean at the cathedral and the father of H. N. Clausen. In his church there were several painful episodes where parents or relatives protested against his form of baptism, with the final result that the authorities were compelled reluctantly to reprimand the dean. They had favored Clausen in the controversy, but could not be strict in some affairs and lax in others.

This disciplinary triumph was logically a victory for Grundtvig's point of view, but he did not consider it as such. He had come to see that the cause of the church was not furthered through legal triumphs and the compulsion of ecclesiastical authority. The only condition under which there could be growth in spiritual life was freedom. The church was the body of Christ and not an organization guaranteed by the state. On the other hand, Grundtvig nourished an inherent antipathy toward conventicles. In England he had learned that there could be justification for several forms of church life and that no one group could claim that they had the only true form.

Circumstances had prevented Grundtvig from making an impulsive decision in these matters and had given him time and opportunity to develop his views at leisure. For a while after his journeys to England he had toyed with the idea of leaving the church and forming a free church body, but an application to the church authorities for permission to do this was turned down. When therefore Grundtvig and Lindberg started a devotional group, Grundtvig was permitted to preach at vesper services. For the moment the pressure had been relieved, and when, later on, his desire to officiate at the sacraments grew, the authorities again relented and gave Grundtvig the regular appointment at Vartov. His ideas of church government were therefore not forced into a solution motivated by personal dissatisfaction with his own treatment.

Grundtvig expressed himself in several documents during the early thirties but his most important statement is *The Danish State Church, Impartially Considered*, a booklet he published in 1834. The state church, he claimed, was not identical with the body of Christ. It is not a church-state but only an "establishment," an English word he actually used in the text. This establishment may be ordered and arranged in any way bishops, pastors, and professors deem practical, just so it does not trespass upon freedom of conscience, a fundamental right of all religion as well as of all citizenship. What was wrong with the present situation was that the common belief actually was that there existed a church-state within the legal state. Of this the clergy was the soul, the government the administration, and lawyers the fingers. The reason was that the church had been mistakenly identified with theology on the one hand and the clergy on the other. As a result freedom had existed only for an authorized religion regardless of dissenting opinions. What Grundtvig wanted now was not a tightening of the authoritative bonds of the church, which he had demanded a decade earlier, but a continuation of the doctrinal tolerance shown toward the Rationalists. He had learned in England that dissenting voices could be an advantage to the state, that outward authority could never be a guarantee of true religion. It was certainly not his desire to change the traditional doctrines. He only insisted upon freedom for those who wished to make a change. Then the natural solution to the practical difficulties of the moment was that each individual be loosed from his parish bonds.

Grundtvig's proposal was a radical departure from existing conditions and from the prevailing theory that the pure doctrine of the church was to be protected and guaranteed by the state. He did not himself desire any release from a single point of Lutheran doctrine. For his own situation he wanted freedom for the traditional views where they had been jeopardized by liberalizing tendencies within the church. This freedom was given when he was appointed pastor at Vartov with full rights of pastoral services. But he wanted freedom also for the common members of the church to choose the minister they wanted, and he claimed freedom for all pastors to preach and serve according to their own conscience and the guidance of Scripture. It was the latter demand, not only asking for the same freedom for his opponents as he wanted for himself, but including a completely new program for the church, that exploded the traditional concept of the state church. The state establishment for ecclesiastical affairs should, according to his demand, only be a civic arrangement by which the security of the pastors was guaranteed. The content of preaching and the ritual of the service should no longer be the concern of the establishment, giving complete freedom to the ministers in doctrinal and liturgical affairs. This freedom was necessary, not only because compulsion was in itself an evil and freedom the necessary atmosphere in spiritual affairs, but because the only guarantee for the spiritual life of the church is the spirit within the church.

Grundtvig's program was not accepted and carried out at the time. In 1834 J. P. Mynster was appointed bishop of Sjaelland. He quickly conducted an orthodox reform requiring that all ministers hold strictly to the ritual. The lay demand that the children be baptized according to the ritual was therefore complied with, and popular pressure for action disappeared. Grundtvig's liberal and even radical demand for freedom, grown out of a conservative request for conformity, was thus left hanging in the air. For the moment even his suggestion of emancipation from parish bonds was scuttled. But once expressed, his new proposal was not forgotten. It is outside the realm of this study to detail the church history of Denmark in which his theory over a century of development won almost complete victory. The first step of emancipation from parish bonds was legalized in 1855—after the death of Mynster.

In 1839 Grundtvig wrote "An Open Letter to an English Clergyman," addressed to a Rev. Mr. Wade who had been in Denmark a number of years and had returned to England. In this he gave a summary of his ecclesiastical development and included the notes for his first sermon at Vartov. The sermon posed the question of who he was and whence he had come to his new office, and among other things he said: "I do not come from a sect in any spiritual or Christian sense, for I come from the holy 'universal' church which shall last forever and which has one Lord, one faith and one baptism. I come from that house of the Lord which is built on the rock and which according to his promise shall resist even the gates of hell. I come from that house which always has been and always will be foreign to the world but which never can be foreign to anyone who really believes what we all at baptism confess. And where could we with greater certainty say about the holy, universal church that it is 'not far from any of us' than among the spiritual children of Martin Luther? Is it not in this church that Martin Luther's name will be immortal, and was it not here that God made him a priest of the order of Melchizedek, so that he was without father, mother, and family tree? Is it not in this church that we 'live and move and have our being' as long as we retain our Lutheran childhood faith and have been baptized as our Father revealed it through Christ, not in His name but in the name of the Father, the Son, and the Holy Spirit."

The next year, 1840, Grundtvig submitted a series of three articles, "Ecclesiastical Information, Especially for Lutheran Christians," to *Nordic Journal for Christian Theology*, edited by his friend and follower Peter Christian Kierkegaard, brother of Søren Kierkegaard. These articles leave the subject of the form of the church, with which he had been concerned for some time, and return to the matter of the inner character of the church. In the first article he discussed the church itself. He defined it as a fellowship of faith of living people. It is, he said, a community of faith and hope, founded in baptism and knowable by the oral confession of faith which is its condition for membership and therefore for baptism. He refuted alike the Catholic concept of the institutional church and the idealistic Protestant concept of an invisible church which has no "reality." True to his previously developed philosophical concepts he claimed that a church must be "knowable." Although it is "invisible" in that its "evidence" is not "cross or tower, mitre or cowl, custom or ceremony" or even a book, it is nevertheless known to the human ear, through the "plain, public, spoken word by which its members confess their faith and hope." This word is the word of truth by which Christians confess their Lord and by which they know one another. Grundtvig argued his case with the obsolete propositions of Wolffian logic, grating on modern ears. But this should not obscure his message that the church lives by a word, its covenant and confession, mediating the grace of God to man. He went on to denounce all forms of compulsion, including that of the confessional documents of the Lutheran church, tying the word of confession inseparably to baptism as the entrance into Christian life, and to communion as the nourishment of the same life. Faith and baptism form the foundation of the church, and the church is known by its word of faith and baptism.

In the second article, concerning baptism, he committed himself to the unfortunate doctrine that the Creed was given to the apostles by Jesus in the forty days between the resurrection and the ascension. This shift from his original emphasis has more than anything else been a barrier to the understanding and acceptance of Grundtvig's views. For the exposition of the development of this assertion we are particularly indebted to Høirup's research and analysis.[4]

Grundtvig's dynamic concept of the church as the

[4] Henning Høirup: *Grundtvigs Syn paa Tro og Erkendelse* (1949).

effective vehicle of revelation had led him to the insight that there must have been a living response to the revelation of God in the body of Christ, the church. This response he had found in the confession of faith which accompanied baptism throughout the whole history of the church. He had expressed this idea in *The Reply of the Church*, 1825, and developed it in the articles "Concerning True Christianity" and "Concerning the Truth of Christianity" during the next few years. At that time he was concerned with the content of the confession and not with its literalism, maintaining that the origin of the Creed was apostolic.[5] Partly under the influence of Lessing, however, he soon started to toy with the idea that the actual wording of the confession had come from the Lord himself. During the years 1827-30 he began to identify the confession of the baptismal covenant with the Apostles' Creed. At first this idea occurred mostly in sermons—Høirup calls it a "homiletical by-product" of these years.

In the thirties he was busy with studies in England and with historical writings, but his friends carried his doctrinal suggestions further. A discussion of them broke out in the *Nordic Journal*, and when Grundtvig was pressed for a stand by friends and opponents alike he finally came out with a clear statement in the article about baptism. He now abandoned the emphasis upon the content of the confession and on its apostolic character. Categorically he pronounced that Jesus must

[5] Cf., pp. 51-52.

have given the exact words of the Creed during the forty days (*evangelium quadraginta dierum*). Grundtvig in this dogmatization moved from the strong ground of a spiritual understanding of the nature of revelation and the church to the static and historically indefensible postulate of a verbatim dictation of the Creed. This dogmatization does not necessarily obscure the original insight, which has emerged to renewed prominence in our own day while the dogmatization has been given up by even the most ardent followers of Grundtvig. But it has caused much confusion and misunderstanding. The cause of the shift might be the pressure exerted by his disciples, but it is mainly, as Høirup has demonstrated, Grundtvig's fascination for the Wolffian logic, which claimed to prove realities by logical deductions. Grundtvig argued that "if our Lord Jesus Christ has instituted baptism as a bath of rebirth and renewal in the Holy Spirit, then he must also have given definite and unchangeable conditions for the gift. These must either have been the same ones the church requires in its baptismal covenant today, or the church must have falsified the genuine apostolic baptism." We are not impressed with the form of the argument and less with the result, but Grundtvig did arrive at this conclusion.

The status of the church was not Grundtvig's only concern during these years. He was vitally interested in the fate of his people, but his attitude was far removed from the apocalyptic judgments of the war years. Economic conditions had improved and there was a growing interest in national and political affairs. Grundtvig's faith in the common people had been strengthened by his experience in England, leading him to look forward to national and democratic growth. He was still a royalist convinced that the most desirable form of government could be established under a benevolent monarch guided by the voice of the people. He was therefore delighted when the old king yielded to popular pressure and established three provincial assemblies of the "estates." Although these assemblies were only to be advisory bodies, they were elected through a limited franchise and proved to be excellent proving grounds for a growing democracy which demanded and finally adopted a democratic constitution in 1849. At that time Grundtvig became a member of the constitutional assembly, taking an active part in the enactment of the new instrument.

Meanwhile he was convinced that the greatest need of the people, in order to become an effective participant in government, was education. He therefore developed further the idea of an academy of the people which he had proposed in the introduction to *Nordic Mythology*. Now he no longer called it an "academy" but a "civic high school," calling it a "school for life" in contrast to the sterile intellectualism of the university with its emphasis on the "dead" languages of the classical tradition. It was not his intention that it should be a school for children, and the term "high school" was not identical with a secondary school or a school for adolescents. "I am not advocating a school for boys, for as the Englishman says, one should not discuss affairs of state with women and children. It is a high school for young citizens where the education desirable in the representatives of the people as well as their electors can be promoted. The only boy's school for citizens I know is the home of capable and progressive citizens." [6] Inasmuch as life can be divided into religious, civic, and scientific parts, he advocated three types of schools for life; the church school, the school for citizenship, and the university.[7]

During the next few years he wrote a number of articles and pamphlets advocating a high school for the people as a school for life, discussing in detail the features he believed should be included in it. Not an academic institution in the sense that it required examinations and handed out degrees, it should not only accept anyone who wished to come but be unhampered by formalities. To equip the students for citizenship, it should teach them knowledge and love of their country through its history and literature. Naturally it should emphasize their own language, a demand far more radical in a day when intellectual groups favored French and German and when all learning was steeped in the classical languages. Finally it should be a school with a living, i.e. oral, communication between teacher and

[6] *Det Danske Fiir-Kløver* (1836), p. 40 f.
[7] *Skolen for Livet og Akademiet i Soer* (1838), p. 21 f.

student to counteract the deadening influence of the printed word.

There was no letup in Grundtvig's pressure for a school for the people. Not only did he advocate the general character of such a school; he recommended the place where it could be put into practice. His suggestion was excellent. At Sorø, an idyllic provincial city located about fifty miles from Copenhagen, King Christian IV had founded an academy for young men of the nobility two hundred years earlier. This academy had been richly endowed a hundred years later by the noted playwright and philosopher, Ludvig Holberg, but had failed to attract students though it had been thrown open to all. It had been closed in 1793 but reopened in 1822. A reorganization in 1827 had been only partly successful, leaving buildings and funds available for another purpose. Inasmuch as the purpose of the academy originally had been to supplement the university, the situation seemed made to order for Grundtvig's ideas. The place was no less attractive because Grundtvig's good friend, the poet B. S. Ingemann, was a professor at the college.

Despite the new advisory assembly of the Estates, the king still held the purse strings and made all decisions of importance. The old monarch, Frederik VI, was not interested in innovations of this character. His reign, as sovereign and as regent for his father, reached back to the days of revolution and unrest in Europe. He had been a willing co-operator in the reactionary policies which had dominated Europe since the Treaty of Vienna. Upon his death in 1838 new possibilities opened up. The new king, Christian VIII, was more progressive and listened to Grundtvig. With relative speed, for bureaucracy, a decree was issued in 1847 stipulating the conditions of the new academy at Sorø. Although it did not seem to catch the spirit of what Grundtvig wanted, he was overjoyed at the possibility that a practical step would finally be taken. Unfortunately the king died in 1848 and the cabinet member for education under the new king, a university professor of Latin, hastily scuttled the whole project. Grundtvig's plan for a college, or "high school," at Sorø was thus never realized. His educational ideas were to germinate in a way he had not envisioned or suggested.

Grundtvig's educational activity during these years was not limited to theoretical writing or political pressure. In a fashion he set an example for the personal communication of ideas which he so strongly advocated in his Folk School program. The lectures he gave at Borch's College in 1838 about contemporary history set a new precedent for popular lectures. When a lecturer can start with two hundred and fifty in the audience and end, after fifty lectures, with an overflow crowd of six hundred, he has demonstrated the lectures' appeal.

Political developments also created an opportunity for lecture activity. In a fusion of liberal, political, and nationalistic activity public meetings were held during the forties, the most important of these being the meeting at Skamlingsbanke in 1844. It was purposely held on the American Independence Day, July fourth. Here Grundtvig was asked to speak to ten thousand people, which he did in an inspirational address, using the opportunity to call for a school for the people. More than anything else this address was the direct cause of the founding of the first Folk School according to the proposed general outline. The school at Rødding was begun in the fall of the same year.

Many influences merged in Grundtvig's educational program.[8] His ideas emerged in line with his total development from the early days of his interest in national affairs. They reflect his philosophical struggle even in the days when he was most interested in religious affairs. But they are primarily an expression of the influences Grundtvig felt in England at a time when he was ready to accept them.

[8] Chapter X.

7

Freedom

In many ways, Grundtvig was a "new" man after 1832. Most of this change of attitude can be ascribed to his journeys to England. There he became acquainted with a more active and free society than he had known in the stuffiness of Copenhagen. The whole experience emancipated him and opened new perspectives. But for him to be satisfied with this explanation would be superficial. There were deeper currents of personality development involved. The new and more "free" attitudes are inseparably bound to the religious and philosophical struggles of the earlier years. It was fortunate for Grundtvig that he had a long life. He was fifty years old before his personality was completely mature. Only then did he enter actively into educational and political work. At an age when many people retire he started upon twenty to thirty years of public activity.

Until he was more than fifty years old, he was hampered by being compelled to struggle for recognition and even for income. He could, of course, have buried himself in an out-of-the-way parish or a teaching position and found security at the cost of obscurity and ineffectiveness. But his spirit drove him to the capital where doors to office in the church as well as the university were slammed by irritated officials who had been hit by his barbs. Only the benevolence of a monarch who was elevated above bureaucratic pettiness kept him and his family alive during a long and turbulent period, although he did receive some private support. He also lacked scientific recognition as antiquarian and historian, which posterity has so richly bestowed on him. His idiosyncracies and his irritating accurate criticisms, blinding most of his colleagues to his real worth, caused his enemies to ignore him when they were not lashing out at him in retort or ridiculing him for his peculiarities. Even in England he felt their personal resentment. His failure to conform to social standards handicapped him here and hindered the recognition which he should have been given for his scholarship.

In a sense Grundtvig escaped all this irritation and criticism only by outgrowing or outlasting it. He was in his sixties when the relentless resistance to his person let up somewhat and was replaced by admiration in a majestic loneliness. At that time his older opponents had passed away, his contemporaries had been mellowed in their dotage, and the younger generation looked upon him more as a phenomenon than as a person. He was like a giant oak that loomed up over the newer growth, and his odd behavior was what could be expected from a man of his temperament and stature. He made few friends during his lifetime, but he gained many admirers. It is one of the tragedies of history that he and Kierkegaard could not get along, but he was seventy-two years old when Kierkegaard died at the age of forty-two.

Even this explanation of the more emancipated activity of his later years is not sufficient. The maturing of his ideas and his liberation from older patterns of thought came gradually and only after a struggle. His views of society and of the nature of man were the result of the strenuous philosophical spade work he accomplished during 1816-19, also the outgrowth of the religious development which took place before and after that. To dismiss the religious side of his growth as something irrelevant to his historical, social, and educational work is to disregard the wholeness of his personality. Dogmatic and philosophical concepts had threatened to wrap his philosophy of man in the tentacles of stereotyped thinking. It was only because he struggled and fought his way through them that he could retain a Christian foundation for a modern point of view. And it was only because he insisted, in the face of anti-Christian and irreligious developments, that man was created in the image of God, that he could hold to the Christian view over against the nineteenth-century biological, naturalistic, and psychological developments.

For Grundtvig the starting point of all thought and all activity was God. It was not a God concerning whose existence he had reached definite conclusions through thought, like Descartes; through experience, like Hume and Locke; through conscience, like Kant; or through vital dependence, like Schleiermacher. It was a God in whom he believed through Christian faith. This foundation is not a recognized philosophical point of departure, but for Grundtvig it was a reality on which all his thought and activity were founded. His faith was a Christian faith, which again meant that he believed God had revealed himself in history through Christ; that it was a personal relationship to this revelation which was the basis of his faith. He believed firmly that faith was a gift from God.

From this conviction of the existence or reality of God Grundtvig asked himself the question: How can we know God of whose reality we are convinced? This approach is different from the philosophical. The problem which ordinarily is the primary one in epistemology became a secondary problem or a derivation from the starting point. But though the question of knowing God was secondary, it was no less important for him to find an answer. We can, of course, know God through the created world, the physical world. This he took for granted. He did not spend much time on it, for he was interested in the problem: How can we know God in the life of man? His answer was first that we can know God's creation of man through the living word which is in the power of man, i.e. through human speech. Secondly, we can know God through the signs of his work in history.

Grundtvig's concept of God was thus a dynamic concept. He abandoned the exclusively static concept of God which claims that he can be known, and only known, through a written record. The written record is a source of information of inestimable worth, but it is not the source of our "knowledge" of God. All "knowledge" of God must be living, contemporary, dynamic.

Grundtvig's first liberation was from the tyranny of philosophy. Next he freed himself from the static authority of biblical and creedal orthodoxy. The third step was emancipation from a static concept of history, i.e. that the Christian life should express itself in set and definite forms which should be equally valid at all times and all places. He was opposed to reliance upon forms of office and organization. He rejected not only the episcopal claim of the significance of the apostolic succession and the Roman claim of the authority of the pope and the hierarchy, but also any claim of the spiritual authority of office whether in an official state church or in a freely organized church. The basic feature of Christianity, the one which can be abandoned only at the cost of Christianity itself, was the living confession of faith in God, in his revelation in Christ, and in his contemporary activity through the Spirit. But this faith could never be guaranteed through any external show of authority, and it could live and grow only in freedom. We can know God through the historic reality of his church. We can live in that reality by sharing its community of life. But we can never guarantee that reality by any human arrangements, and we can destroy its dynamic by compulsion and by reliance upon externalism.

On the basis of this faith man must be free and active. He must not be bound by static notions of what a Christian must do and should not do. His only compulsion, religiously speaking, is the compulsion of God himself as revealed through Christ. Religiously speaking man is not free, for he is bound to God, but humanly speaking and in the development of all his God-given faculties and possibilities he is and must be free.

So far, so good. To this logical development of his ideas we must now add another important feature. Man cannot live and grow to the full extent of his possibilities as an individual; he must live in community with others. This means that religiously he must live in the corporate body of a religious fellowship, and for Grundtvig this religious fellowship was, as a matter of course, the Christian church. Here we have the fundamental difference between Grundtvig and Kierkegaard. But it also means that the individual must live in a community of his practical and human interests. Grundtvig distinguished between the community of the church and the social community, and he resented an identification of the two. He therefore opposed labelling as "Christian" any national, social, or political activity, but he did not create an unbridgeable gap between them, as some of his interpreters have believed. In his opinion, both activities had their motivation in the faith in and reliance upon God. There was a difference, for the religious community was the fellowship of those who through faith in Christ and thereby through his redemptive activity had been brought into a new relationship with God. The human community was the fellowship of those who had been created in the image of God. But the dynamic for all activity was faith in God.

The human community in which a man must live in order to fulfil his purpose was, for Grundtvig, the people. When he spoke of a people, he did not mean the lower stratum of society in contrast to an upper or privileged group, though Grundtvig worked hard for the "common people" in the development of their rights. Nor did he mean people in a nationalistic or chauvinistic sense. A people was for him the natural group in which man found the community of life without which he could not realize his purpose. When he spoke of a "school for the people" he did not mean the common people differentiated from the intellectual class. He meant a school for all Danish people where they could learn the things necessary for growth and development.

Grundtvig's homeland was Denmark, but due to his interest in history and his absorption in the ancient tales and mythology he extended the boundaries to include the whole North, which he considered to be of common origin and to have a common spirit. Even England, for which he had much sympathy, was included in the

North. But he excluded the German states with the possible exception of Saxony. The latter was the country of Martin Luther and it was the Saxons who had conquered England together with the Angles, a Danish tribe. The Nordic people, Grundtvig felt, had a cultural content and a spirit of which he felt a part and which was the necessary condition for future growth. It had, in his analysis, a heroic and vital quality of which he had found evidence in the ancient Nordic and Anglo-Saxon tales. This heroic quality of the myths, which showed itself in a battle of good against evil, he found to be akin to the spirit of Christianity, which for him was primarily a battle against evil and death.

When Grundtvig entered public life to take an active part in political and social problems, he believed that he was serving his people in accordance with the principles we have outlined above. But the picture of this activity is somewhat obscured by another element. The Danes of the forties and fifties were not interested exclusively in cultural and social problems; they also became nationalistic. This was inevitable, for Denmark became involved in a threat of revolution on the part of the provinces of Slesvig and Holstein. This revolution eventually developed into an open war into which Prussia also entered. Therefore, when Grundtvig was elected to the constitutional assembly in 1848, he also became a member of a legislature which made decisions concerning the war. Grundtvig took an active part in the war program as well as the constitutional work.

The nationalistic problem which came to a head in the middle of the century was that of the relationship of the provinces of Slesvig and Holstein to the kingdom of Denmark. Slesvig was ancient Danish territory which had been partially separated from the crown when it was made into a duchy during the Middle Ages. In the course of time the Duchy of Slesvig and the Duchy of Holstein had come into the possession of the same ducal line which owed fealty for both duchies to the king of Denmark, although Holstein was a member of the German confederation and Slesvig was not. In the nineteenth century, when nationalistic sentiments were in the ascendancy, conflicting loyalties developed in Slesvig. The one was a Germanizing movement maintaining the right of an inseparable union of the two provinces, resisting the sovereignty of Denmark, and promoting the German language, even in Danish-speaking northern Slesvig. The other, a growing Danish consciousness, emphasized the ancient relationship of Slesvig to Denmark and resisted the spread of the German language. It was as an outgrowth of the latter sentiment that the first Folk School, founded through the inspiration of Grundtvig, was built at Rødding in the fall of 1844.

The conflict of the two movements was sharpened when the problem of a constitution became acute in the forties. One group wished to unite the provinces constitutionally and effect a separation from Denmark. The other group wished to tie Slesvig constitutionally closer to Denmark and loosen its ties with Holstein.

Under the influence of revolutionary movements in Europe, particularly in France and Germany in February, 1848, a revolt broke out in the duchies, followed by intermittent warfare during the years 1848, 1849, and 1850. Supported by Prussia, the revolt, though somewhat successful, was eventually put down. Attempts at constitutional solutions during the next decade were futile, and in 1864, when the matter became acute upon the death of King Christian VIII and the end of a royal line, open warfare again broke out. Bismarck used the occasion for a test of his new military machine, and Denmark, abandoned by other powers, was quickly defeated. The whole province of Slesvig was subsequently annexed by Prussia. This whole situation quite naturally evoked virile patriotism in Grundtvig. He was a member of parliament, his sons were in the army, and sentiment ran high. Even as England had been the archenemy in his youth, Germany now was the great foe and usurper who threatened the existence of his small country.

The problem that has greater universal interest was the development of democratic ideas. These took the form of a demand for a new constitution with a parliamentary and representative form of government. The step taken in the establishment of the advisory Estates in 1835 had only whetted the people's appetite, and during the reign of Christian VIII, 1839-48, the demand grew stronger. It reached a climax upon the accession of the new king, Frederik VII, 1848-63, coinciding with the revolutionary movements in Europe that also inspired the Slesvig revolt. Frederik VII consented to the wishes of the people and called a constitutional assembly. The new constitution was signed and became effective June 5, 1849, changing Denmark from an absolute monarchy to a democratic monarchy. The legislative power was placed in the hands of the people through representatives elected by universal male suffrage in the lower house and a limited suffrage in the upper house. The problem of whether the executive branch should be exclusively responsible to the people or to a combination of the people, the royalty, and the privileged classes became pressing during the remainder of the century. It was eventually determined completely in favor of the people.

Grundtvig was originally not in favor of a democracy. He believed in a benevolent monarchy advised by the best intellect of the people and limited only by the freedom of popular criticism. Therefore he was in favor of freedom of expression. In this he was a true son of the eighteenth century. The establishment of the advisory Estates he considered an excellent move by the king, but he did not favor the agitation for the next step of parliamentarianism. The country should be ruled by "the hand of the king and the voice of the people, both strong and both free." He therefore worked hard to have his Folk School ideas promoted by the chief executive to whom he ascribed wisdom enough to see the value of such an institution.

Though Grundtvig changed his views, he never became democratic in the modern sense of the word. He was aristocratic by nature, but he believed in the people. He was suspicious of intellectual aristocracy and classical learning. He believed that the sturdy and natural impulses and cultural values of a nation came from the common people, who had retained the natural vigor and soundness of the ancient North. He was convinced that he was in contact with this folk life. When therefore the king called a constitutional assembly, he considered himself well qualified for membership, especially as a student of history. He sought election in Copenhagen, but in vain. He was finally elected in a supplementary election in Præstø, the district in which he was born and where he had twice been a pastor for short periods. After the constitution had been adopted he was a member of the lower house 1849-53 and 1854-58. In 1866 he was elected a member of the upper house and served a few months. He was then eighty-three years old.

Grundtvig's parliamentary activity can in no way be called brilliant. He was cast in a different mold from that of most politicians, finding it difficult to conform to the routine and pettiness of political debate. As a historian he enjoyed a perspective which often carried him far beyond the limitations of an agenda, and his eye for details was a handicap in obtaining practical results. A foe of parliamentary double-talk, he disdained compromise. As a result he refrained from voting for the final draft of the constitution, but he could not oppose it, because it contained much good, so he stayed away from the adoption. Realist as he was, he strongly opposed a conservative revision of the same constitution in 1866. It was for this reason that he sought election to the upper house then. An example of his argumentation was his plea for one chamber in the parliament. To the claim that there was greater security in two chambers, he replied that there was no security in driving a team of two horses of which one balked while the other ran away.

The most interesting point of his political development was that although he never abandoned his confidence in the monarchy, he gradually let himself be convinced that a new age required new methods. He therefore became much more friendly toward parliamentary representation. He was a liberal who believed in free enterprise, and freedom of the press, as opposed to government restrictions, particularly in religious and spiritual matters. He was disappointed because he never succeeded in provoking government action to establish a college for the people. He did succeed, however, in effectuating in legislation his old demand that the parish bonds be severed. This law was passed in 1855. Subsequent church legislation as well was greatly inspired by the ideas he had expounded.

Most of his influence was indirect. The only direct impact he made upon the new constitution was the adoption of his motion that legal procedure should be oral and public. For four years, 1848-51, he published a magazine, *Danskeren*, most of which he wrote himself, discussing all the current national and political issues in a lively and refreshing way.

8

A Song to God

> Give me, God, the gift of singing
> That in phrases full and ringing
>   I may sing Thy praise!
> Grant me that, Thy joy possessing,
> In acclaim of Thy great blessing
>   I my voice may raise!

To move into the realm of Grundtvig's hymns is to move into another world. The fiery gleam of the historian and reformer is supplanted by the dreamy vision of the prophet and the inspired glow of the bard. As a hymn writer Grundtvig demonstrated a tremendous range, from the humble petition of the sinner and tender care for children to the majestic vision of the land beyond the seas and the apocalyptic expectancy of the return.

Grundtvig wrote more than two thousand hymns, of which two hundred are included in the official hymnal of Denmark. He wrote his first hymns during his religious crisis of 1810 and continued writing them as long as he lived. Most of the hymns were written after 1832. In 1835 he accepted the offer by a good friend, Pastor

Gunni Busck, of financial assistance so he could take several months' leave of absence from his church to write hymns. The result was the first volume of *Work of Song—for the Danish Church* which was published in 1836. A second volume came in 1870, followed by three volumes of hymns published after his death. Many of the hymns were first introduced in his congregation at Vartov. The memoirs of several church leaders bear witness to the fact that its powerful singing was one of the most vigorous features of the life at this church as at others influenced by Grundtvig's ideas.

Quite a number of the hymns were translations or recreations of other hymns. He was least successful in his attempts to improve older Danish hymns, although one of his greatest hymns, "O day full of grace," is based on a medieval hymn. Far greater was his success with Greek and particularly Latin hymns. Two of his best-known hymns are recreations of songs by Bernard of Clairvaux and Adam of St. Victor. From Anglo-Saxon he translated several songs by Caedmon, and a number of modern English hymns, including Montgomery's and Wesley's, have won prominence in his versions. These English hymns, reproduced in meters and rhythms different from their original, are not immediately recognizable in their Danish form, but their content has been transplanted. Several of them are highly cherished.

However, the greatest single source of inspiration for Grundtvig's hymns was the Bible. He wrote scores of

songs in which he retold biblical events in verse. The
children of Denmark have become familiar with these
events as much through his songs as through any other
source. "Of tales that to the Book belong, he trans-
ferred half to verse and song." His hymns are so permeated with biblical expressions that even the careful
Bible scholar is constantly surprised to find so many in
them. Only a constant and thorough reader could be
thus saturated with the words of Scripture. Most of the
hymns are direct rewritings of biblical passages such as
Isaiah 35:

> Blossom as a rose shall here
> All the desert places,
> Blossom when the golden year
> Shines on saddened faces.
> Glory crowns proud Lebanon,
> Carmel's height has splendor won,
> Flowers bloom in Sharon.
>
> Sight is given to the blind
> And their eyes shall glisten;
> Every mute his voice shall find,
> All the deaf shall listen;
> Like the hart the lame shall leap,
> Zion nevermore shall weep,
> Peace shall reign forever.
>
> Thus Isaiah prophesied
> In the days of sadness.
> Ages passed, then far and wide
> Spread the news of gladness;
> Christ is here, with us He stands,
> Changing with His loving hand
> Desert wastes to Eden.

Hail our King at God's right hand,
Jesus and His Spirit
Lead us to the promised land
We by faith inherit.
And though death be drawing near,
Words of life the deaf shall hear;
Mutes shall sing His praises.

Translation by S. D. Rodholm

Others are based on a word or an act of Jesus, such as Luke 10:23-24.

Blessed were the eyes that truly
Here on earth beheld the Lord,
Happy were the ears that duly
Listened to His precious word,
Who revealed the wondrous story
Of God's mercy, truth, and glory.

Kings and prophets long with yearning
Prayed to see His day appear,
Angels with desire were burning
To behold the golden year,
When God's light and grace should quicken
All that sin and death hath stricken.

He who, light and life revealing,
By His Spirit stills our want,
He who broken hearts is healing
By His cup and at the font,
Jesus, Fount of joy incessant,
Is with life and light now present.

Though the world cannot perceive Him,
He is near to yearning hearts,
And to all who here believe Him
His blest word sweet grace imparts,
Making bright the gloomy spaces,
Paradise of desert places.

Eyes in deepest darkness blinded
May now see His glory bright,
Hearts, perverse and carnal minded,
May obtain His Spirit's light
When contrite and sorely yearning
They in faith to Him are turning.

Blessed are the eyes that truly
Here on earth behold the Lord,
Happy are the ears that duly
Listen to His blessed word.
When His words our spirit nourish
Shall His kingdom in us flourish.

Translation by J. C. Aaberg

The great events of Christian history, and above all the great events of the life of Jesus, were treated in many hymns. A number of Christmas hymns, such as "A Babe is born in Bethlehem," the translation from Latin, and the tender and beautiful "Be welcome again, God's angels bright," are among the favorites of his countrymen at Yuletide. His great Easter hymns include "From the grave remove dark crosses." Pentecost and the coming of the Holy Spirit brought forth some of his best efforts. He translated Luther's "O Holy Spirit, come, we pray," and wrote the flowery "The sun now shines in all its splendor." Quite naturally the church was the subject of several hymns, best known of which is "Built on the Rock the Church doth stand." "Fair beyond telling" extols the worship service, and "This is the day which the Lord hath giv'n" is in praise of the day of worship. In line with his theological emphasis he naturally included baptismal and Communion hymns,

and some of his most intimate hymns are songs of the
sacraments, especially of Communion. One of these is
a translation of Noel's "If human kindness meets return." Grundtvig's rendering reads, in translation,
"Mindful of a constant friend." Other church functions
such as ordination, confirmation, church dedication all
were subjects for hymns.

Most of the songs are written in major keys, songs of
praise and joy, songs of the mighty works of God. But
the humble and penitent note is found in such lines as:

> Weeping, despairing,
> Judgment preparing,
> Fate of the sinner who wakes to repent.

His tender baptismal hymn, "Oh let Thy Spirit with us
tarry," has the verse:

> The angels sing when babes are sleeping;
> May still they sing when death draws near.
> Both cross and crown are in Thy keeping;
> Lead Thou us on, we have no fear.

His song to the church bell, "Hallowed church bell," is
also in a minor key, as is the soft "Sleep, my child, now
be quiet," written in a mental crisis, as profound and
intimate an expression of utter confidence in God as has
ever been written. The same childlike trust is in his interpretation of the exhortation in the Sermon on the
Mount not to be concerned about food and clothing.

> God's little child, what troubles thee?
> Children may to their Father flee;
> He will uphold them by His hand;

None can His might and grace withstand.
The Lord be praised.

Raiment and food and counsel tried
God for His children will provide;
They shall not starve, nor homeless roam,
Children may claim their Father's home.
The Lord be praised.

Clad are the flow'rs in raiment fair,
Fairest to see on deserts bare;
Neither they spin, nor weave, nor sew,
Glory like theirs no king can show.
The Lord be praised.

God's little child, do then fore'er
Cast on the Lord thy ev'ry care,
Trust in His love, His grace and might,
Then shall His peace Thy soul delight.
The Lord be praised.

Raiment and food, thy daily bread,
He will provide as He has said,
And when His sun for thee goes down
He will thy soul with glory crown.
The Lord be praised.

Translation by J. C. Aaberg

An Anglo-American reader might find an emphasis missing which is prominent in English-language hymnology. It is the note of exhortation to practical Christian living. Grundtvig did not think this to be a particular emphasis of the church. The exhortation and the inspiration for living is found in the common grace of God given to us in the creation. But it is doubtful whether there can be found a more forceful single admonition than the one he gives, inspired by Luke 9:62.

Hast to the plough thou put thy hand,
Let not thy spirit waver.
Heed not the world's allurements grand,
Nor pause for Sodom's favor.
But plow thy furrow, sow God's seed,
Though tares and thorns thy work impede;
For he who sows with weeping
Shall soon with joy be reaping.

But should at times thy courage fail,
For even strength may falter,
Let not the tempting world prevail
On thee thy course to alter.
He that would win must forward go;
Retreat can bring thee naught but woe;
When foes bid thee defiance,
On God be thy reliance.

Press onward then in Jesus' name,
Though thorns and rocks inclose thee;
Yea, forward, though with sword and flame
The foe should here oppose thee.
Most precious is the victor's prize,
And open is God's paradise,
Where God on Zion's mountain
Has opened wide life's fountain.

Translation by J. C. Aaberg

The majestic note is probably most prominent in the great hymn to the light which is a re-rendering of a medieval "Song of the day." It is a long hymn with a crescendo of power, but three verses of C. Doving's translation can give an impression of it.

O day full of grace, which we behold,
Now gently to view ascending;
Thou over the earth thy reign unfold,

Good cheer to all mortals lending,
That children of light in ev'ry clime
May prove that the night is ending!

How blest was that gracious midnight hour,
When God in our flesh was given;
Then flushed the dawn with light and pow'r,
That spread o'er the darkened heaven;
Then rose o'er the world that Sun divine
Which gloom from our hearts hath driven.

Yea, were ev'ry tree endowed with speech,
And ev'ry leaflet singing,
They never with praise His worth could reach,
Though earth with their praise were ringing.
Who fully could praise the Light of life,
Who light to our souls is bringing?

Grundtvig's language was revolutionary when he first used it in hymns. It is still revolutionary to one unaccustomed to it, but it has become accepted and appreciated in his native country. There is nothing stiff or stilted about it. He filled his verse with comely expressions and highly poetic imagery. He was not afraid of ornate language, and while he often erred in his taste, his good hymns are inspirational gems; the bad ones are forgotten except by literary critics. Many of the boldest expressions are toned down in translation, for they are often idioms whose finesse is untranslatable. These have been best rendered in S. D. Rodholm's translation of the great Pentecost song.

The sun now shines in all its splendor,
The light of life with mercy tender;
Now bright Whitsunday lilies grow

> And summer sparkles high and low;
> Sweet voices sing of harvest gold
> In Jesus' name, a thousand fold.
>
> The peaceful nightingales are filling
> The summer night with music thrilling,
> So all that to the Lord belong
> May sleep in peace and wake with song,
> May dream anew of Paradise
> And with God's praise at daylight rise.

His boldest imagery is found in the song of the expectation of the return of Christ, but the overwhelming power of his vision and imagination has not been retained in Aaberg's loyal and competent translation.

> Lift up thy head, O Christendom!
> Behold in heav'n thy blessed home,
> For which thy heart is yearning,
> There is thy Joy and soul's Delight,
> Who soon with pow'r and glory bright
> Will be for thee returning.

Doctrinally Grundtvig's hymns are much more precise and powerful than his prose writings. This is partly due to the fact that the polemics are missing, but it is also due to the discipline of the form and the genius of inspiration. Nowhere in the church can be found a stronger tribute to the power of the cross and a clearer statement of an acceptable doctrine of the atonement than in his hymn, "Hail Thee, Savior and Atoner." He speaks of the victory that was won, adding a supplication that the life-giving power from the cross may enter our lives, melt away the iceberg of indifference, and carry away the mountain of sin. Unfortunately, the commonly used translation misses the essential point and changes his atonement doctrine from one of victory through battle to one of victory through submission.

The greatest distinguishing mark of his hymns is perhaps his fundamental trust in the power of the Spirit. He has written more hymns about the Holy Spirit than about anything else and they are among his best. Besides those already mentioned there has been translated "Holy Spirit, come with light," and "Holy Spirit, still our sorrow." In doctrine the soundest of them all, "Kaerligheds og Sandheds Aand" ("Spirit of love and truth") has unfortunately not been rendered into our language. But we can get a glimpse of his ideas.

> Holy Spirit, still our sorrow,
> In our hearts Thy light reveal,
> Turn our darkness into morrow
> And the fount of life unseal;
> Give us comfort, strength and breath,
> Light in darkness, life in death.
>
> God's eternal might and glory
> Lie revealed before Thy sight,
> And salvation's wondrous story
> Thou alone canst bring to light
> When to us from heav'n above
> Thou descendest with God's love.
>
> Maker of the new creation,
> Prove in us what Thou canst do,
> Save us from the foe's temptation,
> Through God's Word our faith renew,
> Build Thy temple in our breast,
> Fill Thy house with peace and rest.
>
> *Translation by J. C. Aaberg*

But faith in the Spirit must not be isolated from faith in God.

> We are in our Father's hand,
> Wisely led at His command,
> By His grace and to His pleasure
> We His keeping gladly treasure
> In the name of Christ, our Lord.

Translation by P. C. Paulsen

Man's nobility lies in the fact that he is created in the image of God. The distinguishing mark of this nobility is, in Grundtvig's mind, the human word, and he sings in tribute to this in one of his songs (which has been corrupted in the only available translation). In paraphrase his tribute goes thus: "My soul, of all things on earth thou hast been given the best wings in thy thoughts and in thy words. But thou art most free to breathe when thou drawest thy breath in song so that it resounds beneath the skies." This thought is repeated in the hymn "Fair beyond telling" in which he states that our greatest moment on earth comes when we gather in praise of the Lord and are "lifted on wings of the word far beyond the stars." To this "lifting" of the soul he has mightily contributed.

Grundtvig sang in praise of God and His mighty works, and his one purpose with his song was expressed in his rendering of the last verse of Luther's "Mighty Fortress." He sings about God's Word, by which he meant the living Word of God.

God's Word is our great heritage,
And shall be ours forever;
To spread its light from age to age
Shall be our chief endeavor;
Through life it guides our way,
In death it is our stay;
Lord, grant, while worlds endure,
We keep its teachings pure,
Throughout all generations.

Translation by O. G. Belsheim

9

Last Years

Grundtvig's years of parliamentary activity were also years of more strictly private concern. He was approaching the "days of our years" and the thought of old age and death depressed him. Death was always a dreaded reality for him, theologically as well as personally, and he fought against the dread as he encountered its power in his aging body. A poem from 1847, "Skies now are graying and leaves are falling," bears witness to the struggle, but it is also a testimony to the resurrective power of the Christian faith and hope.

> Wintertime comes, but although we fear it
> Springtime through faith is reborn.
> Cradled and nourished, it cheers our spirit;
> New Year is daytime at morn.

At an age when most men are compelled to recognize the eventide he still had a "day" full of activity before him. He even experienced a new morn of personal happiness, but it came after a night of sorrow.

Fru Lise, his faithful wife of thirty-three years, became ill and died early in 1851. She and Grundtvig had been loyal and devoted to one another, but their spirits had been quite different. She could not follow him on his flights of inspiration and had contented herself with the cares of the household and her "old-fashioned" piety. As a result she could not comfort him in moments of distress, and when gloom settled upon her in her declining years, he could not help her. This fact was a burden to both which they carried in solitude. For a while, in England, he had been attracted to another woman in whom he found a sympathetic friend and kindred spirit, but he had disciplined himself and shut her out. During the last years before Fru Lise's death he had found inspiration in the friendship of Fru Marie Toft, a leader of conventicles in southern Sjaelland, gradually moving her to share his point of view in regard to church life. In the lonely days of 1851 their mutual sympathy blossomed into love, and in the fall they were married. He was then sixty-eight years old.

This second marriage was radiantly happy. Fru Marie owned a country estate at which they spent a good deal of their time. They shared ideas and insights, and despite an age difference of thirty years they found complete satisfaction in one another's company. There was, of course, some criticism and grumbling among his friends, but this subsided. His opponents had always thought him odd! May 15, 1854, they were blessed with a son, Frederik Lange Grundtvig, who became his father's consolation and comfort, for Fru

Marie lived only two weeks after the birth of her son. Grundtvig was prostrate with grief, but learned to channel his emotions into a more active fellowship with his friends and his congregation. In 1858, at seventy-five, he married for a third time. His wife was a friend of Fru Marie who sought Grundtvig's help when her first husband died in 1857. Her name was Asta Reedtz, like Fru Marie of noble birth. Grundtvig and she lived together harmoniously for the remainder of his life, and the spiritual strength of their home life was a joy to their friends. They had a daughter, Asta Marie Elisabeth, named for each of Grundtvig's three wives.

As the dynamic decades of development and creative activity faded into the reflectiveness of old age, Grundtvig gave more thought to revision, consolidation, and clarification of his views. In some respects the consolidation was unfortunate insofar as it led to a dogmatization which formalized and thereby altered an original idea. The most important instance of this took place in regard to the origin of the Apostles' Creed. In other instances the reflection clarified issues in a fruitful way. One of the most beneficial clarifications took place in regard to his view of man.

It was inevitable that Grundtvig's wide scope of ideas should cause confusion, and in 1847 he was accused of compounding an undesirable mixture of ideas concerning Danish and Christian living. He immediately responded with an article in *Danish Church Tidings* called "Folk Life and Christianity." He vigorously denied that he had confused the two elements, showing what he considered to be the right relationship. In a famous statement he began by saying that Christianity is a "heavenly guest in an earthly home." It enters the life of a people by the power of a living word, and disclaims by its very nature all use of compulsion to maintain itself. On the other hand it does not suppress the life of the people. It fosters such a life, because it needs it and uses it. The sixteenth-century reformers in reviving the gospel in their native tongue, recognized this. Man does not live in heaven or in the air. He always has a human home, which must be a living home for Christianity to be alive. Grundtvig compared the life of a people to the situation of the widow's son at Nain whom Jesus raised from the dead. It was hopeless to proclaim the kingdom of God to him before he was physically brought to life. In the same manner a people must be alive and alert before it can appreciate a living gospel. He refuted the opposing idea that true patriotism requires a Christian awakening. "If the Word of God is to find a well-prepared people, then a 'folk word' in the native tongue must first have turned the hearts of the children to the parents and the hearts of the parents to the children, that they might realize that death in all its forms is their enemy and that of all mankind; that He [Christ] alone is the rightful Saviour who can and will give us life eternal." Thus, he maintained, he did not confuse Danish and Christian living but kept them apart, because "people must be alive before it is of any use to speak to them about temporal or eternal life."

The article caused a sharp rebuttal by an old German friend, Dr. Rudelbach, who accused Grundtvig of introducing nationalistic elements into Christianity. Grundtvig replied, again in the *Danish Church Tidings*. He denied that he had claimed that folk life was to replace Christianity or that it qualified a people for Christianity. He claimed that as the life of the people of Israel had been necessary for the coming of Christ, so the life of a people is necessary for Christianity today. An argument for this he found in the blossoming of the faith in the sixteenth century when Christianity became an integral part of the life of the people. His main contention was, however, that the living word of God's revelation had to become a human word, and no human word exists outside the language of a people. Christ became a man through birth by a woman. Therefore we must all be born in a people or we will "have no living concept of the relation between God and man, time and eternity, life and death in a spiritual way, and between the kingdom of God and the kingdom of this world." A Christian life is a life in Christ, but Christ lived among men. "If 'folk life' was of no importance in the household of God's grace, 'humanity' was in the same situation and the incarnation of the Son of God was superfluous."

There are two elements in this argument of Grundtvig's. The one grew out of the polemical situation in which, as usual, he found himself. The other is the more basic argument about the nature of man. The first was caused by his reaction to the sanctimonious attitude which identified Christianity with outward appearances and which regarded human nature as an evil which must be combatted, or at least sanctified, in order to be acceptable. The polemical argument led to the more basic contention, however, that humanity is a necessary requirement for Christianity.

Grundtvig's spirited emphasis on the separation of folk life and Christianity, caused by the accusation that he confused the two, was a reaction to a Pietistic and quietistic depreciation of human activity and a further development of the ideas expressed in his introduction to *Nordic Mythology*. There he had maintained the significance of folk life for Christianity, and pleaded for a recognition of the value of the created life of man. He had argued against the (false) synthesis of Christianity and culture which had existed since the Renaissance, but also emancipated his concept of humanity from a (false) subjugation to an orthodox theology which did not recognize the inherent worth of man. Subsequently he had so vigorously taken a part in the political and civic life of his own people, particularly in folk education, that he seemed to have broken loose from traditional concepts of the influence of the church and Christianity. He had argued so much against the traditional controls of the church that his motivations appeared to be purely secular.

In his battle against the entrenched interests of the church, Grundtvig's emphases and arguments had become one-sided. Other emphases that balance them are primarily in his unpolemical poetry, which is difficult to translate. A few prose expressions from this period, however, state that humanity and Christianity are not only two separate concepts but are intimately related and in some respects identical. The motivations for dynamic human living are also Christian, or, to turn it around, Christianity provides a dynamic for human living. The expressions for this point of view are not numerous, for Grundtvig's polemics were turned more against formalism than against secularism. Their scarcity has led some interpreters to maintain that Grundtvig had created an unbridgeable gap between Christian and human living.

In 1854 Grundtvig wrote a letter to a friend, Peter Larsen, in which he answered Larsen's questions in regard to the folk high school. In this connection he wrote: "I consider the cause of education from the so-called 'purely human side,' in my style called the 'Christian side.' " Thus he equated human activity with Christian activity. In 1855 he wrote a series of articles, "The Danish Cause," in a weekly called *Dannebrog* in which he stated: "My view of Christianity is first and last the human view which merges with the divine just as surely as, according to the thinking of our Lord, man is not made for the sake of Christianity but Christianity for the sake of man." Furthermore, Christianity "is not

139

only the fruit of God's love for man, given in the fulness of time, but the action of God's love for man through history." In an article of 1857 incorporated in *Elemental Christian Teachings*, as a counterargument to Kierkegaard's claim that there had been no Christian life on this earth, he wrote: "We have gained the right and living view of the Christian life as a spiritual human life, just as real and much more human than our physical life . . ." Also from *Teachings* comes this assertion. "When we now by the help of the Lord see the light in the Lord's light, . . . then all our secular, human living will gain a spiritual and renewed form, whose Christianity cannot strictly be proved but which nevertheless is certain. For this noble and renewed form of life will be found only where the Christian confession, preaching, and praise is vitally present." About the same time he wrote the following verse:

> Let us go
> Our task to do,
> Relying on God's blessing.
> Through grace we then shall be alive;
> His will to do with joy we strive,
> His power and peace possessing.

It is hard for the English reader to grasp the Danish (and German) distinction between "human" and "Christian." The Danish word "Menneske" (German: "Mensch") is not covered by the English term "human being," while "menneskelig" (German: "menschlich") is still farther from the adjective "human." While both languages make a distinction between man and animal, the distinction between "human" and "Christian" looms up much more forcefully in the Danish language. Behind words lie concepts, and behind concepts lie attitudes and practices.

Grundtvig's fourth and final major effort at a systematic presentation of his ideas in regard to Christianity and the church was a series of articles written 1855-62 and printed in a periodical called *Churchly Gatherer*. They were published in book form in 1868 and again in 1883 under the title *Den Kristelige Børnelaerdom*. This is literally translated *The Christian Childhood Doctrines* but a better translation would be *Elemental Christian Teachings*. [1] The articles did not follow an outline or cover all the subjects usually contained in "systematics." Nevertheless it is the most complete statement of Grundtvig's doctrines. The spirited polemical tone which characterized and to some extent marred Grundtvig's earlier writings is much softened in these articles as could be expected from a seventy-year-old man. A more calm and deliberate presentation, it may lack some of the fire of the earlier arguments, but has gained in insight and reflection. The first articles especially demonstrate a heroic effort at expression in simple, short phrases, a determination that seems to fade later in the series. But the talkativeness of old age is so evident in the style throughout that his drive toward the

---

[1] The others were: *Concerning the Truth of Christianity* and *Concerning the True Christianity* (1826-27); *Shall the Lutheran Reformation Really Be Continued* (1830-31); and *Ecclesiastical Information, Especially for Lutheran Christians* (1840).

goal suffers. It might be said that the *Teachings* contain more wisdom and less force. If Grundtvig ever wrote "dogmatics," this is it.

Oddly enough he never wrote a formal history of the church. He was always intensely interested in the subject, and had often discussed the idea that such a history could be undertaken in connection with the letters to the churches in the Book of Revelation. When he finally carried out this idea, it was in poetic form. In 1854 he published a long poem, about 850 seven-verse stanzas, in successive issues of *Danish Church Tidings*. Called *The Seven Stars of Christendom*, it dealt with the idea that the seven letters of Revelation were visionary utterances concerning the churches that were to develop in the course of time. Grundtvig identified these churches with the language groups that had developed in the history of the church, the three classical communities, Hebrew, Greek, and Latin, and the three modern communities, English, German, and Nordic. The seventh church was an unidentified church yet to come. Within these categories he then described church history, but the general hypothesis of the poem is obviously mistaken. The Book of Revelation was not intended for this type of prophecy, nor does the history of the church particularly help us to understand John's epistles.

The main merit of the poem lies in a realm other than the prophetic. Grundtvig saw plainly that we must "let every creature rise and bring peculiar honors to our King," identifying these "peculiar honors" with the religious expression of a people in its native language. "The peculiar character of the present survey of the history of the church," he wrote in the introduction, "is not that it is connected with the heavenly letters of Revelation. It is that the Christian life throughout is considered as a spiritual folk life which has been in living and reciprocal relationship to the characteristic development and language of all the main peoples in which the Christian life has been revealed as Christian confession, proclamation, and praise. This reciprocal relationship is the cause of the intricate pattern of their history as well as the key to the understanding of the Christian churches with all their confusion.

"It follows naturally that the Christian confession, proclamation, and praise, which is the only plain sign of life in the Christian people, can neither be purer, warmer, nor clearer than the language of the people which the gospel . . . in the course of time borrows as an expression of its life. Since history teaches us that the language of every people corresponds to its expansion and development, a living Christianity must always, at a given place and time, be identified with the folk life of a people, and it can only develop as the people and its language becomes Christian . . . Living Christianity does not have its own language but borrows the language of every people which it visits. This has not been understood well enough in the history of the church, which is the reason why this history has been unintelligible . . . This is what the Lord meant when he enjoined the apostles to make disciples out of all nations. Folk churches are in the right spirit of Christianity, just so they . . . never become state churches or instruments of spiritual compulsion . . . for the Lord Jesus Christ . . . is a sworn enemy of all confession without faith and especially of all compulsion to a certain confession of faith."

Grundtvig's work with the poem led to a further effort in church history. In 1861-63 he gave a series of lectures for a private group in his home. The resultant survey of the history of the church was published in 1871 under the title *A Mirror of the Church*. A lively and interesting account, the survey reflects the informal character of the lectures. It presents what Grundtvig considered to be the nature of church history, as he stated it in the first lecture, "a sure account about the Christian revelation, the Christian faith and fellowship, their witness and fate in the world from the ascension of our Lord to this day."

During the last two decades of his life Grundtvig had the satisfaction of seeing the movements which he had stimulated grow to become formidable forces in Denmark. Though the Folk School had not been established by government effort at Sorø, it had been given practical form by Christen Kold. The combination of Kold's and Grundtvig's example and inspiration had led to the establishment of an increasing number of schools throughout the country. In the parishes of the church Grundtvig's emphasis upon the living congregation and its sacraments, and upon a cultural awakening, had given new life to both church and community. The center of influence for this growth was the congregation at Vartov where the university students especially became inspired by Grundtvig's sermons, his new songs, and the congregational fellowship.

As Grundtvig was the patriarch of the movement, the greatest tribute paid to his influence was the growth of the life he had worked to foster ever since the time of the Napoleonic wars. But he also received official recognition in 1861 on the fiftieth anniversary of his ordination. Fifty ministers and high church officials were present at the service. At a private celebration in the afternoon the Secretary for Church Affairs announced to Grundtvig that the king had honored him by giving him the rank of bishop. A public meeting in the evening with thousands of participants honored him with songs and speeches and a gift of three thousand dollars for a new edition of his hymns.

Out of this meeting and a series of Scandinavian church meetings, held biennially but discontinued when the war crisis caused an annulment of the Copenhagen meeting in 1863, grew the idea of a "Meeting of Friends." The first one was held in September, 1863, in the days following Grundtvig's eightieth birthday, attracting seven hundred participants. The war with Prussia prevented a meeting in 1864, but they were resumed in 1865, becoming annual events. Having given the introductory lecture at all the meetings, the last time he spoke was at the meeting in 1871. His death came a few days before the scheduled meeting in 1872 which then took the character of a gigantic memorial service.

Though Grundtvig's lectures at these meetings were given from notes, the talks were recorded and are available. They were concerned with review and consolidation of his ideas, important through so many stormy and fruitful decades, which were to become a treasured heritage of the Christian church and the Danish people. He talked about the tension of the war but the most burning issue was the growing demand for freedom within the church and the legislation to implement it. Of particular significance was the meeting in 1866 when Christen Kold was invited to present his philosophy of folk education.

Active to the very last, Grundtvig died September 3, 1872, failing by a few days to reach his eighty-ninth birthday. A nation mourned his death as did many friends in other lands. The greatest tribute he was given at his death was perhaps by the Norwegian poet, Bjørnstjerne Bjørnson, who called him a prophet and predicted that his vision would not be exhausted in the nations of the North for a thousand years.

Education

Grundtvig's most widespread fame has come from his contribution in the field of education. He is often called the "founder" or the "father" of the Danish Folk Schools, and most of the biographies of him in English have dealt mainly with this feature of his work. The tribute to Grundtvig is well deserved, although he must share laurels with Christen Kold. But Grundtvig's educational ideas are often presented apart from his religious ideas and conception of man, also essentially religious. This leaves a one-sided or distorted picture of his genius, for his educational views grew out of his thinking in the other two fields and cannot be understood without them.

From his youth Grundtvig was interested in and familiar with education. His first position was that of a private tutor, from which he moved to that of teacher in a school for boys in Copenhagen. As a parish minister he supervised common school education, giving much effort and attention to the confirmation classes. Years later his pupils testified to the vivacity of his instruction.

He was never in charge of a Folk School, nor did he regularly teach in one, but the lecture series he gave during the winter of 1838-39 proved him to be a versatile and interesting educational lecturer. He was therefore no novice at teaching. Although the ministry and his literary and historical efforts absorbed most of his time during his mature years, he always retained his interest and contacts in education.

During the latter part of the eighteenth century there had been a rising interest in education in Denmark. It had been stimulated by the ideas of Rousseau and by the practical program of Pestalozzi. School reforms were carried out on the manors of the young radicals in the government; teacher-training schools were established; city schools were built; and finally, in 1814, a new national decree established schools in all communities of the country. The purpose, as expressed in a Copenhagen ordinance, was that the children "by the correct development of their mental and physical faculties should become good, enlightened, and industrious human beings and citizens, and to that end early be kept from idleness and vice, become accustomed to morality and order, and be subjected to such knowledge and skill as is necessary for a man and a citizen." The utilitarian character of the reform is easily detected, and there is a line of influence from this to Grundtvig's educational programs.

Grundtvig believed that education was an important factor in the national recovery which he promoted after the Napoleonic wars. His intense work with the translation of medieval histories was intended as a part of the moral uplift of the people. Like his other humanistic interests he shelved his interest in education during the years in which he was engaged in ecclesiastical controversy, reviving it only when he journeyed to England in 1829. Prior to this journey he had been interested in certain English institutions, notably the University of London. He never visited the University of London, however, and in 1839 a remark of his showed that his interest in it had waned. He did visit the Central School in Southwark and was impressed with its monitorial system of instruction where questions and answers by the students of one another to a large extent replaced the use of textbooks. The novelty, replacing the deadening memorization and examinations of his own youth, attracted him.

It was the old universities at Oxford and Cambridge which inspired him the most. He never ceased his praise of them, although he was critical of certain features. What fascinated him more than anything else was the free and unhampered inquiry and method of study and the deep fellowship which developed among the men who taught and the men who learned. The taste of English college life he obtained while living for a time at Trinity College in Cambridge reminded him of the valuable years he had spent at Valkendorff College at Copenhagen as a graduate student. He was also much impressed with the English emphasis on freedom. The contrast of the free English method to the compulsion of examinations, which he had experienced in Copenhagen, could hardly be greater. In many ways the British college became the prototype of the Danish Folk School, but with some differences, especially in entrance requirements.

Upon his return from the third trip to England, when Grundtvig wrote *Nordic Mythology*, launching his new views of man, he proclaimed the idea for a civic academy, a higher institution for folk culture and practical efficiency. The school was thus to have a dual purpose. One was to create an institution independent of the academic tradition of the university, based on real learning and having a living connection with science and research to prevent it from becoming inimical to them and static or stereotyped. It should maintain an independent position in order not to become a "tail or an empty shadow." An institute for learning, based on and founded in the knowledge, common sense, and spirit of the people, where the real requirements of life and the demands of the moment assert their rights, can and will become a real spiritual force.

The second purpose was to promote practical efficiency. It was Grundtvig's long-time complaint that the university occupied itself with theoretical matters of little value to the common life. He therefore proposed that all servants and officials of the state, who need "life perspective and practical efficiency," and all who wished to belong to the cultivated classes, should have an opportunity for purposeful development and mutual acquaintance. Then the literature of the people would find the practical application and encouragement it deserved, "without which it will soon become a dying display flower." Science, while applying its benefits to the people, would in turn be stimulated and enriched by its contacts with everyday life.

Grundtvig wrote these lines under the stimulus of the ideas discussed in the introduction to *Nordic Mythology*. Because he believed in freedom, he was willing to co-operate with the "naturalists" in joint efforts within the great field of human affairs, particularly in education. Of even greater significance than this field of common endeavor was the fact that he had seen the inherent value in general human endeavor, again particularly in edu-cation. Education does not have to be doctrinal in a narrow sense. It can promote its goals without the specific interpretations and requirements laid down by the church. In fact, true education must operate in freedom and not in bondage to theologians.

This emphasis on general and civic purposes and his demand for freedom of thought must not be construed to mean that he was departing from the Christian goal of life. As a bold advocate of freedom for all points of view, he was definitely opposed to a narrow, doctrinal circumscription of the goal of common living as well as of education. A Christian could live his faith and pro-claim it without imposing it upon others. Faith is to be confessed, and confession can never be gained through compulsion. But without the Christian faith all education and all explanation of life falls short. This was expressed in 1839 in one of Grundtvig's most important educational treatises, *Concerning the Scientific Union of the North.* One's relationship to heaven and eternity, he said, is the highest relationship of life, and "any explanation of life in which this relationship is unappreciated or unclear is necessarily basically wrong."

Because Grundtvig was so excited about his new ideas and the new emancipation he had gained that he overemphasized them, he gave the impression for the moment that he had departed from the Christian interpretation of life, relegating religion to a narrow concern for man's eternal destiny. A dynamic character who gave himself heart and soul to a project in which he was interested, he pursued his goals with complete disregard for supplementary points of view. This drive was his strength as well as his weakness. He lived in a world of stereotyped prejudices and strong animosities to his program, not immediately obvious to us. It would be a mistake to judge his educational program as purely secular, especially in view of the things he wrote about it later.

For ten to fifteen years after his return from England Grundtvig pressed hard for a school for the people, writing a number of treatises and letters on the subject. The first one, written in 1834, was "The Latin Composition," a sharp attack upon the stereotyped classical tradition of the university and its reliance upon examinations. The election of the advisory "Estates" in 1835, which he with his monarchistic loyalties had not favored, convinced him that the voice of the people must be liberated. He very soon became an enthusiast of the "Estates." In 1836 he wrote a treatise recommending to the assembly the establishment of a "high school" at Sorø. The title of the treatise was *The Danish Four-Leaf Clover*, the four leaves described as the king, the people, the country, and the mother tongue. In 1838 he contributed another booklet on the same subject: *The School for Life and the Academy at Sorø*. He was then in a jubilant mood because he had finally been released from the censorship imposed upon him after his attack on Clausen in 1825. He introduced the discussion with one of his most beautiful songs, a tribute to the mother tongue, "Mother's name is a heavenly sound." He now spoke not only of a school for citizenship but of a school for life as distinguished from a school for death, as he labeled the university.

Probably the most convincing of the series of articles, or booklets, was the one published in 1839, *Concerning the Scientific Union of the North*. It was an eloquent plea for a closer co-operation between the Scandinavian countries, and for the foundation of a common university for the people. Patterned to a large extent on Cambridge, this center of learning should be a living and life-giving institution. His free Nordic university was never established, nor was the folk high school at Sorø, but the ideas he expressed have stimulated educators to this day. King Christian VIII showed great interest in the project for the school at Sorø, but died before the plans could be carried out. Grundtvig had appealed to him in another treatise, published in 1840 and called *Prayer and Concept of a Danish High School at Sorø.* Taken up with politics shortly after this, he gave one of his most enthusiastic statements of the Folk School in an address at Skamling July 4, 1844, to a large assembly interested in political freedom and national security. The address was one of the direct causes of the foundation of the first Folk School at Rødding in North Slesvig.

Inspired by these writings Christen Kold in 1850 started his first Folk School at Ryslinge. Kold was a quiet, frugal, and persistent schoolteacher, as bent upon the religious and national welfare of his people as Grundtvig. On trying to introduce Grundtvig's ideas in the elementary school, he had run into opposition and emigrated to Turkey. Upon his return he was engaged as a private tutor in the household of Vilhelm Birkedal, a follower of Grundtvig and pastor at Ryslinge. Shortly afterward the school was started under primitive circumstances.

It was this school and Kold's administration of it that set the pattern followed by the great majority of the Folk Schools established during the rest of the century. A private school, stressing the inspirational rather than the practical, under the direction of one man, it was quite different from the pattern Grundtvig advocated. As Kold had a tenacious faith, inspired by Grundtvig, in the power of the living or spoken word, he used the lecture method almost exclusively. Kold emphasized history, but also gave his school a definitely religious character. Though he did not preach, he conducted daily devotions, and made Bible history an important part of the curriculum. The one respect in which Kold changed his early pattern to conform to Grundtvig's suggestions was in regard to the age of the students. He started with sixteen-year-olds but soon gave in to Grundtvig's advice, shifting to those eighteen or older.[1]

After Grundtvig's political enthusiasm waned he returned to religious and educational writings. This was when he produced his *Elemental Christian Teachings*. In these reflective essays he again stated his case for education, this time more in consideration of the church and religious requirements. The presentation is not com-

[1] F. Skrubbeltrang, in his book, *The Danish Folk High Schools* (Copenhagen, 1947), calls Kold "a kind of Jutland Hans Andersen, cheerful and ardent, yet possessing a subtle humor and self-irony." He continues: "In the day-to-day life of the High School his students must have gained a still more vivid impression from the personal form in which he clothed his thoughts, and the way he always kept his feet on the ground even when speaking of higher things . . . Kold hardly read anything, and there was very little plan or method in his teaching. But, like no other Danish High School leader, he knew how to turn the small observations of daily life to account in his lectures on historical, religious, or moral subjects. He drew his figures of speech and his examples from everyday life, and so was always understood even when most profound. He was in contact with his audience; his eyes seemed to pierce through them, and in simple speech he went straight to the heart of his subject. Hating all learning by rote, he yet spoke many a time so his hearers remembered his lectures for the rest of their lives, so sure and so vivid were they in every detail, and so captivating the impression of his personality." pp. 15-16.

pletely in accord with the more fiery and one-sided statements of the 1830's, and there are those who maintain that these views should be discounted and discarded in favor of the earlier writings. Others maintain that the *Teachings* convey the real Grundtvig. It is difficult to grasp the whole Grundtvig, warrior as he was, in a single and consistent presentation.

Grundtvig distinguished among three kinds of education; we might call them scientific, theological, and general. He gave them various names, depending upon his interest and emphasis at the time. The last category in particular was named in different ways. At first it was called a civic school, then a folk school or a school for the people, then a school for life. In *The School for Life and the Academy at Sorø*, 1838, he wrote: "Inasmuch as the life of man in all its diversities can be classified in three main ways; the religious, the civic, and the scientific, we can also imagine three types of schools for life; the church school, the citizen school, and the learned school." Of the three he gave by far the greater attention to the school for the people.

The prevailing university training and university preparation was long a target for some of Grundtvig's severest criticism and heaviest satire. He deplored its emphasis upon Latin, the dulness of its instruction, and the heavy burden of examinations. It was, in his opinion, the poorest possible training school for men of practical endeavor, including the officials of the government. In calling it a school for death, he did not mean that he was opposed to an institute for science and research. On the contrary, he wished to liberate this institution from the obligation of training ministers, teachers, doctors, civil service functionaries, and even lawyers. For such men he advocated training in what he called seminaries or nurseries (in the horticultural sense of the word). Science needed an institution of its own. "For if science was only a mass of knowledge and an inter-related system of teachings from Greece and Rome which should be perpetuated unchanged from generation to generation, preferably by the pen, then we can easily see that all universities have long been super-fluous." But science means more than this. "Mathematics and science can be exhausted neither by the training of officials nor by the general education of the people. They deserve the attention of all major peoples for their great practical usefulness and for the insight they give us, or promise to give us, into the secrets of nature." He added a plea for historical research, not limited to practical instruction. He considered it even more necessary, because "all human knowledge is basically historical, and knowledge about the past is the only means of understanding the present and planning for the future . . . We must therefore do our part that the individual who has the desire and the ability can accumulate thorough knowledge and acquire deeper insight into all phases of human knowledge and science."

His interest in the field of general education was expressed as early as 1804 in an item in his diary. Later, his demand for a civic school or a training school for the leaders and officials of the people developed into a demand for the education of all adults. He called his dream school a "high school," explaining that it was a school which should give "higher" insights to mature people, in contrast to the elementary school. He soon called the "high school" a school for life, not "a house of book-learning in which people were instructed and trained in the rules by which life can be adjusted and improved," but a school which was "alert to the demands of life and which takes life as it really is." "All true science is enlightenment and explanation of the life of man." One of his educational songs, which has been sung by four generations of Folk School people, goes: "Enlightenment shall be our goal, even about the blade of grass, but first and last, with the voice of the people, enlightenment about life."

Grundtvig was interested in promoting the educational welfare of the underprivileged, as well as in training better those who could afford academic training. When he spoke about folk education, or education of the people, he meant primarily an education that would promote, encourage, and develop the inherent, historic, and cultural values of the people. In each people there are peculiarities of attitude and understanding which reflect their basic values. As far as these are good, they should be promoted. They will to a certain extent be good, because the individual not only is created in the image of God, but is born into a natural fellowship of interest and concern. Therefore the people's values should be promoted and developed that they might grow in such a way as to fulfil their destiny. This was no political nationalism leading to aggrandizement or super-ciliousness. Grundtvig claimed the same inherent rights for other people that he claimed for his own, but asserted the absolute superiority of his people's culture for themselves.

Cultural values are developed through history and expressed through literature. "To understand a people that we may speak from its heart, the people must possess our heart and lend us its tongue." Grundtvig wanted the curriculum of his school to be comprehensive. "If we raise the question, . . . what is to be conveyed to the young people at a folk high school, it does not help much to say: by no means everything we know but all that profitably and joyfully can be held in common." But he is as sure that the curriculum should include history and literature. "Both by the nature of the case and according to the characteristics of our people we can predict that it will be history and poetry, and particularly our national history and our ballads, which will be prominent at our folk high school." In history he included current history, and civics, "the present condition of the country, including its constitution, laws, and institutions as well as its commerce and trade, resources and industry."

The Folk School ideas were first launched in connection with the comprehensive treatment of Nordic my-

thology, and the ancient myths were used in the instruction in the schools. It may seem strange at first glance
that pagan stories of imaginary gods and their activities
should play a prominent part in a nineteenth-century
educational program. But Grundtvig did not regard
the myths as distorted history or superstitious nature
explanations, as was the custom of his time, but as expressions of an attitude of life. They are images which
reflect the concepts of good and evil, life and death,
held by a people living at the height of an ancient and
fine culture. The images were the words of the ancients,
and a word is more than a sound or a communication.
It is always a living thing, a manifestation of the spirit,
and therefore creative. Even the human word, which is
the evidence of man's creation by God, has power and
expresses the realities of the spirit. In their spoken
imagery the ancient Nordics expressed their spirit. But,
we might ask, of what concern is this to us except for
the fact that we can find an interesting and entertaining
study in the old tales? And here Grundtvig answers:
The spirit which is the power in the word and culture of
the ancient people is the spirit of man, given to him by
God in his creation. It is of significance for us that this
spirit of our ancestors, expressed at a time when they had
established a great culture, speaks about the real issues
of life.

Grundtvig found that the myths of Greece as well
as the myths of the North had a valuable message for
modern man. He did not consider them primarily as

evidence of a life that had been lived. They were prophetic, turned toward the future. Therefore they have something to say to us about the conditions of our life. They fall short, because they have only the inborn spirit of man, given to him by God, to rely on. Therefore we must maintain a Christian "Anskuelse," or attitude toward life, founded on the revelation in Christ. If the two are at odds, we quite naturally rely on the Christian view. But Grundtvig found to his delight that the Christian and the Nordic point of view often corresponded in their evaluation of life and of the forces at play, perhaps because of a penetration of Christian views into the far North before Christianity was officially taught or accepted. But this is not the whole explanation. The fact was that the ancient Nordics had a sound and significant concept of the conditions of life from which we can profit. Using our imagination, then, we can use the stories as lesson material for our edification, judging them and correcting them by the Christian orientation. The myths are the literature of the ancient people which has a living and creative significance even today. "Why do we need the myths when we have the Christian 'Anskuelse'? Why clouds and stars when we have the sun and the moon?" The imagery of the church, he answered, given through the revelation in Christ, casts light upon the things of eternal life. "We have, however, also a secular life which needs the light of the spirit. Our soul, as well as our body, has secular needs, and it is the intention of the Creator that we shall

161

work for these by the light and power which he has given us. For well does he let manna fall to his people when they are in the desert but not in a fertile land where they can sow and harvest."

The significance Grundtvig placed upon the living word made it inevitable that this expression should assume an important place in his educational plans. It is, of course, an excellent expression for the oral communication of ideas which loomed so large in the program, but the term means much more than an ability to speak freely and interestingly. It should be related to Grundtvig's whole realm of ideas, especially his religious concepts. Basically it is an expression of God's creative and redemptive power. God acts in his word, and when he acts his word is a living word. He said: Let there be light, and there was light. God let his Word become flesh to dwell among us as a Living Word which is Christ. He still dwells among us in a living word which is Christ—in the church or in the gospel. He speaks a living and creative word to us in baptism and Communion, and our response in the confession is the word which has become activated in us. From this understanding of the living word of God we proceed to the spoken or living word of man, the sign or evidence of his creation by God. Man's word is also creative. It creates spiritual realities which can become alive only through the word. Through the word God speaks to man; through the word man speaks to God; through the word man speaks to man.

The Folk Schools of Denmark have emphasized the lecture method of teaching so much that the school and the method have become almost identical. Grundtvig himself provided the emphasis. In *Prayer and Concept* he discussed the teaching methods of the proposed school: "It is easy to say that it is first and last the mouth which will be used, partly because it is the only living instrument of the spirit on earth and partly because we can never share more with the people than that which can be contained in the mouth and can go from mouth to mouth. It is also easy to say that only as talk becomes conversation,[2] partly between the old and the young and partly between the young people themselves, will the instruction succeed. But whether the parties will be willing to co-operate and bear with one another until their mouth gets going, we shall have to wait and see." He was insistent that there should be a free exchange of ideas between the students. "Whether I go back thirty years to Valkendorff College or seven years to Trinity College, I have a living conception of the marvelous banquet which could be offered daily at a free Nordic high school." He claimed that "my guest appearance at Trinity College . . . showed me what a fellowship could be when it was characterized by a true scientific spirit, with eyes opened for all of life, its great laws of nature, its forces and its goals."

As a final characteristic of the Folk School, fostered in the mind of Grundtvig, we must mention freedom.

[2] With a play on the words "Tale" and "Samtale."

This element has a negative as well as a positive side. Grundtvig reacted strongly against the compulsory character of the education to which he had been subjected in secondary school and in the university. He found that the main result of compulsion had been to kill interest in subjects and in life in general. Compulsion leads to spiritual death. The positive side of the argument for freedom had been inherent in his long battle for human rights, but it had attained full status during his journeys to England. From the early thirties he was a crusader for freedom in the church and politics, especially freedom of expression. He never forgot that he had been shackled by censorship for a dozen years during the most productive period of his literary career. Quite naturally he carried his concept of freedom into his educational proposals.

Freedom meant more than anything else, liberty from examinations. A student should have the privilege of accepting and assimilating whatever was of value to him. Freedom from examinations did not mean, of course, freedom from work. Grundtvig took for granted that the impact of the spirit would be enough of a motive for work. But freedom also meant free admission. There should be no entrance requirement other than eagerness and desire for learning. It is in this respect that the Danish Folk School differs most widely from the English college which in so many ways is its prototype. It became the actual practice to welcome into the schools any person who wanted sincerely to come, no matter what his previous training was, or what his status. For the instructor, Grundtvig advocated freedom of expression, unhampered by any censorship.

The question, facetiously asked, whether the "four freedoms" include freedom *from* religion, might seriously be applied to the program of the Folk Schools. At any rate, the question of whether the idea and spirit of these schools include a direct religious influence has become a controversial issue during the last few years. A majority of the Folk School administrators maintain that such an influence is inherent in the whole program. They insist on the religious character of the school, maintained, of course, in an atmosphere of freedom. Others hold that the emphasis on freedom should be made paramount, even to the extent of presenting the religious point of view impartially and without pressure, leaving the student free to choose. Both parties in the dispute refer to Grundtvig and both parties quote him to prove their point. On the surface Grundtvig apparently favored the neutral position. He emphasized the national and humanistic side of his educational program to an extent suggesting he was not in favor of permeation of the school by a religious point of view. But Grundtvig was always polemically inclined and was not only fighting for something, he was also fighting against something. In the eighteen thirties and forties he was fighting for a free program of national education and against an ancient, rigid, and doctrinaire system. He was therefore likely to become one-sided in his emphasis and biased in his whole discussion. Probably he would have been equally vociferous in support of the thesis that instruction in the Folk Schools should have a Christian basis, if such a proposition had been attacked. But he was certainly not in favor of any particular doctrinal commitment for the director and faculty of the schools. Grundtvig wrote for a particular situation in a particular century. The special emphases this provoked must not be absolutized, nor must the universal truths of his program be obscured by the special features. They cannot be dismissed because they were clothed according to the need of the time.

This brings us to the third type of school which Grundtvig advocated, the church school. His ideas concerning it were set forth in *Elemental Christian Teachings*. Again one of his first concerns is freedom. The church must have teachers, and to get them it must train them. If the state schools do not provide adequate instruction for them, the church must create its own seminaries. The teachers of the church must be bound by the gospel and be responsible to the Holy Spirit, but not bound by doctrinal precepts. Consequently they must have freedom of speech and freedom of interpretation. How this would work in practice Grundtvig had no opportunity to find out. His discussion of the needs and requirements of a seminary are theoretical only, inasmuch as there was no real movement in Denmark to emancipate the training of ministers from the university.

If anything, the Danish university has proved to be a strong protector of academic freedom.

But freedom was not his only demand. He was strongly convinced that a seminary must guard against academic narrowness. "The goal must be to include all treasures of knowledge and wisdom." Through the ages the Christian church has inspired the progressive knowledge which has given society its common concepts of life. It must continue to "light up the horizon to the utmost limits of the human spirit and human living." Secular knowledge is important for the church. Moses benefited by the fact that he had been given the wisdom of Egypt. Scripture can only be understood and rightly interpreted by the aid of human knowledge and the exercise of human ability. Contrariwise, Scripture must not dominate science and knowledge, for then the free relationship is perverted. The church will then be tempted to operate without knowledge and even denounce it as dangerous to the faith. "The faith in Christ could not be true faith concerning the basic relationship of truth and falsehood, light and darkness, life and death, or concerning God and the world, God and man, spirit and flesh, time and eternity, if the spirit of faith, which is the spirit of truth, did not develop and clarify human understanding about all these relationships." But the church must fight against all spiritual darkness with spiritual weapons alone.

"Christian education starts with the proposition that creation and time itself have their origin in the eternal

Word of God, which was with God, was God, and is the Light of life. Therefore Christian education as well as the Christian life have their origin in the spiritual fact that the Word of God became flesh in order to win a faithful church, which in fellowship with Him receives spirit of His Spirit and flesh of His flesh. It must therefore be the goal of Christian education to show how all the secular world is clearly bound to the eternal Word of God and how it, in the course of time, is gathered in Christ Jesus and lives and moves in his church." For this point of view the church must go to battle against those who deny it, and for this purpose the Spirit of truth will provide the teachers.

But knowledge must be mobile and progressive. The Christian faith, founded on the rock, is unchangeable. It is the same today as it was in the days of the apostles, and it shall ever remain the same. But the understanding and interpretation of life, which is the task of Christian teachers, must change with varying circumstances. Their task is to testify about the faith to the world and to shed light on the present world of the spirit. This latter task has been neglected by Christian teachers. "This is the reason why I have sought so eagerly to illumine the relation between the Christian life and the folk life of man. Although I could not foresee that because of it anyone but Turks would call me pagan, I knew well enough that all the hypocrites would be shocked by my secularism." But misunderstanding still leaves a task to be done. "Just as the Christian church, in order to rest securely in the faith in the Holy Spirit and in the Word from God, needs to be educated about the spirit of man and the word of man in activity and power, so does the Christian church, for the sake of its Christian life, need to be enlightened about the human life of a people."

The task of the school is not to defend the faith, for "no one but Christ himself can defend his Word, his faith, and his church against the spiritual evil under the skies." Therefore we must be on guard against the effort to "defend the faith and the church by any kind of book-writing, by dogmatics, or by our knowledge and wisdom. There is no strength in them against the tricky wiles of the devil."

11

The Church

Ours is a bewildered generation. The great certainties and optimisms of the nineteenth century have been replaced by caution and questions. Dreams of peace have not come true, and despite all his material gains western man is ready to admit that he does not know how to control his own creations. Forces of race and nationalism and the tremendous upsurge of underprivileged groups have destroyed our familiar patterns. A tremendous effort is made to stabilize them by consolidation and by the exercise of authority.

Through all this we are led, however, to examine and question not only the structures of society but the very purpose and goal of life itself. We seek answers, and we search for those who can give answers to basic questions. The very nature of human existence is in the crucible of investigation and analysis. The rise of authoritarian systems of government and the spread of materialistic and secular philosophies of government and society show how deep-seated the quest is and how great the need for authoritative answers.

In this dilemma it is only natural to look to the church for authority and guidance. Basically our problem is a religious one, and therefore the church should be able to tell us the true character of our nature and destiny. The matter should be simple. Christian people confess faith in God who has created the world and has revealed his will and his way through Christ. But the response of the church has become the response of the churches, and this response is so varied and contradictory that, on the whole, our bewilderment is increased. The reason for this lies in the fact that we have no clear and unified concept of what the church is, nor of its message. The problem of authority thus becomes a problem of the nature and the function of the church. This is where Grundtvig enters the picture. His major contributions concerned the nature of the church and the nature of man. The pertinency of his views for us today hinge upon their value in these two areas. If Grundtvig said something important to his own age in these realms, possibly what he has said, if removed from nineteenth-century garb, may speak to our generation.

For a long time Grundtvig was not aware that he was searching for an answer to the problem of authority. He asked the questions his contemporaries asked. The age was philosophically minded, and he followed the patterns of its thoughts. The important philosophical problem had to do with "knowledge" and "certainty." Essentially this problem is the same as ours, but the philosophers of that day had a different background and spoke a different language. They asked the question: "How do we know? How do we know the world round about us, and how do we know the world beyond our senses? How do we know God?" In the early nineteenth century these questions were vital, and the problem of knowledge was still new—only two or three centuries old. Before then, before the Reformation and the Renaissance, it had not even been permitted open discussion. In the Middle Ages the authoritative Roman Catholic Church had assumed the role of question-answerer even in science. Its claim of absolute authority had been dismissed by the heroes of the sixteenth century, the scientists, reformers, and humanists, but for a while, and quite naturally, confusion prevailed as to the authority or authorities to replace the one rejected.

The Protestant church had established the Bible as the authority in religious, moral, and even practical affairs, and, feeling the need for guidance, had interpreted the Bible in doctrinal statements. In many places this authority was backed by the power of the princes. But many intellectuals refused to be bound, seeking other avenues for a criterion of and an authority for knowledge. They found them essentially in two ways. From these two schools of thought developed: Rationalism, emphasizing the mind and reason, and Empiricism, emphasizing practical experience.

By Grundtvig's time these two approaches to knowledge had shown their limitations, as pointed out by Immanuel Kant. But his refutation had not made any immediate impression upon Grundtvig, trained as he was in the eighteenth-century school of logical thought. He was still impressed with the significance of the quest for knowledge, particularly the problem of knowing God. His concern for knowledge, for that which is "knowable," though emancipated from eighteenth-century philosophy, shows up in much of his writing. He was influenced by both Rationalistic and Empiricist schools of thought, learning the significance of each. Added to these two was the influence of Romanticism, the main cause of his keen interest in history and in growth or development. It explained the world as growing according to certain inherent principles and striving toward a goal identified with God.

Grundtvig rejected the basic principles of all three approaches to an understanding of the world because they included in their very nature a search for God. For him that search had come to an end, because he had found God (or God had found him) in a personal experience of the Christian faith. All search for God was futile, for God's revelation of himself was the one known and basic factor of all existence. He was known through the faith of the Christian. Any attempt to identify him with a principle of thought or a philosophical goal was out of the question.[1]

[1] At this point the fundamental difference between Grundtvig and Schleiermacher begins. Both lived in the same age and environment and reacted to the same forces and problems. Both wished to build a positive Christianity which could answer the problems of the day. But Grundtvig had experienced a struggle with sin and guilt while Schleiermacher had not. Grundtvig based his whole theology on a

In spite of this, the problem of knowledge was still a vital one for Grundtvig. He was fascinated by the problem of how we come to "know" the God in whom we have believed and to whom we have committed ourselves in faith. The reality of God rather than his existence became his major inquiry. How does God manifest himself? How can we find evidence of his Being and his activity? By what authority does he speak today?

Grundtvig might have followed two ways in his quest for evidence of God in the world in general. He might have sought the evidence in the created world of nature, a field of interest dear to Henrik Steffens, the Romanticist who had first inspired him. But Grundtvig was little interested in natural science and chose to follow the other way, history. In God's action among men, Grundtvig found the evidence he sought. Through history we can know the God in whom we believe.

At the time of these speculative answers to the problem of knowledge Grundtvig was not actively engaged in the work of the church. He had been excluded from

concept of faith identical with Luther's, a dynamic acceptance of the grace of God coming unmerited to the repentant sinner. For Schleiermacher the problem of sin and guilt was more an intellectual problem, and he resorted to the answers of Romanticism for his basic concepts, whereas Grundtvig reacted against Romanticism for the very reason that its concept of sin and of God were inadequate. Schleiermacher defined religion in terms of "feeling" and Christianity as the feeling of absolute dependence upon God. Unfortunately, Schleiermacher became the teacher of the nineteenth century, and for a hundred years Protestant theology was given direction by his subjectivism. Grundtvig's answers to the same problem were different, and now that the period of "psychologism" has come to an end, Grundtvig comes into his own.

the pulpit and had occupied himself with historical writing and research. The time came, however, when he again needed the answers to the direct problems of Christian authority, and it was the necessity of preaching that made him think about the content and pertinency of his faith. A man may have faith and still lack ability to analyze or explain it, but when he has to proclaim the faith to others he must be able to. In his search for clarity he will scrutinize the sources and the authority for his convictions. When Grundtvig, after an absence from the ministry, found himself in a parish, he centered the problem of knowledge on the evidence for the Christian revelation in the world. By what means do we know the content and power of the Christian faith?

If we were to put the question in terms of our own day, we would not ask for "knowledge" or "evidence" of God. This terminology belongs to the early nineteenth century or perhaps to the eighteenth. Our own age is not so concerned with speculative questions or with abstract intellectual problems. It is more practical, and its practicality is manifested also in its religious concerns. Its question might be: What does God mean to me personally and how does he work in the world today? Christianity is not a theoretical doctrinal matter for modern man; it is a matter of practical existence. Therefore the challenge to Christianity today is whether or not it is existential or contemporary. In this setting Grundtvig's problem was existential, his answers were existential, and he was an existentialist twenty years before Kierkegaard raised the same question in a different way.

Traditionally a Lutheran would have a ready answer to the question. The evidence, and therefore the authority, for faith lies in the Bible. There is also adequate explanation for understanding and clarity in the confessional documents of the church. The second part of the answer was not obvious in Grundtvig's day, however. Pietism had weakened the concern for doctrine, and Rationalism had undermined the respect that was left. Grundtvig did not resort to the authority of the Lutheran doctrinal statements of the sixteenth century, but the Bible became authoritative for him during the first years after his conversion. He took its authority for granted and never doubted the significance of the New Testament.

The difficulty he met as he once more preached the gospel was that the Bible was subject to interpretation, that every group presented its interpretation as the authoritative expression of Christianity, even those who denied the central truths of the incarnation and the resurrection. When a dispute arose, seemingly there was no other arbiter than the learned man or professor. This puzzled and frustrated Grundtvig. On the one hand orthodox conservatives interpreted Scripture on the basis of agreements about the nature of Christianity adopted beforehand. On the other hand scholars interpreted Christianity in terms of the learning and the philosophical ideas of their time. Both parties used the Bible with an equal assertion of authority. Was there no evidence of the Christian revelation that avoids these human extremes? Was there no expression of Christianity unshakably the same in its essence, but with a message for modern man in terms of his problems?

In this dilemma Grundtvig resorted to the same answers he had found as to the evidences of God in the created world. The same criterion that was valid there must be pertinent to the validity of the revelation in Christ, as found in the historic expression of the revelation which is the church. Thus the church became the answer to his whole quest for authority and certainty. The church is the body of Christ in which he is alive and active. It is the church that makes Christ contemporary. The church carries the gospel. He looked for an expression of the church that conveys, in a living and dynamic manner to modern man, the essence and content of faith. He found the answer in the living response of the church to God in its confession of faith, basically the same today as it was in the beginning days of the church. Unfortunately, Grundtvig later identified the confession with the literal formula of the Apostles' Creed in such a way that he made the Creed into a doctrinal statement, but at first it was only the content that counted. This confession of the Triune God and of Christ as divine Lord and Saviour formed the essence of the revelation of the church.

The basic factor in his point of view was not that Grundtvig found a historic evidence of the faith, but that he saw the church as a living, dynamic, creative continuation of the revelation in Christ. God operates, God creates, God works in and through the church. The body of Christ is more than an organization of men; it is the vehicle of God, the active community of God and men. Its secret is the Word of God, a dynamic, creative word. When God meets his people in the church, the life from God becomes a living reality for them. The church is the Holy Spirit's creation and realm of activity. Through the church we are brought to the glory and blessing of the kingdom of God which Jesus founded and which is a living reality today. We can live in this realm, we can receive the forgiveness of our sins, we can be given power to live as God's children, all accomplished in the living community of Christian fellowship in the church.

The church not only brings us the witness of salvation through the confession and through the testimony of Scripture; only the church brings salvation itself. "Outside the church there is no salvation," Cyprian wrote, for the church is *the* vehicle of salvation. It is the vehicle, because it possesses a *living word*. The word acts through the sacraments, creative acts of the living Word which is Christ, creative acts of God through his Holy Spirit. At baptism, God acts to make us his children, heirs of salvation. When we receive communion, God acts creatively and dynamically, restoring us to the right relationship to him, giving us power and strength to live our daily life. The basic gift of life is in baptism.

Communion renews and restores that life. But baptism and Communion are part of the church's organic relationship to God. The worship of the church expresses and nourishes the Christian life, and its signs are preaching, prayer, confession. But the inner life and secret of all this is the living and creative word of God.

The church, God's realm of creation, makes but one requirement of man—response. The response is the confession of the church, and through the church of the individual. "The word is near to you, on your lips and in your heart (that is, the word of faith which we preach) because, if you confess with your lips that Jesus is Lord and believe in your heart that God raised him from the dead, you will be saved" (Rom. 10:8-9, R.S.V.). Confession is the activated word of God which takes possession of men. Its inner quality is not its form nor the historic correctness of all its elements but the living response to God who has revealed himself in Christ. It is therefore a confession of Jesus Christ as Lord and Saviour, the same today as it was in the days of Peter and Paul. It is not just repetition by rote; it is a living and dynamic response to and acceptance of life from God.

This response in confession is organically connected with God's act of baptism. When at baptism we confess our faith, we become partners in a covenant relationship, a mutual relationship. It is God who acts in his church, in a community where there is a confessional response. Grundtvig said, and often implied, that "only at baptism

and Communion do we hear the living Word of God."
This exclusiveness has been criticized, and if it were to
mean that we cannot hear God speak to us any other
way, it would be wrong. But his intention was to place
the convenant and creative relationship of the sacraments in a unique place, where God's gift meets man's
need in a special way, according to God's promise and
as a historic revelation of God's creative and redemptive act.

Grundtvig emphasized the *reality* of the church.

> Most wondrous is of all on earth
> The kingdom Jesus founded,
> Its glory, peace and precious worth
> No tongue has ever sounded.
>
> As breath of wind invisible,
> Its signs are yet revealed;
> A city set upon a hill
> From men is not concealed.
>
> Its secret—God's almighty word
> Which heav'n and earth created,
> The valleys when His voice they heard
> Were filled, the floods abated.

Another:

> God 'mongst us His kingdom founded
> By His Spirit and His word,
> Gave us all His invitation,
> In His church His voice we heard.
>
> Visibly is never present
> God's eternal grace and love
> Which with peace and joy abundant
> Came to us from heaven above.

180

When the Spirit ever calls us
With the voice of God to come,
In our hearts we know, however,
That God's kingdom is our home.

Or the famous:

Built on the Rock the Church does stand,
Even when steeples are falling;
Crumbled have spires in every land,
Bells still are chiming and calling;
Calling the young and old to rest,
But above all the soul distrest,
Longing for rest everlasting.

Surely in temples made with hands
God, the Most High, is not dwelling,
High above earth His temple stands,
All earthly temples excelling;
Yet, He whom heav'ns cannot contain,
Chose to abide on earth with men—
Built in our bodies His temple.

The kingdom of God is not visible, yet it is known to men. It is more than the ephemeral church of the idealists. It is a reality in which we can live.

He also emphasized the *historical character* or the continuity of the church. In doing this he restored to Lutheranism a dimension which had been somewhat lacking since the time of the Reformation. Martin Luther, of course, was very much aware of the historical character of the church, but he battled against the Roman church with its claim of history and tradition as the basis for the authority of the hierarchy, and the times were too confused to draw the fine line between various types of historicity. As a result, he fell back on the authority of Scripture. This one-sided emphasis was perpetuated and formalized by Lutheran orthodoxy. Laying aside the continuity of the church, the theologians of orthodoxy emphasized doctrine. Minimizing the flow of the church's life, they established a hop, skip, and a jump from Scripture to the confessions to present-day commitment. Grundtvig remedied this by returning to the original emphasis upon the living body of Christ as a historical reality down through the ages. It would have warmed his heart to read the statement made by the Faith and Order meeting at Lund in 1952 about this continuity: "All agree not only upon the continuity assured by the constant action of the risen Lord through the Holy Spirit, but also upon the value of some form of continuity in history, assured by some means under the action of the Holy Spirit. All would emphasize the apostolic continuity of Christian life within the Christian community of men and women, redeemed by the one Cross of Christ, seeking to follow the example and teaching of the same Master and inspired by the continuing presence of the same living Lord. Most would also regard the preaching of the gospel and the ministration of the sacraments as essential means of continuity." [2]

Finally, he emphasized the *corporate* character of the church. The church is a community of believers. It is a fellowship of faith. The church is the corporate body

[2] Report of the Third World Conference on Faith and Order, p. 14.

to which all confessing Christians belong no matter what their organization. For Grundtvig this feature was of tremendous significance. The individual cannot live by himself but must share with others. Only in the sharing of experience and the sharing of tasks does a Christian grow to full stature. In fact, a man cannot become a Christian except through the corporate body, for it is the church which baptizes and presents the sacrament of Communion. In contrast to Kierkegaard who stressed the importance of the individual, Grundtvig maintained that the individual must find the Christian life in the Christian congregation. The church is a fellowship in faith of living people, a community of faith and hope, founded in baptism and known by the oral confession of faith which is its condition for membership and therefore for baptism.

The basic elements of his concept of the church came to Grundtvig in the period 1823-25, first expressed in *The Reply of the Church*. Many years were to pass before he fully developed his ideas. When he attacked the "heretical" views of Professor Clausen he still identified the universal church and its confession with the state church of Denmark. The basis for the action, Grundtvig maintained, was the confession of the church which Professor Clausen had violated in his interpretation of Christianity.

When the authorities reprimanded Grundtvig, he concluded that the authorities were not true representatives of the church. He was sorely tempted to break with the state church and join like-minded, "old-time" Christians of the revival movements in the formation of a "pure" church unsoiled by the heretical and radical ideas of the corrupted state church. He appealed for permission to do so, but it could not be granted under the laws of the time. Grundtvig was not too eager to step out, however, for he did not entirely approve of the revival groups and had an innate reluctance to break with the fellowship in which he had been reared. Furthermore, he still believed that the authority vested in the bishops would move to cleanse and revive the church. At that stage he might be called an episcopalian.

After his journeys to England and under the influence of English church life, particularly the broad church movement, Grundtvig rejected the authority of the bishops and the secular administration of the church in matters of faith, calling for a church "establishment" with freedom of faith and worship. No longer did he ask that the heterodox be dismissed from the church nor did he wish to leave the state church. The establishment and its purpose should be secular, providing the moral force which the state needs for its life, and taking care of the practical matters of organization and finance of the church. Within this framework each clergyman should be free to preach and conduct the services as he wished, responsible only to the congregation he served. Freedom was the essence of the establishment, with the Spirit as the only authority in matters of faith and practice.

Grundtvig's final definition of the church was in terms of a spiritual fellowship rather than any form of organization. Calling it a "heavenly guest" in an earthly home, he refused to identify it with any earthly form it might take. Necessarily and unavoidably, the church formed organizations, but they were only practical steps taken to relate the church to the world, never one with the church itself. Their significance is in the realm of human society. The real church is built of living stones, of people. Even the local congregation cannot claim to be *the* church. The church—real, historic, and corporate —is a fellowship of faith guided by the Holy Spirit.

This view of the church was Grundtvig's answer to the problem of authority. Without realizing the significance of each step in its solution, without putting the problem in terms of authority, he had nevertheless in the course of two decades met, tried, and rejected three types of authority: Scripture, holy orders, and subjective individualism. In their place he set the historic and confessing church, guided and given power by the Holy Spirit.

Lutheran orthodoxy regarded the canonical books of the Old and New Testaments as the only norm and source of Christian faith and life. This attitude in its exclusive form dates back only to the period of orthodoxy which followed the death of Luther. It is not found in any doctrinal statement formulated during the lifetime of Luther, including the Augsburg Confession, and does not represent in its exclusiveness the conviction of Luther himself. He had a more vital concept of the character of the Word. But in Grundtvig's time it was accepted, though not practiced by that large segment of the Danish church given over to Rationalism. The fact is, of course, that all people interpret the Bible. All those who believe that the Bible is the only norm and source of faith and life interpret the Bible according to standards they have adopted or accepted. The criterion or the basis of the interpretation is generally a doctrinal statement or commitment, in the case of Lutheranism primarily the Augsburg Confession.

Rationalists did not subscribe to the exclusiveness of the orthodox Lutheran statement about the Bible, but nevertheless used it as a chief source. Contrary to the orthodox they were open and frank in their interpretation based on current philosophical ideas. Therefore when Grundtvig argued from Scripture against Rationalism and Professor Clausen, he was disturbed to find that his opponents used not only the same Bible as he, but also the same method of interpretation, though they began with different premises. He realized then that as a vehicle of revelation the Bible was not adequate. Using it exclusively left the church open to biased interpretation, varying with different premises.

Grundtvig did not reject the Bible as a vehicle of revelation nor as a source. He was an avid Bible reader and based his teaching and preaching on it. What he did was assert that there was a source of life which was not subject to interpretations as the Bible was. A book can never be a source of life. The Bible is a fruit of the faith. It is a source of information and of doctrine, a guide for Christians, but the source of life must be a living word. This living word was the living Christ in his body, the church. Through the sacraments of the church his life becomes ours, and when we confess our faith in him at baptism a covenant of life is made. Out of this life the Bible grew.

The second type of authority with which Grundtvig dealt was the authority of office or orders. In the first flush of his battle against "false" teachings he depended on this authority for a purification of the church. He leaned heavily for a few years to the episcopalian (or Catholic) idea that the purity of doctrine and life is maintained and guaranteed by the authority of office in the church. Some years later, he not only rejected this idea but took great pains to make plain that his emphasis upon the historic church must not be identified with the emphasis upon the hierarchy and tradition which characterizes the Roman Catholic Church. This de-lineation was particularly important inasmuch as Grundtvig strongly emphasized the sacraments, an em-phasis paralleled by the Episcopal and Roman Catholic churches. For Grundtvig the validity of the sacraments was not vouched for by the office in the church but by the corporate life of the church itself.

The authority of office had a peculiar manifestation in northern Europe, particularly in the Lutheran countries. From the time of the treaty of Augsburg, 1555, the principle had been invoked that the prince or ruler of a country should determine its religion ("ejus regio cujus religio"). For some generations this secular authority had protected the "pure doctrine" of the Lutheran church in Denmark, and at the time of Grundtvig it was supposed to be a protector of practice as well as doctrine. Strangely enough, it was less a protector of doctrine than of practice in the early nineteenth century. It allowed individualism in preaching and teaching, but not freedom of worship or of participation in the sacraments. Grundtvig eventually also became an energetic antagonist of this type of authority. Purity of doctrine or correctness of practice can never be guaranteed or conveyed by any show of external authority.

The positive side of this rejection was Grundtvig's insistence upon freedom in the church. In many ways a conservative, his unfaltering devotion to the basic ideas which he maintained drove him to be a champion of religious and political freedom. There can be no other authority than the Spirit. No individual can be bound to certain doctrines and practice by ecclesiastical or political authorities, nor should any minister be bound. If he is not bound by the Spirit to confess the Christian faith and to preach and practice accordingly, no outward show of authority can put him right; if he is bound by the Spirit, then no form of coercion is necessary. Departments of church affairs, bishops, deans, and councils, have a necessary practical function but they must never become a spiritual police force.

Grundtvig's battle for religious freedom had a tremendous influence in shaping the affairs of the Church of Denmark. Although it probably will not acknowledge it officially, nevertheless the state church is largely dominated today by his ideas of freedom.

The third type of authority, individual subjectivism, Grundtvig met first in the teachings of Professor Clausen. Clausen, under the influence of Schleiermacher, maintained that the true character of the Christian faith, while drawn from Scripture, should be determined by the interpretation of scholars who alone were able to read and understand the Bible. Grundtvig protested against what he called this "exegetical papacy," maintaining that the Christian faith must be something definite and unchangeable, not subject to the whims and wiles of changing generations of intellectuals. The authority for what we are to believe and live by can never be a purely personal matter. It is a concern of the church which lives and confesses. This rejection of subjectivism and emphasis on the corporate body of the church later on placed Grundtvig in almost automatic opposition to Kierkegaard with his contention that "subjectivity is the truth."

It was not only intellectual subjectivity as represented by Clausen and Kierkegaard that Grundtvig rejected, but also the experiential subjectivity of Pietism represented in his day by the revival movements. Grundtvig was, as a matter of course, in favor of a personal commitment to the Christian faith. He had undergone a profound conversion, the basis for his Christian life, and advocated personal commitment to the faith, especially through the confession. But he did not believe that a Christian community could be built on religious experience. In fact, he was opposed to the conventicle or free-church concept of the church, built on the idea that the church is essentially a group of people who have had a certain experience. He therefore refused to join the revivalistic groups, resisting the temptation, prompted by the restrictions placed upon him by church authorities, to revolt against the church and join in forming an independent church. Eventually his influence was largely instrumental in assimilating the revival groups into the general body of the church.

Grundtvig certainly would have been strongly opposed to the neo-pietistic movements of today which place so great an emphasis upon a certain type of experience or commitment or upon the observance of certain forms of worship or organization. For him the church was a fellowship of faith, and his concept of faith was the Lutheran concept that faith is not an accomplishment of man but a gift by the grace of God. It is given to us through the church, expressed in the common confession of the church. Therefore since a faith-experience is not meritorious, it cannot be called for in a formalized way. It is misleading to make a certain experience or even a certain type of experience the criterion for the faith or the authority for doctrine and practice.[3]

In place of the three types of authority he rejected Grundtvig placed the authority of the living church. But how, we might ask, can the church be an authority, how can it be a source and norm when it has no visible concrete form? The church is an association of people, a fellowship. From Grundtvig's point of view it is a spiritual fellowship the outer forms of which must not be considered the same as the spiritual reality. How can it be authoritative when it is only a means or a vehicle? Grundtvig's answer would be: The church is more than a fellowship. It is the means and vehicle of God, his continued creative and redemptive act. It is the body of Christ with the power of the Holy Spirit. In the church, during the worship and especially at the sacraments, we are in a living, dynamic relationship to God who forgives, guides, comforts, and revitalizes. In the church we have Christ, the Living Word. But we cannot exclusively identify this church, the fellowship

[3] Although Grundtvig believed that the church expressed itself in its visible form primarily in the fellowship of the individual congregation, he was no "congregationalist" in the denominational sense of the word. His polity was congregational, but his concept of the church could not be contained in that which limits the church to the local congregation, maintaining that only in the immediate experiential fellowship of those who have joined for worship do we have the church. According to Grundtvig, the church is the universal church, the body and home of the resurrected Christ, with a spiritual but historic existence from the time of the apostles, taking shape in human society. The earthly home of this heavenly guest is not the organization of the hierarchy or the organization of the state church. It is primarily the congregation in its fellowship of faith, with its preaching, praise, and prayer, and with its God-given expression in the sacraments. But the congregation is only a finite expression of the living and universal church.

of faith, the body of Christ, with any particular organization which gives human form to the fellowship. Nor
should we exhaust its authority with any statement of
principles or convictions, no matter how excellent these
may be.

The authority for the gospel, for the kerygma, belongs to the church and only to the church. Therefore
the church is the source of the faith. What Jesus lived
and taught, and what the church believed and preached,
comes to us with authority, not because it was written
down and perpetuated by even the most faithful but
because this was and is the testimony of the church. In
a day when scholars distinguish between the "mythos"
and the "kerygma" of the New Testament and when
there seems no other choice than a defiant literalism on
the one hand and a scientific exegesis on the other, here
is Grundtvig's third alternative, the witness of the
church. This would not be the church of bishops nor
the church of doctrines but the living and confessing
church, which testifies to us through its confession and
through the Scriptures that it believes in and has built
its life on the Christ, who as Jesus of Nazareth has revealed God and has become the risen Saviour. He conquered death and is now at the right hand of God, which
means that he is living in his church. This testimony,
this confession, this continued, creative, and redemptive
life, is the norm and source, and for that reason the authority of Christian life. Its gospel (kerygma) stands as
a witness to God despite all the exegesis, explanation, and

even elimination of scholars. The New Testament is the church's testimony, and therefore it is our sacred Scripture, our guidance and our source of life.

The church, as it has been given body through the ages, as it has met with many and varying situations of tension and victory, has time and again put its testimony into words of explanation, argument, and clarification. Doctrines are necessary and important, but the church must not be limited to them, nor must they ever be made the authoritative voice of the church. Only the living word or the living spirit can be authoritative. All else is guidance. Correct doctrines are the concern of the school, a vital concern of every outward form of the church, but school and church must be kept separate. There is a great difference between teaching and preaching. We preach, creatively, from the gospel. The church brings us the gospel. Therefore the church is our authority. It instructs us through the Holy Spirit, but it does not lay down an authoritative set of statements. Its only definite expression is its confession.

Grundtvig's belief that the church was a heavenly guest in an earthly home led to the conviction that it found such a home in the various people of the earth. In order to create the best conditions for expressing itself the church must adapt itself to the varying conditions of the different peoples. It must use to its advantage the conditions which it finds, particularly the language of the people in which the church must proclaim the gospel, developing them to make the atmosphere the best possible for the unfolding and development of the Christian life. Each country must respect other countries and allow them to develop their Christian life according to their own cultural leanings. Grundtvig has been called a nationalist, but his active interest in his native land and native language did not lead to arrogant proclamation of the superiority of Scandinavian Christianity. The fact that he proclaimed certain ways to be best for himself and his people led him to recognize that native folkways would be better for the people of other countries.

His emphasis upon the folk character of the church was not meant to obscure its universality. Grundtvig constantly emphasized the Creed in which the third article confesses faith in the holy catholic (universal) church. He did not speak about ecumenicity, for he lived long before the ecumenical movement, but he would certainly have been in favor of any emphasis upon universality.

12

Man

What is man that thou art mindful of him,
And the son of man that thou dost care for him?
—Psalm 8:4

The cry, "What is man?" is an ancient one. It is inherent in all religions and essential to all philosophies. In our modern world it has been parceled out in separate sciences, which have obscured the totality of the inquiry, but it has not been eliminated. The timeless question is as pertinent as ever.

Essentially the problem of man is a problem of good and evil, of man's worth in relation to his purpose and possibilities. For those who believe in God it is a problem of man in his relation and response to God, or in his failure to respond. It becomes a matter of that which hinders man's purpose and is therefore a problem of sin. Can man overcome the power of evil and fulfil his purpose? Most often the answer has been negative. Man is caught in the power of evil and needs help to reach his goal. This leads to the further question: Has man been corrupted and is his very nature contaminated so that it has become evil?

195

Historically two main answers have been given to the latter question. The one minimizes the power of evil and attributes to man the strength to overcome it—or at least to initiate the victory. The other admits that man is in the grip of a force which he cannot conquer. His liberation depends upon a power greater than his own, upon divine help or divine action. Within the framework of the latter answer men have differed concerning the condition of human nature, with extremists maintaining that man is completely depraved and that there is nothing good in him. The fall into sin, they maintain, has deprived man of any goodness with which he has been endowed by the Creator, and the natural activity of man is not only inadequate but is to be condemned. Part of Grundtvig's legacy through the church of the eighteenth century, this view has been held by orthodox Lutherans and Pietists.

In his youthful enthusiasm for Romanticism Grundtvig had adopted its philosophy and therefore its view of man. This view has been expressed by Hal Koch in the following way: "In its essence the world is life and spirit, fire and power, and the soul of man is a spark of the eternal fire. Therefore life demands of man that he unqualifiedly accept the urge for living, which is the divine quality of his soul, and commit himself to life and its longings, so that he is carried by his passion toward totality and eternity and thus fulfils his destiny." [1] Grundtvig's conversion released him from this mystical

[1] *Vaerker I Udvalg,* II, vii.

and pantheistic nonsense, and he quarreled with the philosophy of Romanticism because its view of man and of sin was inadequate. He also condemned the view of Rationalism which, although differently expressed, fell into the same category with its underestimation of the power of evil in the world.

After his conversion experience of 1810-11 and during the ensuing apocalyptic period, when he sought to save his people by a religious conversion, Grundtvig readopted the orthodox Lutheran view. He regarded man primarily as sinner, believing that true life is found only in Christ. Consequently all features of life, of the individual, of science,[2] and of national life, must be redeemed and sanctified in order to attain its true nature. In this respect Grundtvig shared the view of the Pietists, but he could not align himself with a small and select group. He could not agree that the life in Christ only concerned the life of the soul, since for him it touched all features of living.

As doors of activity were closed to him, and as the recovery after the Napoleonic wars dissipated the fear of doom, Grundtvig's zeal for conversion flagged and he occupied himself with other interests. In 1821 he returned to the ministry, and the problem of church and authority became paramount. For the time being his concern for the status of man was relegated to the sidelines, but inherent in his newly developed ideas about the

[2] "Unless old-fashioned Christianity returns, all scientific work is lost for the generation as it obviously is for the individual." *Ibid.*, II, 214.

church were new ideas of man. His emphasis upon the evidence in history of God's creation and his emphasis upon a living participation in the faith-fellowship of the church were bound to broaden and change his concept of man. It took some time for the new ideas to develop. He was ostensibly so influenced by outside stimuli that those new attitudes seemed to have formed an entirely independent phase of development. But there was an essential relation between Grundtvig's view of the church and his view of man.

From his youth Grundtvig had been vitally interested in national affairs, and his religious conversion had only spurred him to greater activity on behalf of the nation and the people. His methods were overzealous and he repelled many people. Eventually he withdrew temporarily in frustration from public affairs, but his Christianity never let him withdraw completely from public life. On the contrary, it drove him to a constant concern. This concern was expressed in writing; it was a commonly accepted idea that literary discussion was a form of action.

Then, 1829-31, Grundtvig visited England and was jolted into an understanding of activity which far surpassed the customary comprehension in Denmark. The hustle and bustle of British common life, its commercial enterprise, the momentum of its industrial revolution, its liberal political development, the broad church group, all these impressed him with English activism. He discovered a whole new type of activity and a new attitude toward work. Practical living assumed a new significance, and out of this understanding grew a reconsideration of the basic spiritual questions concerning man. The question emerged and became pertinent whether man really needs a religious conversion in order to live a true and valuable life. Might not even the reverse be true, that it is necessary to live a sound and active human life as a natural-born human being in order to live as a Christian?

His concern for the problem of human nature came up with a demand for solution. The problem was first treated in the introduction to his *Nordic Mythology*. This was not by accident. For Grundtvig, mythology was a philosophy of life, a cosmology, an explanation of the nature of life and the circumstances of good and evil under which it is lived. The drama of the myth was the drama of man; the inner secret of the myth was the secret of life as it was understood by the spiritual man of ancient cultures. Grundtvig was impressed by the soundness and strength of the philosophy of ancient mythology. It saw the issues of life and of death in a simpler but more realistic framework than the philosophies of modern civilization, and its answers were, apart from the problem of the ultimate destiny and salvation of man, in many ways more sound and genuine. Life is a battle between good and evil, life and death. It is the drama of man. If the ancient Nordics could see this, and if they could suggest the solutions in terms of battle and victory, why then must life be redeemed and sanctified in order to be true and real? Does this not mean that the orthodox concept of the depravity of man is wrong and that there exists in natural man a condition and quality of striving for good which has not been totally destroyed by the fall?

Grundtvig did not give up his conviction of sin nor his faith that only through Christ can man be made right with God and possess the eternal life which is mediated by Christ. The fall of man makes it necessary for a divine Saviour to rescue him from death by making atonement for his sin. But he was released from a narrow traditional concept of man, growing to understand that man, as he was created by God, created in his image, had a life and a nature which not only had significance in itself but had importance also for the redeemed life of the Christian.

Some scholars maintain that Grundtvig at this time (1832) made a clean break with previously held ideas and instituted a new and entirely different philosophy of life. But obviously his new ideas were contained in his previous opinions, only to emerge now. There is no conflict between Grundtvig's Christian convictions and views of humanity. Rather, his philosophy of man is a logical consequence of his basic Christian ideas. The conflict is found in the difference between his view of man and that held by orthodox Lutherans and Pietists.

The problem is complicated, however, by the fact that Grundtvig's expression of his viewpoints was dialectic, emphasizing different, and apparently even contradictory, features of it in different situations. For the most part he was turned in polemics against his own previously held orthodox view of the total depravity of man, which insisted that man must be redeemed and sanctified in order to live as man should live. He fought orthodoxy and Pietism in their narrow condemnation of secular life and their narrow insistence upon the sanctified and spiritual character of the redeemed man. Therefore many of his writings heavily stressed the natural— or created—man. The opposite polemical situation occurred less often, and it is therefore harder to find expressed in writing. But whenever he was up against the view that natural man is sufficient unto himself and that he does not need God in order to live a true life, he emphasized the need for God and for the guidance of the Spirit. "When we, by the help of God, see the light of the Lord, then the confession will become more vital, the preaching more simple and strong, and the praise more clear and sweet, and our *whole human life will gain a spiritual and renewed character whose Christianity cannot be proved but which is nevertheless certain, because this noble and sincere nature will only be found where the Christian confession, preaching, and praise is actually present.*" [3]

When Grundtvig wrote the introduction to *Nordic Mythology*, he envisioned the whole of life in what he called "universal-historical development." The key to his new understanding was found in the combination of

[3] *Ibid.*, Vol. VI, p. 81.

Christian revelation and the insights into the condition of man given by the ancient Nordics. The result was visionary. "When we consider the spiritual world with Nordic eyes and in the light of Christianity we grasp the concept of a universal-historical development, an art and a science. This concept includes all of life with all its forces, conditions, and results. It liberates, strengthens and illumines everything in accord with the earthly welfare of the individual, the people, and the whole of mankind. This must necessarily lead to the most perfect explanation of life that is possible on earth."

Basic to this panorama of life was the Christian "Anskuelse," [4] which was emancipated from false intellectualism, proclaiming that man was endowed by the Creator with a life that was truly wonderful. "The Mosaic-Christian 'Anskuelse,' whether it be historic or

[4] "Anskuelse" is a philosophy, an idea, a point of view (German: "Anschauung") which must be distinguished from faith. It is an explanation of life, not a commitment. It can be shared by those who have not committed themselves to the revelation in Christ, whom Grundtvig calls the "naturalists." For Christians the "Anskuelse" grows out of their faith in the revelation. For the "naturalists" it is simply an explanation. The result is that the Christian may change the explanation with equanimity, because a change of explanation does not change his faith, but the "naturalist" must take it seriously, because he has to rely on his explanation of life. Cf. *Nordic Mythology*, p. 64. According to Grundtvig, faith is unchangeable but explanation (theology) is progressive and polemical. Cf. *Elemental Christian Teachings*, V.U., VI, 261. See the discussion of this problem by Regin Prenter in *Die Frage Nach Einer Theologischen Grundtvig-Interpretation* in *Theologische Aufsätze, Karl Barth zum 50 Geburtstag* (München: Chr. Kaiser Verlag, 1936), p. 505-513. In it Prenter calls Grundtvig's discussion in *Nordic Mythology* and his world histories "secondary theology," which is a "necessary function of the church which proclaims the incarnation of the Word to the world."

poetic, whether it has come naturally or through a revelation, is the only true view of human life which has . . . amply proved its own divinity and that of Christ. This view therefore must guide us in science as well as in life itself . . . It was the higher Christian 'Anskuelse' which in the day of Rome miraculously shattered the chains of mankind and, reborn in Luther, struck down the power of the Pope. It is this view alone which has given the thought, culture, and knowledge of the new folk world its universal-human character."

The fundamental character of man was therefore not dependent upon theology or religious experience but was inherent in the creation. "One is not necessarily a monkey or a Roman because he is a heathen, as it has been sufficiently demonstrated by the poetry and history of Greece and the ancient North. One need only be a real person essentially different from dumb animals, marvelously related to the immortal gods, addressed by the spirit of man and God in all known languages. One bows deeply in reverence for this spirit which from the inspired lips of the apostles was spread as a living word from Jerusalem and accomplished miracles to the end of the earth."

Grundtvig found that he had no argument with the "naturalists" in regard to the divinity of Christ and the divinity of the Christian "Anskuelse," but he saw clearly the gap between them and himself in the view of man. Both parties agreed that man was created in the image of God and that he had had a "misfortune" which brought him into the wrong relation to eternity, but the "naturalists" called this "misfortune" an "aberation" and claimed that the damage could be remedied in a "natural" way. Grundtvig disagreed. "For Christians believe that the nature of man has become so corrupted through the fall that a real remedy is impossible. They praise baptism as the washing of regeneration by which the man of faith is re-created. To nurture this new man toward a divine union with the God-man and Saviour, Jesus Christ, is their churchly task." The basic question is "whether God's Son became the son of man or the son of man became the Son of God."

Grundtvig clearly took exception to the view of the "naturalists" in regard to salvation. He maintained the traditional faith in Christ as God and Saviour and in the reality and necessity of salvation through Christ. But he also took exception to the orthodox view of man as totally corrupted by the fall,[5] claiming that man, created in the image of God, is able to live a true life by the character given him in creation. "Man is no monkey destined to ape the other animals, . . . but a matchless and marvelous creature in whom divine forces shall proclaim, develop, and clarify themselves through a thousand generations as a divine experiment. It will demonstrate how dust and spirit can interpenetrate one another and emerge with a common divine consciousness."

---

[5] When Luther claimed that the whole man was corrupted, he did not mean that man was completely depraved in all respects but that there was no part of man which was not touched by the corruption.

Natural man, while shackled by the power of sin in the fall, nevertheless has retained the image of God and is in possession of his God-given abilities. They enable him to live and grow and work. He is the *created* man. He can build his culture and civilization by the strength of his created nature. The distinguishing mark of the created man is the living and spoken word by which he is distinctive from animals. He cannot by his own strength attain the right relationship to God and his eternal values. He must be saved to this life through faith in Christ. The most he can do by his own power in this respect is to "long" for God, i.e. he can be aware of his sin and shortcoming and he can desire God's help. But he does not need to be "saved" in order to live as a human being and in order to build a human society. For this his created nature is sufficient.[6]

The introduction to *Nordic Mythology* goes on to discuss the problem of culture. Grundtvig denounced the false synthesis existing in the previous four centuries between Christianity and the intellectualism developed since the Renaissance, resulting in a denial of the true spirit of man. Reason had dominated the realm of secular culture as well as the theology of the church to the detriment of a real understanding of life, resulting in a loss of the personal values that alone can build a true culture. He called for a new synthesis of the ancient Nordic spirit and the Mosaic-Christian "Anskuelse" in

---

[6] It was in this connection that Grundtvig first launched his ideas about a school for the people. See Chapter X.

order to build the dynamic and positive culture of the future.

The next important expression of Grundtvig's view of man was given in a poem written in 1837, which became a highly controversial statement discussed widely even today.

> Man first and then Christian
> This is the order of life;
> Even if we are called sheep we must not think
> Of adding animals to the flock (of God)!
> Even the Almighty cannot remake
> Devils into Christians;
> Therefore, do not throw pearls to swine.

The second verse elaborates the theme that devils cannot be made into Christians, and the third verse condemns missionaries who give superficial instruction to heathens without a thought to their human development. The next two verses call attention to the fact that Adam, Enoch, Noah, Abraham, and David were faithful men of God but not Christians. "If there could be Christians before Christ, then Christianity is false and foolish."

> The Baptizer was the greatest man
> Among all the peers of David,
> But greater yet than he
> Is the smallest in the kingdom of God:
> I.e. everyone who believes and is baptized,
> Who is given the swaddling clothes of Christ,
> In other words, every Christian.
>
> Man first and then Christian,
> This is a main article,
> Christianity is given free,

It is purely our good fortune,
But a good fortune which only comes to him
Who already is the friend of God
By being of the noble tribe (or body) of truth.

Therefore every man on this earth
Must strive to be a true person,
To open his ears for the word of truth,
And to give God glory!
As Christianity then is the truth,
Even if he is not a Christian today,
He will be one tomorrow.

There are two things which Grundtvig does *not* say. He does not say that being a true person will make a man Christian. He believed that salvation is a gift from God.

From earth and to heaven
But one man was given
The power to raise up himself.

And Grundtvig does *not* say that there can be a growth from the one condition to the other. Therefore man cannot by moral effort or by evolutionary process become a Christian. What man can do, however, is to strive to *be* a true person.

Man belongs to the noble tribe (or body) of truth because he is created by God. By his creation he is already the friend of God. It might be said that he is eligible for salvation. He is created in God's image, raised in his possibilities far above animals, and of a different quality from devils. He only becomes Christian through faith and baptism, but even this is not his own accomplishment. What he can do is open his ears for the word of truth and give glory to God. He does it by living the best possible life as a human being. Not by denouncing his humanity but by developing it to the fullest and best extent, does he place himself in a position where he is receptive to the word from God.

The most complete discussion of the nature of man is found in *Elemental Christian Teachings*, particularly in the two essays, "The Christian, the Spiritual, and the Eternal Life," and "The Innate and the Redeemed Life of Man." Grundtvig started his whole argument with the premise that man is created in the image and likeness of God.[7] "If man had not been created in the image of God, he could never have fallen away from it nor be restored unto it." He believed that there was a fall, but he did not believe that "this fall has so corrupted or erased and completely destroyed man and his life in the image of God that there is not a vestige left of the inborn glory and the original relation between God and man." The corruption of evil must not be underestimated, "for if there were no devil—then there would not be a word of truth in the gospel of Christ." On the other hand, man could not be totally corrupted and demonized, for if "all that is human had become demonic in the fall, then the Son of God could no more have become a real man than he could have become a devil, and then no new man could have arisen in the image of God through the rebirth and renewal of the old man."

[7] Genesis 1:26. Unlike other theologians, Grundtvig does not distinguish between "creation in the image of God" and "creation in the likeness of God."

The "new man" is not a different man. That is important. "Naturally, it is the same human life that fell which is to be raised up, the same prodigal son who was lost and was found, was dead and became alive. It was the same lost sheep which suffered from exposure and was carried home on the shoulders of the shepherd. Therefore the new man is not, strictly speaking, another man than the old. He is only a different man according to the figure of speech that was used when it was written that Saul became another man when he was anointed and the spirit came upon him . . . The robber on the cross shared the same human life as the only begotten Son of God . . . Even the new body with which the Lord was resurrected was essentially the same that was nailed to the cross." But the "scribes," who "have emphasized the Christian life as the life of our Lord Jesus Christ and of no other man, have misunderstood." They have "severed the so-called new life in Christ and his church from the old life as a sinful life in the flesh, which must be destroyed or eradicated in order that the new life, which is something entirely different from the old, can succeed it."

Grundtvig was severe in his criticism of the orthodox doctrine in regard to this problem. He continued the quotation above with the following blast: "Out of this basic error emerged not only all the monastic rules but also all our so-called orthodox dogmatics. In them the basic corruption of human nature and its spiritual incapacity toward good was made the foundation for the whole work of reconciliation. It was obvious, however, that human nature, which needed salvation and redemption, rebirth and renewal in His image who created us, thereby would be destroyed. The result was quite naturally that the old life, which was thus forsaken, more and more went to the dogs. That which was called new life either had no life and power and did nothing except, perhaps, write dogmatics and memorize them. Otherwise it became an inhuman, demonic life, which battled against humanity and elevated, under pretense of false names, the wilfulness and self-conceit which belongs to the devil, the murderer of men."

Grundtvig looked for that distinguishing characteristic in man which was indicative of the fact that he was created in the image of God, finding it in the word of man, in human speech. "It is the word and speech which essentially and obviously separates us human beings from all the dumb creatures." The concept of the word was not accidental. It was intimately connected with his basic theology of God and of the church. God creates by his Word. He has revealed himself in his Word, Christ, and comes to us through a living word in the Christian church. What would then be more natural than to believe that God has given man the spoken word as the mark of distinction for that which makes him an image of God? Grundtvig maintained that the Word is "not only the one means of creation— and that the Word is the light of life that enlightens every man coming into the world." [8] He considered "the Word furthermore as the only expression of spiritual life, so that man's word is not only the image of life but the image of light in which God created man."

While Grundtvig did not believe that sinful man had lost the image of God, he spoke of the captivity of man who has "lost the power to do His will and thus has been deprived of communion and fellowship with Him." [9] Like the prodigal son man must repent and acknowledge his guilt before God. He does have the power to do this. He has a longing for God as the prodigal son had the desire to return. This longing and desire is an indication that he is still the man who is created in the image of God. Grundtvig spoke of a "remnant," an expression that suggests that the image of God is a quality *in* man instead of being man himself. Nevertheless it indicates the absence of total depravity and destruction. Here he mentioned the possession of the spoken word: "just as man in his word retained a recognized likeness to God, so a remnant of faith, of hope, and of love followed the fallen man from paradise into the wilderness." [10]

[8] John 1:9.

[9] cf. Luther's discussion of the bondage of the will in *De Servo Arbitrio*.

[10] Michelsen contends that a difference in Luther's and Grundtvig's view of man is to be found in varying views of the creation and the fall. "For Luther the creation was an incessantly continuing but the fall a completed event which determined the character of human nature prior to all history. In contrast, Grundtvig regarded the creation as the first fact of history and the fall as a progressive process." *Op. cit.*, p. 160.

Since he did not consider man's part in salvation in terms of human accomplishment, he spoke of the response of the fallen man in passive terms. "In this presentation of the relationship of the fallen man to God and to the image of God within himself, all thought of merit, self-justification, and power to save oneself falls away, while the *readiness to be comforted, pardoned, reborn, and renewed* has been retained." Describing these problems is a delicate matter which can best be approached dialectically, but it is quite plain that while Grundtvig does not believe that the image of God is totally destroyed, he does not believe either that man can initiate salvation or contribute to it in any way.[11]

The value of Grundtvig's view of man is that, while he retains the concept of the sin and guilt of man and believes that the burden of this guilt cannot be overcome by man's own effort, he nevertheless believes in and forcibly emphasizes the inborn or created nature of man as a wonderful gift from God. This conviction adds

[11] The problem of whether Grundtvig's anthropology was in accord with Luther's and that of Lutheran orthodoxy has been discussed by Regin Prenter in an article, "Grundtvig's View of Man" in *Kirke og Kultur* (Oslo, 1948), pp. 209-226. Prenter maintains that despite apparent differences there is much agreement between the first two and that they primarily agree as over against Lutheran orthodoxy. Grundtvig exaggerates the views of orthodoxy, and formally he is unfair to it. "If we essentially regard the evil in man as a corruption of nature, then we are led, if we are consistent—this is the element of truth in Grundtvig's criticism of orthodoxy—to place evil within man himself rather than to understand it as an objective power outside of man. The result of this will be either that we minimize the evil in man and make it a simple fault in man, as was done in the Age of Enlightenment, or that we tend in the direction of that demonizing of man of which Grundtvig accuses orthodoxy and of which the cynical contempt of man in our own day is an effective illustration."

new significance to the fact that God became man in Christ, for the incarnation is thus a recognition of man's God-given nature. But it is also verified by the fact of the incarnation. Christ would not have become man if there had not been a wonderful life to save. It is also a denunciation of and a liberation from Pietism which completely condemns or minimizes man's human or secular activity and places the stress upon some sort of religious or sanctified activity where human nature allegedly is cleansed or liberated from the corruption of human activity. In the final analysis, the only activity at which man can possibly work is one which rises out of his natural being. Claims of sanctification by abstinence from certain human activities, by personal commitment, or by participation in certain religious forms, can only lead to self-righteousness and sanctimoniousness rather than sanctification. The only one who can sanctify is God, and the only performance of which we are capable as human beings is development and appreciation of the qualities and abilities God has given us.

From the viewpoint of Pietism Grundtvig's conclusions are negative, for he spurned and scorned all their forms and results. Grundtvig, they say, is a heretic, because he did not conform to their schedule and framework or procedure. His emphasis was on the joy and happiness of life, springing out of a genuine appreciation of the created world and of a Pauline and Lutheran recognition that man's salvation and ultimate destiny is taken care of by God, given unmerited to those who accept God in faith and are baptized into the fellowship of the church. Pietists represented this as a sinful and heretical secularism which did not appreciate the seriousness and narrowness of Christian living. It seems quite safe to say, however, that Grundtvig's concept of Christianity not only is in conformity with Luther's basic ideas, but forms the soundest continuation of Luther's great work. This needs to be emphasized today, when a part of the Lutheran church has substituted pagan, self-righteous, and narrowly exclusive Pietism and austere orthodox intellectualism for the original dynamic of the Reformation.

The greatest benefit of Grundtvig's view of man is that it restored the dynamic of Christendom in a church that had largely lost it. It offers this dynamic to a world in which the motivation for action and progress comes either from non-Christian sources or from a Christianity that has lost the original concern of the church for the salvation of man from sin and guilt and has substituted a superficial social action.

Grundtvig's view of man is dynamic, eliminating the checkrein of religious exclusiveness and permitting full freedom in human activity in the name of Christianity. But besides freedom of action it offers a double motivation. First there is the motivation of the gift of creation. We have received life from God and therefore we are responsible for its use. Secondly, all activity is Christian activity, insofar as it is not sinful. Man cannot achieve his salvation but he can develop his humanity, a necessity for salvation, inasmuch as man has to be man in order to be saved. Grundtvig calls attention to the fact that Jesus could not save the widow's son until He had called him back to life. When this view is combined with the emphasis upon the Spirit, so important in Grundtvig's view of the church, the dynamic quality of Christianity is fully brought out, challenging legalism, doctrinalism, and religious exclusiveness.

Grundtvig's view of man does not mean that the tension of Christian living and Christian thought have been relieved. No one will ever be able satisfactorily to explain or resolve the tension in his own life caused by the fact that man is at the same time a child of God and a rebel against God. The New Testament itself is filled with this tension. Man can do nothing to make things right with God. The miracle of salvation is entirely one of God's own making. Yet man must do something. He is responsible to God and will be held responsible for his failures and his wrongdoings. In this tension Grundtvig constantly lived. What he did was to release the dynamic of Christianity and to clarify the relation between the created nature of man and the life of the redeemed sinner. Kierkegaard was caught in this same tension. While he explored to the innermost chambers the intricate problems of the tensions and called attention to the fact that they can be resolved only by the leap of faith, he failed to find the peace and dynamic of faith.

In *Elemental Christian Teachings* Grundtvig opposed

215

Kierkegaard. Some of the essays were written shortly after Kierkegaard's last attack on Christendom, in which he claimed that the Christianity of the New Testament had never existed. "It was not difficult for Søren Kierkegaard, with the loud acclaim of the world, to describe our Christian sermon, Bible study, and service, baptism, and Communion, as a great foolishness, as a merry comedy, which not only became tragicomical but tremendously sad and highly blasphemous when many people grew to believe what we so-called ministers, we 'black-gowns,' taught them. We taught them that when they listened to us and accepted our teachings, had their children baptized, and went to communion occasionally, they really, though in a hidden manner, took part in Christian, spiritual, and eternal life. This life our Lord Jesus Christ lived on earth and promised to share eternally with all his faithful followers.

"No, this was not difficult. Søren Kierkegaard was very careful not to write that out of himself or the New Testament he had received the life and power to live a real, Christian, spiritual, and eternal life, or that he could convey this power to others. He wrote that, out of himself or the New Testament, he had learned and could prove that the Christian, spiritual, and eternal life presented to us and described in the New Testament, is a lie, an illusion, and even blasphemy. Therefore he has pledged his own honor and the New Testament to the fact that there is no Christian, spiritual, and eternal life on this earth. It is up to us, the Lord Jesus Christ we confess, and the Spirit who directs and comforts us, to prove to the world that there is such a life on earth, though it has long been difficult to ascertain." Grundtvig answers that the "signs of Christian life" were confession, preaching, and praise.

In 1841 Grundtvig wrote a poem entitled "An Open Letter to My Children." In this he expressed his philosophy of life, perhaps the best short statement he has given. It has been translated, but the translation misses several vital points, and it is therefore necessary to render it in prose.

> A simple, joyful, active life on earth
> Which I would not exchange for the life of kings,
> An exalted life in the tradition of the fathers
> With equal worth given to cottage and castle,
> With eyes turned heavenward, as in our birth,
> Alert to all that is good and beautiful,
> But well acquainted with the deep longings
> And only perfected by the glory of eternity,
> Such a life I desired for all my loved ones
> And strove diligently to prepare,
> And when my soul grew tired of the struggle,
> It found rest in the prayer of our Lord;
> Then I felt the comfort of the spirit of truth,
> That blessings abound in the vineyard of life,
> When dust is given into the hands of the Creator
> And we await the natural course of events.

Our life must be simple, joyful, active. It is the life of a people in which equality reigns and life is inspired by the traditions and the experience of mankind. Its basic worth is given to us in creation when we were born with an appreciation of God and with alertness to that which is good and beautiful in the world.

So far Grundtvig has been describing the created man, made in the image of God. He says little in this poem about sin and the fall, but the inference is found in the line, "well acquainted with the deep longings." "Longing" is the condition of man imprisoned by the power of evil. Liberation is in the next line, "only perfected by the glory of eternity." Perfection, or righteousness with God, comes only through him who is the glory of God and whose glory comes as an after-glow to man. Those who claim that Grundtvig failed to recognize the necessity of the Christian events of salvation, fail to read the poem aright. Grundtvig took it for granted that the readers knew what he meant when he spoke of the deep longings and the glory of eternity.

By all my strength and power, Grundtvig continues, I tried to realize such a life on earth. I could see its significance and fought for it. But I could not attain it by my own strength. Then, as I grew tired, I prayed the Lord's own prayer, the prayer of hope, and the Holy Spirit came to me to comfort me and give me strength. When that happened, I realized that God had given his blessing to our human efforts. Our whole "garden of life," our human fellowship and activity, was given power by the Spirit. We can therefore rest assured that by his help things will grow, blossom, and bear fruit. We must learn to have trust and confidence in God who will take our best efforts and use them.

Appendix

The Background of Grundtvig's Time

THE ENLIGHTENMENT AND CHRISTIAN WOLFF

The latter half of the eighteenth century was the period of the Enlightenment, or Rationalism in its religious form. This movement had its roots in the Renaissance and the personal and intellectual emancipation of the individual which took place at that time. Its modern form originated in the philosophy of Descartes (1596-1650). His point of departure was reason. When he said: "I think, therefore I am," he emphasized both the faculty of reasoning and the significance of the individual person. The trend which he started was further promoted by philosophers such as Leibnitz and Spinoza. It was given its eighteenth century expression in Germany by the philosopher Christian Wolff (1679-1754). Although the famous playwright, Ludvig Holberg, introduced the Enlightenment to Denmark, it was the Wolffian form that prevailed. Wolff's philosophy was predominant at the University of Copenhagen in the beginning of the nineteenth century.

It is not difficult to understand why the eighteenth

century placed so great an emphasis upon human thoughts and the fruits of speculation. The excellent faculty of logical reasoning had been restricted during the Middle Ages by the authoritarianism of the church. It had been permitted to function only within the limits of accepted general truths concerning God and the universe. When the great revolt against this authority took place in the sixteenth century, the champions of new ideas in the realm of science and philosophy lagged behind the Reformers in finding sponsors and protectors for their revolt. Protestant forces on the continent even found it necessary, in the face of military threat, to fortify their cause with a new authoritarianism which was intellectually intolerant. It was not until the Netherlands wrested their freedom from the Hapsburgs of Spain that a real haven was created with freedom for nonconformists. In the seventeenth-century religious and imperialistic wars and the totalitarianism of absolute monarchies still blocked the advance of science and thought, but in the eighteenth century they came into their own.

The new primacy and independence of thought proclaimed by Descartes, the advance in natural science demonstrated by Newton, and the new basis for social relations championed by Grotius, gave tremendous impetus to the thought and practice of the new century, and many remarkable accomplishments for the bettering of human conditions must be ascribed to this period. The social and political ideas, proclaimed in the American and French revolutions and practiced in the founding of the new American nation, were inspired and formulated by the social philosophers of the eighteenth century. Great social and political reforms, though obscured by the excesses of the French Revolution, were promoted and carried out. In Denmark striking agricultural reforms were effected. What wonder then that the age indulged in great optimism and confidence in the power of intellectual accomplishment. Resentment against the traditionalism of the church and its outmoded theology led to an almost exclusive emphasis on the secular or material features of life, while emphasis on the laws of nature led to an eclipse of interest in and need for the divine. In fact, one modern historian of the age has proclaimed that God died about 1770.

The century was a peculiar mixture. In our criticism of its excesses we are apt to forget its valuable contributions, but we can hardly overemphasize its great humanitarian character, its many practical advances, its creative and inspirational genius, and its great unfolding of human ability in the free and unhampered atmosphere of progress. True, it underestimated the forces of evil in the world and its optimism fell flat and was discredited, but who are we in our century to blame the eighteenth for such shortcomings. When therefore we are compelled to point out the limitations of the Enlightenment, we do so primarily to explain the reactions of the nineteenth century in their search for a more profound understanding of life.

As mentioned above, the philosopher of the Enlightenment whose ideas predominated in Denmark was the
famous German philosopher, Christian Wolff. He made
no particular original contribution to the thought of his
age, and he was completely overshadowed and refuted
by Kant's demonstration of the impossibility of gaining
a real knowledge of the world through reason and the
senses, but he was cock of the roost in Copenhagen in
Grundtvig's university days. It is therefore necessary
to make brief mention of his ideas. Wolff believed with
his age that the reality of the world and of God could
be penetrated through rational processes which func-
tioned logically and with almost mathematical precision.
Although God was above the limitations of reason, man
could nevertheless prove His existence from the orderliness of the world. There arose from this conclusion a
strong identification of thought and existence.

As it has been brilliantly analyzed in a dissertation by
Henning Høirup,[1] Wolff's method of reasoning was
the one used by Grundtvig. He had been taught the
method by his philosophy professor, Børge Riisbrigh,
and although he rejected the philosophy of Wolff, he
retained Wolff's epistemology, especially after he in
1812-13 again had become aware of its potentialities.
The main feature of the method is the so-called Principle of Contradiction, one of the three basic principles
of classical logic, which states that a thing cannot
simultaneously be itself and its opposite. The statement

[1] Henning Høirup: *Grundtvigs Syn paa Tro og Erkendelse* (1949).

222

is in itself indisputable; its limitation lies in its application. This was especially true in the belief of Wolff and his followers that reality could be grasped through rational processes. The problem lies in the exact establishment of alternatives. Only when true and exclusive alternatives are present can the principle be used, and since the time of Kant it has been evident that theoretical alternatives do not necessarily cover real alternatives. The application of this principle in the so-called Principle of Exclusion, the theory that the verity of a principle or the reality of a phenomenon can be proved by disproving the opposite, leaves room for great doubt and uncertainty. It is extremely difficult to be sure that true alternatives exist. When, therefore, a philosophy maintains that logic or reasoning is identical with reality, the weakness of the process is apparent.

Grundtvig indisputably used this form of argumentation to prove some of his main theses, as Høirup has demonstrated in his book. But it is not true that the use of an antequated system of logic as proof or demonstration discredits the proposition which is proclaimed. Grundtvig used the logic of his age to validate the truths which had become apparent to him. These truths rest in themselves and cannot be discarded merely because they were argued by an obsolete method of reasoning.

THE ENLIGHTENMENT AND ORTHODOXY

Of far greater significance than the logic or method of reasoning employed by the philosophers of Enlightenment was the influence of the ideas of the moment on their understanding of Christianity, or more narrowly defined, on the field of theology. The forceful emphasis upon the faculty of reasoning was a blessing in the field of natural science and social relations, and it was the natural tool and object of philosophical speculation, but it posed special problems within the realm of religion. Reason was not a stranger to theology before the eighteenth century, for the practice of orthodoxy had been to expound authoritative ideas in intellectual terms, but whereas reason had been the slave of theology in the period of orthodoxy, it now became the master.

To give the devil his due, Rationalism did bring a welcome and blessed relief from the yoke and shackles of the orthodoxist demand for conformity. Whenever the theologians of an age develop self-worship to the extent that they identify their particular formulation of Christian insights with the truth itself and impose a static lid of doctrine upon life, they expose themselves to an inevitable explosion of accumulated resentment which not only blows off the lid but is apt to hinder the acceptance of the truths which the doctrines try to express. All compulsion in the realm of the spirit will eventually and inevitably lead to revolt. The tighter the lid, the greater the explosion.

The Enlightenment with its belief in science and in the orderliness of nature had little difficulty in blowing the lid off traditional orthodoxy, but it went beyond this to a practical elimination of God. God could be proved from the orderliness of nature, and he fitted admirably into the system as a First Cause. His ancient function as Judge and Redeemer was unnecessary, for with his common sense man could take care of the minor obstacles of evil. If man thus lived a good life according to his conscience and the wise ethics which Jesus had given us, he would be in harmony with eternal values and would therefore live on after death. Theoretically God was still a necessary part of the system, for there had to be a first cause and a promoter of values, but the religious slogan of the age became: God, Virtue, and Immortality. Of the Deity there was little left.

In our understanding of the relationship between God and man there often seems to be a sort of cord-and-pulley connection. When one is elevated the other is lowered and vice versa. We can debate whether the one movement is the cause or the result of the other, but the fact is that as the Rationalists lowered the significance of God they raised the estimate of man considerably. Rousseau made an essential contribution to this attitude by proclaiming the innate and natural goodness of man and maintaining that he was spoiled by civilization. In line with this is the predominantly British interest in so-called "natural" religion which allegedly was basic to all expressions of religion.

The stress on science and common sense and the general skepticism of the age quite naturally led to an upsurge of historical criticism, unfortunately accompanied by a lack of historical appreciation. The combination of the two is vicious.[2] In the religious field this criticism was chiefly directed against the Bible. The result was devastating. Controls and inhibitions were shattered and Scripture was used to defend or prove whatever beliefs were held to be reasonable. This use of the Bible was, of course, the same as that of orthodoxy, but the results were widely different. Christianity was reduced to motivations and justifications for practical problems, and skepticism grew. One Danish theologian published a notorious periodical called *Jesus and Reason*, and the ministers who were founded in traditional and orthodox views fought a losing battle. The alienation of the people from the church which was begun during the time of sterile and static orthodox preaching was intensified. One man in Copenhagen stood out as a pillar of strength against the flood tide. He was N. E. Balle, professor and later bishop, called "the lonely champion of the Bible." He published a magazine as a counterbalance to the one mentioned above. It was called *The Bible Defends Itself*.

Lest it be forgotten, however, in the impression left by the negative features of Rationalism as it influenced Danish theology, the total picture of Enlightenment must not be obscured by the excesses of one phase. The practical and social reforms which took place in Denmark during the latter decades of the eighteenth century, especially the agricultural reforms, had tremendous,

[2] "Revolutions are fostered in periods that are blind to history." Alf Ahlberg, *Historiens Filosofi*, II, 83, Danish translation.

beneficial results which blessed the nineteenth century and even the twentieth. Like any age, this one had its contradictions and its many nuances of light and shadow. On the whole it was an active, fruitful, and creative century. It contained also and as a matter of course the elements and embryos of the new age which was to succeed it and overwhelm it.

LESSING AND HERDER

It seems to be a law of life that intellectual emphases and emotional outbursts succeed one another, and even as the Enlightenment had pushed Pietism from the scene, it was to be crowded out by Romanticism. Before we proceed to consider the new thunder we should, however, discuss two men who did not entirely conform to their age and who presaged the new. They have particular interest in a study of Grundtvig.

At first glance G. E. Lessing (1729-81) seems to have had exclusively eighteenth-century ideas. He published fragments of a critical attack upon the Bible and proclaimed ethical results as the true criterion of religion dogmatism by Reimarus, he preached toleration and in his *Nathan der Weise*, and he seemed to lack appreciation of history when he stated that "incidental historical truths can never be proof of the eternal truths of reason." Yet in his separation of the truth of Christianity from the literalness of the Bible, in his emphasis upon the Apostles' Creed, and especially in his discussion of the developmental character of history he pointed to considerations that were to become significant in the following century. Grundtvig condemned Lessing roundly in his early historical works, and his positive Christianity never conceded anything to Lessing's more vague and neutral ideas, yet Lessing is one of those who subtly influenced Grundtvig in several respects.

Much discussed in his relation to Grundtvig and of indubitable influence is J. G. Herder (1744-1803). He was a gentle, profound, and poetic soul, and Jean Paul called him a poem rather than a poet.[3] Although he shared many of the limitations of the Enlightenment and even of Romanticism by philosophizing God and man's relation to Him, he was nevertheless a prophet of things to come. He maintained that poetry, history, and the life of a people should be evaluated, not in terms of modern, rational criteria but according to their own situations and inner life. He reached an understanding of the organic and dynamic character of religion and culture which has greatly influenced our own century's studies of religions and folk life, and he also proclaimed the developmental character of history. Herder was much influenced by Rousseau's ideas of the innate goodness of man, believing that cultures develop from a natural goodness toward a humanitarian ideal, but he should not be judged by the limitations which he shared with his age. His insight into the communal character of soul life and his understanding of the harmony of

[3] In commenting upon this Grundtvig suggested that Herder should be called a "prophecy" or, more aptly, a "picture book." *World Chronicle* (1817), p. 551.

cultures and religions have independent value today.

Grundtvig was powerfully influenced by Herder although he does not recognize this formally and sharply criticizes Herder's philosophy. As early as 1808 he praised Herder for his interest in mythology, and in his *World Chronicles* he devoted considerable space to a discussion of Herder, in the *Chronicle* of 1817 ten pages. It is apparent from these and other sources that Grundtvig was acquainted with at least five of Herder's books. In his discussion of Herder Grundtvig condemned him for his lack of a Christian understanding of history and positive Christian insight. But he did give him credit for a poetic appreciation and even a resurrection of the Bible, and praised him for a "more profound view of history." Here again Grundtvig absorbed ideas from a man whose philosophy he rejected, even though he was probably not aware of it. He never conceded a whit to Herder's pantheistic philosophy and his inadequate interpretation of Christianity. But later on, in his introduction to *Nordic Mythology*, 1832, he expounded a view of historical development comparing the ages of culture with the ages of man which is so close to Herder's view as to suggest direct influence. Furthermore, his strong and continuous emphasis on folk life definitely has Herderian elements.

THE RISE OF ROMANTICISM

The beautiful and harmonious world, which the philosophers of the eighteenth century had taken for granted, betrayed them by failing to live up to their analysis and expectations. Nature herself dealt them a cruel blow by destroying the city of Lisbon in an earthquake in 1755, and man proved to be no less destructive when passions were let loose in the French Revolution. It was therefore a shaky intellectual structure which Immanuel Kant (1725-1804) undermined when he attacked the very foundation upon which it was built, the sovereignty of reason. He maintained that the human mind, which explored and described the world about us, was so handicapped by its own limitations of functioning within time and space that it did not necessarily bring us to an understanding of the real world, the Thing in Itself. There is therefore no way from knowledge and speculation to God, and if there be any such way, it can only be found in the God-given moral consciousness within man.

Through the critical genius of Kant and the poetic genius of Goethe, who explored the depth and scope of the human soul, the way was paved for a new poetic and philosophical movement which swept into prominence with the new century, called Romanticism or Idealism. It sought a new harmony of life where rationalistic solutions have failed, leaping the barrier of Kant's criticism by building its insights on other human faculties than logic and the power of reason. It was a time of imagination, intuition, and poetic inspiration or, in other words, of emphasis upon the emotional side of the human soul. The "harmony" of the eighteenth century had been too superficial and had not sufficiently considered the multitudinous character of life, but some sort of totality had to be found. The genius of the age turned toward efforts at finding a satisfactory synthesis into which all the features of living could merge. God was therefore revived, but he was not the living God of the Christian revelation. He was a feature of an artificial synthesis, and it would probably not be entirely wrong to apply the altered modern usage of an ancient word and call him "synthetic." He was not a personal God for the Romantic philosophers; he was part of an explanation. In all his vagueness he became a part of all things, which is the status for which the Greeks had the word "pantheistic." No wonder Grundtvig raged at the philosophy of Romanticism after he had emerged from his first outburst of enthusiasm for it.

The Romantic philosophers were not held back by Kant's contention that man cannot by faculties of his mind penetrate beyond the limitations of experience. They were even eagerly grateful for his claim that the world beyond these limitations was the real world, the Thing in Itself. While this "real" world could probably not be reached by reason in its stricter sense, they believed it could be reached through intuition, imagination, and inspiration. These faculties were of premium value to the Romanticists. Their chief mode of insight and expression was poetic. The poet was a man of deep longings, of penetrating vision, and of creative expression. Basically, even the philosopher had to be a poet, and the religious philosophies of the new age grew out of the longing to create a harmonious synthesis which could adequately explain the problems of the universe.

While one line of emphasis of the Romanticists was poetic, the other was historical. The glory of the past had already been preached by Rousseau and Herder, and the present offered little encouragement in a day when the governments and economies of north and central Europe collapsed under the strain of the Napoleonic wars. The greatness for which the poets sought and longed was therefore found in a distant past, the glory of which deserved to be resurrected in the present, or, at least, in the future. This glory has long since faded and the admiration of the Romanticists for the Middle Ages and for early cultures has proved to be superficial and brittle. But their enthusiasm for history and the inspiration of their effort was highly beneficial for the student of history through the nineteenth century. Interpretations wilted in the light of that historical criticism which also grew to recognition and accomplishment in the nineteenth century, but the historical drive of Romanticism motivated even the critical movement which destroyed its philosophy.

J. G. FICHTE

Romanticism presents as brilliant a bouquet of names as any movement of recent centuries. It is not for us in this connection to make exhaustive mention of these. We shall therefore only consider two whose impact upon Grundtvig was the most powerful. J. G. Fichte (1762-1814) is remembered today for his fiery "Addresses to the German Nation" which inspired the German people in their fight against Napoleon and in their struggle to build a new nation, but his philosophy is all but forgotten. Perhaps justly so. Fichte lived in the shadow of Kant. He struggled with the problems of religion and morality which Kant had raised. He placed an emphasis upon man's faith and moral consciousness, upon human freedom, and upon human activity in the realization of moral values within the world, which greatly inspired Grundtvig in 1806. But his philosophical attempt to explain God and the world from the autonomous life of the individual incurred Grundtvig's severe criticism. In 1815 Grundtvig discussed him in his diary: "Certain it is that Fichte's book about *The Purpose of Man*[4] made a deep impression upon me so that this ponderer ["Grubler"], despite my growing disagreement with him, during the following years continually appeared to be the world's wisest master. I still maintain a strange love for him, of which I do not disapprove, for his speech prepared me for Scripture's message of faith and love. It confirmed me so in a certainty about the bottomless gap between good and evil that I always turned away from the basic views of pantheism with contempt despite my inclination toward it." In the *World Chronicle* of 1817 Grundtvig said that Fichte had a warped brain but his heart was in the right place.

[4] *Die Bestimmung des Menschen*, 1800.

F. W. VON SCHELLING

F. W. von Schelling (1775-1854) was the first of the philosophers of Romanticism to gain real prominence. Later on he was overshadowed by his friend and colleague, G. W. F. Hegel (1770-1831), but the early Romanticists were inspired by Schelling's ideas which brought relief and new impulse after the collapse of the Enlightenment and the rigid limitations of Kant. Schelling himself built no complete system of philosophy, partly because his ideas grew beyond their original scope, and changed somewhat with the years, but he relieved the vague aspirations of the new age. He found a way to put God back in the picture and yet maintain faith in the ability of man to expand and understand. Fichte's emphasis upon the individual and the general interest in nature were absorbed and united in Schelling's proclamation of the identity of the two. This identity exists through the activity of the spirit, which replaced the eighteenth century emphasis upon reason, led beyond the barriers imposed by Kant, and expressed the prevailing interest in intuitive or poetic insight. The inner and "real" character of all life was a spiritual, dynamic force, given expression through the principle of an absolute God, the Being who united all within himself. Having reached this insight, Schelling turned the situation around and proceeded from God to an explanation of the world. Two things caused him difficulty, however. One was the increasing stress upon the evolutionary character of life, while the other was the reality of a destructive or evil force. He "solved" the problem by giving even the Absolute, or God, an evolutionary character. God's nature is not that of "being" but "becoming," and in this "becoming" he absorbs within himself the tension between good and evil. Schelling did not reject the concepts of Christian theology. On the contrary, he adjusted them to his "system" and explained them in relation to his pantheism.

Schelling was not only the leading philosopher of the early decades of the century. He was also the thinker who made the greatest impact upon Grundtvig. In his first enthusiasm for Romanticism during his early twenties he was carried away by Schelling's ideas, and these prevailed in his thinking concerning religion for some time. He even tried to identify himself with Schelling's mysticism. When this failed he saw the inadequacy of the whole system, and his reaction against Schelling's pantheism, especially against the inadequate treatment of the problem of evil, was one of the potent factors in his conversion experience of 1810-11. After that he fought Schelling unceasingly refuting this philosophy competently and completely. Grundtvig fought Schelling even as Kierkegaard fought Hegel. In the battle against the German philosophers of their day they were compatriots.

MILITARY DEFEAT, SPIRITUAL GROWTH

One of Denmark's important sources of income during the eighteenth century had been foreign trade.

Colonies had been established in Asia, Africa, and the West Indies, and a great fleet of clipper ships sailed the seven seas, bringing wealth to their owners. To protect the country as a whole and the maritime interests in particular a powerful navy had been developed, and Danish naval power was of no little significance in northern Europe. In the wars of the 1790's between England and France the navy was used to protect Danish shipping, and Denmark tried hard to maintain its neutral rights even by armed escorts of convoys. As a result relations with England became increasingly tense. When Denmark joined Russia and Sweden in a league of neutrality in 1800, England sent a fleet to Copenhagen to force a withdrawal. The fleet accomplished its purpose in the Battle of Copenhagen, April 2, 1801, and gave the Danes a severe shock. Another result was a moral uplift through their own outnumbered navy's stout defense.

Denmark's history of the next fifteen years is one of war, defeat, and economic collapse. The Napoleonic wars placed the country in an extremely difficult position and the end result of several years of tension was another British action against the country. In 1807 Copenhagen was besieged and bombarded and the entire Danish navy was seized. Denmark was thrown into the war as an ally of Napoleon and suffered the ultimate defeat with him. No campaign was carried out on Danish territory, but Danish shipping was ravaged, and the Treaty of Kiel, 1814, deprived the Danish crown of Norway after a rule of more than four hundred years. The war also played havoc with Denmark's economy, and in 1813 the Danish government went into bankruptcy. Long years of depression followed before the financial situation again started to improve in the thirties. This fact must be kept in mind in an evaluation of Grundtvig's attitudes and his personal struggle to make a living.

Strangely enough the same period was of unprecedented spiritual growth. As national and commercial glory faded cultural values took their place. This was particularly true of literature, the special interest of Romanticism, represented by Henrik Steffens, Adam Oehlenschläger, and other brilliant poets, novelists, and dramatists. The period is often called the "golden age" of Danish literature. In the field of art, with Bertel Thorvaldsen as the leading genius, in music, and in science the men of the age scintillated as never before.

THE MONARCHY

The world of ideas forms only a part of the background of Grundtvig's time. Grundtvig said of himself that he was "half bookworm and half bard," but this characterization does not do him justice. He was interested in public affairs and took an active part even during the most retiring years of his career. His was a stirring age, with revolutions and the campaigns of the Napoleonic wars filling the years from his first childhood recollections through the next quarter century.

After his period of adolescent indifference for three-fourths of the nineteenth century Grundtvig was involved in national affairs.

Up until 1849 Denmark was an absolute monarchy. All political and administrative power was gathered in the hands of the one man who sat on the throne by the right of biological inheritance. Christian VII, the monarch who ruled during Grundtvig's childhood and youth (1766-1808), suffered from dementia praecox and was incapable of even the minimum of administration. The country was therefore ruled by those who wielded influence over the king and controlled his signature. During Christian VII's early years this situation had extreme and tragic reverberations, but inasmuch as the enlightenment of the century also influenced the government through able counselors, the enlightened monarchy produced some results that were quite outstanding.

The inspired advisors of Christian VII, led by the young crown prince who later became Frederik VI, carried through a series of agricultural reforms in 1788 and the following years. These reforms were one of the finest fruits of the philosophy of the century, and the ideas which inspired them are well expressed on a memorial column in Copenhagen to commemorate the event. It reads: "The king knew that civil liberty, determined by just law, inspires love of country, courage for its defense, interest in knowledge, desire for industry, and hope of good fortune." Through these reforms, effected peacefully, the feudal system of land ownership was shattered and a permanent foundation was laid for the amazing technical and social developments of the Danish farmer during the nineteenth century. In addition, the government introduced a complete system of elementary public schools in 1814, establishing potentialities for an enlightened and efficient agricultural society. The Folk Schools which grew out of Grundtvig's educational endeavors in the latter half of the nineteenth century must always be evaluated against the background of these reforms.

By and large the period of reform came to an end at the turn of the century. The crown prince grew more conservative with his years, and when he became king in his own right (1808-39), the government became quite static and even reactionary. This was in accord with the prevailing tendency in Europe at the end of the Napoleonic wars and after the Treaty of Vienna, 1815. Symbolic of this development is the fact that freedom of the press, existing since 1770, was curbed by a decree of 1799, and it was through this decree that Grundtvig's censorship was imposed.

Selected Bibliography

In English:
BOOKS

Davis, Noelle, *Education for Life; a Danish Pioneer.* Liverpool: Williams & Norgate, 1931.

Koch, Hal, *Grundtvig.* Translated from the Danish with introduction and notes by Llewellyn Jones. Yellow Springs, Ohio: Antioch College Press, 1952.

Lindhardt, P. G., *Grundtvig: an Introduction.* London: S.P.C.K., 1952.

Nielsen, E. D., *N. F. S. Grundtvig, an American Study.* Rock Island, Illinois: Augustana Book Concern, 1955.

ARTICLES

Knudsen, Johannes, "Grundtvig Research," *Lutheran Quarterly*, May, 1953.

——————, "Grundtvig and Mythology," *Lutheran Quarterly*, November, 1954.

——————, "Grundtvig and American Theology Today," *Lutheran World*, March, 1955.

In Danish:
SELECTED WORKS

N. F. S. Grundtvigs Udvalgte Skrifter 1-10, ed. by Holger Begtrup. Copenhagen: Gyldendal, 1904-09.

N. F. S. Grundtvig Vaerker i Udvalg 1-10, ed. by Georg Christensen and Hal Koch. Copenhagen; Gyldendal, 1940-49.

Haandbog i Grundtvigs Skrifter 1-3, ed. by Ernest J. Borup and Frederik Schrøder. Copenhagen: Hagerup, 1931.

BIBLIOGRAPHY

Johansen, Steen, *Bibliografi over N. F. S. Grundtvigs Skrifter 1-3*. Copenhagen, 1948-52. (Vol. 4 now in preparation.)

STUDIES

Grundtvig Studier, published annually since 1948 with English summaries by Grundtvig-Selskabet. Copenhagen: Gyldendal.

BOOKS

Begtrup, Holger, *Grundtvigs Danske Kristendom, 1-2*. Copenhagen: G. E. C. Gad, 1936.

Høirup, Henning, *Grundtvigs Syn paa Tro og Erkendelse*. Copenhagen: Gyldendal, 1949.

──────────, *Fra Døden til Livet*. Copenhagen: Gyldendal, 1954.

Høirup and Johansen, *Grundtvigs Erindringer og Erindringer om Grundtvig*. Copenhagen: Gyldendal, 1948

Lehmann, Edvard, *Grundtvig*. Copenhagen & Oslo: Jespersen and Pio, 1929.

Michelsen, William, *Tilblivelsen af Grundtvigs Historiesyn*. Copenhagen: Gyldendal, 1954.

Rønning, F., *N. F. S. Grundtvig 1-4*. Copenhagen: Schønberg, 1907-11.

Scharling, C. I., *Grundtvig og Romantiken*. Copenhagen: Gyldendal, 1947.

Toldberg, Helge, *Grundtvigs Symbolverden*. Copenhagen: Gyldendal, 1950.